Applied Turfgrass Science and Physiology

Jack Fry and Bingru Huang

WILEY

John Wiley & Sons, Inc.

Library of Congress Cataloging-in-Publication Data

Fry, Jack.

  Applied turfgrass science and physiology / Jack Fry and Bingru Huang.

    p. cm.

  Includes index.

  ISBN 0-471-47270-0 (cloth)

  1. Turfgrasses. 2. Turf management. 3. Grasses—Physiology. I. Huang, Bingru. II. Title.

  SB433.F75 2004

  635.9'642—dc22

                          2004003020

PRINTED IN THE UNITED STATES OF AMERICA

10 9 8 7 6 5 4

NATHALIE
thanks for sharing life's adventures and making our children your passion
CLARKE, CAROLINE, AND LYDIA
may you pursue your dreams with energy —**JF**

TO
my parents;
my husband and best friend, Ping Zhang;
our children and joy, Eddie and Lisa —**BH**

Contents

Preface

This text is a result of the natural evolution of the Applied Turfgrass Physiology seminar that the authors teach for the Golf Course Superintendents Association of America. It began as an outline for one full-day seminar, was then expanded into an Internet-based course available through www.gcsaa.org, and has now grown into this text. It is not meant to be an introductory turfgrass text; others have done an excellent job of presenting basic turfgrass management information. Furthermore, the 1992 monograph *Turfgrass,* published by the Crop Science Society of America, provided a review of early literature on some of the topics covered herein. Our goal is mainly to focus on research completed since the monograph was published. This should be a useful textbook for advanced turfgrass management or turfgrass science courses, and a valuable addition to the reference shelf for golf course superintendents, sports turf managers, lawn care operators, and others in the green industry.

Efforts have been made to present research results, in most cases from peer-reviewed scientific journals, that support the discussion. It would be an unusual turfgrass manager who would seek out and read articles in science-based journals, so we have tried to incorporate researchers' findings into a more reader-friendly format in this text.

The book is divided into three sections. Part I provides an overview of carbohydrate metabolism, including photosynthesis and respiration, and discusses how these processes differ between warm- and cool-season grasses. Also included in this section is an overview of turfgrasses and their characteristics.

Part II serves as an introduction to turfgrass stress physiology, covering plant responses to drought, temperature extremes, and shade stresses. Also included in this section is an overview of pests that are influenced by turfgrass culture.

Part III reviews the current information available on how the major cultural practices (irrigation, mowing, fertilization, cultivation, and plant growth regulators and biostimulants) influence turfgrass response to the stresses and pests presented in Part II.

INTERPRETING STATISTICS

Statistics might be considered a necessary evil; there is no avoiding them when it comes to science. Without statistics, there is no way to really know whether a given treatment had any effect. We've all heard a salesperson or colleague rave about a particular miracle product that had such a tremendous effect on plant growth that it might change the world as we know it. This individual may truly have observed an effect, but in most cases a test in which the treatment was replicated several times in a statistically proper way was not conducted.

In this text, there are basically two things about statistics you need to know: (1) how great the difference between results has to be for that difference to be meaningful; and (2) the level of confidence the researchers had in saying that a difference of that amount is significant.

The table below represents a hypothetical study in which three treatments were evaluated. The treatments could potentially be any treatment imposed on turfgrass, such as an herbicide evaluation. The response would be what we measured, presented as a mean of three or more replications. The table's footnote indicates that "means followed by the same letter in a column are not significantly different." In this case, the plant's response to treatment 1, represented by the number 50 followed by the letter *b*, is significantly lower than the response to treatment 2, which is 66 followed by the letter *a*. However, treatment 1 is not significantly different from treatment 3, which also is followed by a *b*. The response to treatment 3 is also statistically the same as the response to treatment 2, as both are followed by the letter *a*.

Authors sometimes leave it up to the reader to determine whether treatments have statistically different results. This is done by providing a least significant difference (LSD) value. In the hypothetical example below, the LSD value is 15. To determine whether the difference between two results is meaningful, subtract the smaller number from the larger one. If this number is greater than the LSD (15 in this case), the difference between the two treatments is significant.

Finally, at the end of the footnote is the notation $P < 0.05$. This reflects the researchers' confidence that there is a statistical difference between treatments. In this case, P refers to probability, and 0.05 represents 5 percent. This indicates that the researchers are at least 95 percent confident that if they say two treatments have different results, they truly do.

Treatment	Response[1]
1	50 b
2	66 a
3	55 ab
LSD value	15

[1] Means followed by the same letter in a column are not significantly different ($P < 0.05$).

ACKNOWLEDGMENTS

We are grateful to Angie Settle for the wonderful illustrations she produced. We very much appreciated Dr. Ned Tisserat graciously allowing use of portions of turfgrass disease descriptions he had written for K-State Research and Extension publications. The help that Qi Zhang provided with some of the figures was very much appreciated. Thanks are also extended to our colleagues for taking the time to review portions of this text: Dr. Greg Bell, Dr. Stacey Bonos, Dr. Dale Bremer, Dr. Bob Carrow, Dr. Richard Hull, Dr. Steve Keeley, Dr. Yaling Qian, Ward Upham.

PART I

Carbohydrate Metabolism and Turfgrasses

Cool-season and warm-season turfgrasses are referred to as C₃ and C₄ plants, respectively, based upon their photosynthetic pathways. To establish a basic understanding of the differences between cool- and warm-season turfgrasses in response to environmental stresses such as drought, temperature extremes, and shade, Chapter 1 addresses differences between each regarding photosynthesis and respiration, the carbon metabolic processes. Photosynthesis and respiration, and their balance, ultimately control turfgrass growth, vigor, quality, and resistance to environmental stresses and pests.

Only a handful of the many grasses that exist on the planet are used in turfgrass culture. Growth habits, characteristics, uses, and environmental stress tolerances of the most commonly used grasses are addressed in Chapter 2.

1

Carbohydrate Metabolism

Cool-season and warm-season grasses are referred to as C_3 and C_4 plants, respectively, based upon their photosynthetic pathways. To establish a basic understanding of the differences between cool- and warm-season turfgrasses with respect to their responses to environmental stresses such as drought, temperature extremes, and shade, a familiarity with their differences in photosynthesis and respiration is needed. The balance between the processes of photosynthesis and respiration ultimately controls turfgrass growth, vigor, quality, and resistance to environmental stresses and pests.

PHOTOSYNTHESIS

Photosynthesis takes place mostly in leaf mesophyll cells, which contain chloroplasts. Chloroplasts are cellular organelles that contain green chlorophyll molecules capable of absorbing the light needed for photosynthesis. Photosynthesis is basically a two-step process whereby green leaves convert solar energy to chemical energy (light reaction) that is used to produce energy-rich carbohydrates (food) using carbon dioxide (CO_2) and water (H_2O) (dark reaction). The first step requires light, and thus is referred to as the light reaction. The fixation of CO_2 into carbohydrates is light independent, and thus is called the dark reaction (even though the process occurs during the daytime).

3

Radiant energy captured during photosynthesis is stored in the form of chemical bonds in compounds such as adenosine triphosphate (ATP) and as reducing power (source of electrons) in nicotinamide adenine dinucleotide phosphate (NADPH), with oxygen (O_2) released as a by-product. Adenosine triphosphate is a high-energy molecule, and the removal of phosphate groups from its structure results in the release of a substantial amount of free energy. As such, ATP is the major energy currency of the cell and is the driving force for most of its energy-consuming activities. The energy contained in ATP is used to facilitate the transfer of electrons in NADPH to CO_2, forming simple carbohydrates that are converted to the sugars, glucose, fructose, and sucrose (abbreviated $C_6H_{12}O_6$ for short). The photosynthesis reaction is simplified as:

$$6CO_2 + 6H_2O \xrightarrow{\text{light and chlorophyll}} C_6H_{12}O_6 + 6O_2$$

Carbon dioxide   Water   Carbohydrates   Oxygen

C_3 Pathway (Cool-season Grasses) A majority of plants assimilate CO_2 via the C_3 photosynthetic pathway, in which the first stable product formed following CO_2 fixation is phosphoglyceric acid (PGA). PGA is a three-carbon compound, hence the name C_3 photosynthesis. When the stomata of C_3 grasses are open during the day, CO_2 enters the leaf and diffuses into the mesophyll cells, where it is fixed in the chloroplasts (Fig. 1-1).

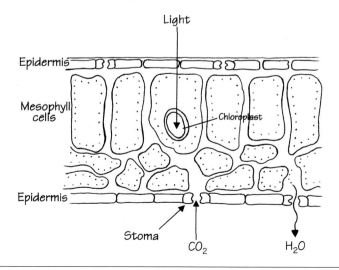

Figure 1-1
Leaf structure for C_3 turfgrasses
(drawing by Angie Settle).

Initially, CO_2 reacts with ribulose bisphosphate (RuBP) to form an intermediate six-carbon compound. This process is called carboxylation. RuBP is a five-carbon compound that functions as the acceptor molecule for CO_2 through a reaction catalyzed by the enzyme ribulose 1,5-bisphosphate carboxylase (rubisco). All enzymes, including rubisco, are proteins and act either to facilitate the interaction of two molecules in a reaction in order to produce new molecules or to break one large molecule into smaller ones. Rubisco is the most prevalent and important enzyme in plants.

The six-carbon compound formed by the union of CO_2 and RuBP is unstable and breaks down into two molecules of phosphoglyceric acid (PGA). What follows is a simplified formula for the C_3 photosynthetic pathway, although many additional reactions are involved:

$$CO_2 + \underset{\text{Ribulose 1,5-bisphosphate}}{RuBP} + H_2O \xrightarrow{\text{Rubisco}} \underset{\text{3-phosphoglyceric acid}}{PGA} + O_2$$

PGA is then reduced using NADPH and ATP to form a three-carbon sugar used as a building block for larger carbohydrates that are produced in a long series of photosynthetic reactions referred to as the Calvin cycle, Calvin-Benson cycle, or photosynthetic carbon reduction cycle (Fig. 1-2).

The final products of C_3 photosynthesis are glucose and fructose, which are used to make sucrose and starch. Sucrose, a water-soluble sugar, is transported to sink tissues such as growing leaves, roots, and reproductive structures through the plant via the phloem, and supplies immediately available energy to nonphotosynthesizing tissues. Starch consists of long chains of glucose that are not readily available for use in cell metabolism. It is often stored inside cells as a carbohydrate reserve. When plants need to use the energy for cell division or growth, they break down starch into glucose.

Photorespiration   Rubisco is a dual-function enzyme. It catalyzes not only the carboxylation of RuBP (the assimilation of CO_2 to RuBP in mesophyll cells) but also the oxidation of RuBP by oxygen molecules (the addition of O_2 to RuBP), which initiates a wasteful sequence of reactions collectively called photorespiration. During photosynthesis, oxygen can accumulate to relatively high concen-

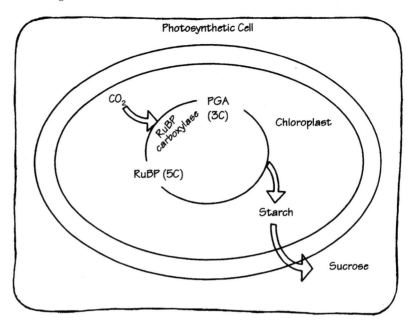

Figure 1-2
The Calvin–Benson cycle simplified (drawing by Angie Settle).

RuBP= ribulose 1, 5-bisphosphate (pentose)

PGA= phosphoglycerate

trations in leaves and chloroplasts, stimulating photorespiration. In photorespiration, O_2 substitutes for CO_2 as a substrate for the rubisco enzyme, leading ultimately to the release of CO_2. In other words, CO_2 and O_2 are alternative substrates that compete with each other for the same binding sites on rubisco. Whether the carboxylase or oxygenase reaction takes place depends on the availability of CO_2 or O_2 to the enzyme. At current atmospheric concentrations (300–400 ppm CO_2, 21 percent O_2), both reactions take place. When the CO_2 concentration is high and that of O_2 is low, carboxylation is favored and carbohydrate synthesis proceeds through the Calvin-Benson cycle. However, when the opposite occurs and the concentration of CO_2 is low and that of O_2 is high, oxidation is favored and photorespiration results. The oxidation process breaks down RuBP to PGA and P-glycolate (a two-carbon acid). Two molecules of P-glycolate are further metabolized to CO_2 and PGA with the consumption of ATP. Photorespiration is particularly problematic at temperatures above 87°F (30°C). The photorespiration reaction can be simplified to:

$$O_2 + RuBP \xrightarrow{\text{Rubisco}} PGA + 2P\text{-glycolate}$$

$$2P\text{-glycolate} + O_2 \rightarrow PGA + CO_2$$

Carbon fixation through the C_3 pathway is most efficient when temperatures are between 60 and 75°F (16 and 24°C). Cool-season grasses are most efficient at fixing CO_2 and making carbohydrates when water is plentiful and stomata remain open, allowing CO_2 to enter the leaves.

C_4 Pathway (Warm-Season Grasses) Grasses that employ the C_4 pathway have a special leaf anatomy, with prominent bundle sheath cells surrounding the leaf vascular bundles (veins) and closely arranged mesophyll cells (Fig. 1-3). C_4 grasses also have chloroplasts in both the mesophyll and bundle sheath cells.

The initial carboxylation process in C_4 grasses is identical to that outlined for C_3 grasses. However, C_4 plants have evolved an effi-

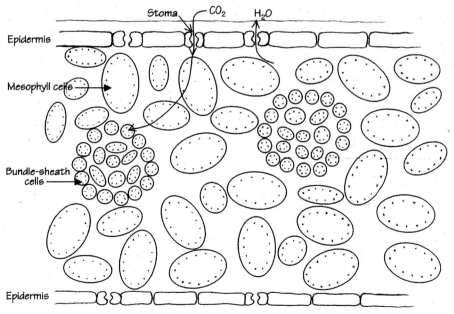

Figure 1-3
Leaf structure for C_4 turfgrasses (drawing by Angie Settle).

cient scheme for capturing CO_2 and creating high concentrations of CO_2 inside bundle sheath cells to react with rubisco in the Calvin-Benson cycle. As in the C_3 pathway, CO_2 enters the leaves through the stomata in C_4 plants. When absorbed into the mesophyll cells, the CO_2 then forms bicarbonate (HCO_3^-) in water. Bicarbonate reacts with a three-carbon compound, phosphoenolpyruvate (PEP), to form a four-carbon compound, oxaloacetate, which is then converted into malate in the chloroplasts of mesophyll cells. This process is catalyzed by the enzyme PEP carboxylase.

$$HCO_3^- + \underset{\text{Phosphoenolpyruvate}}{PEP} + H_2O \xrightarrow{\text{PEP carboxylase}} \underset{\text{Oxaloacetate}}{OAA} \text{ (4 carbon)} + Pi$$

Malate is next transported to adjacent bundle sheath cells and decarboxylated, causing the release of CO_2. A high concentration of CO_2 accumulates in the bundle sheath cells for carbon fixation. This released CO_2 is refixed by rubisco and assimilated using the enzymes and reactions of the Calvin–Benson cycle, eventually forming sugars.

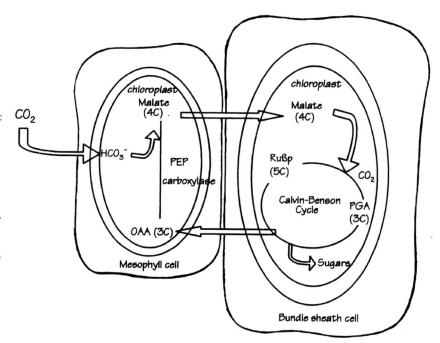

Figure 1-4
The C_4 photosynthetic pathway. The path of CO_2 from air to initial fixation in mesophyll cells to its release in bundle sheath cells and entry into the Calvin– Benson cycle. (PEP = Phosphoenol pyruvate; OAA = Oxaloacetate; RuBp = Ribulose 1,5-bisphosphate; PGA = 3-phosphoglycerate) (drawing by Angie Settle).

Compared to C_3 plants, photorespiration is minimal in C_4 plants. Unlike RuBP carboxylase, PEP carboxylase only catalyzes the carboxylation of PEP (the addition of CO_2 to PEP) using HCO_3^- in mesophyll cells, and the enzyme does not react with oxygen; hence, there is no competition between CO_2 and O_2 in this reaction. In addition, C_4 plants avoid photorespiration by locating the carbon fixation steps or Calvin-Benson cycle in the bundle sheath cells, where the rubisco enzyme is saturated with CO_2, deterring oxygenase activity and any photorespiration. Furthermore, in the cytoplasm of photosynthetic cells, CO_2 is in equilibrium with HCO_3^-, and under physiological conditions, this equilibrium results in a HCO_3^- concentration that is many times greater than that of CO_2.

Grasses that use the C_4 pathway are well adapted to hot and arid climates and exhibit higher photosynthetic efficiency and use water more efficiently than cool-season grasses for the following reasons:

■ Optimal temperatures for photosynthesis are lower in C_3 than in C_4 plants.

■ Photorespiration is greater at higher temperatures, reducing carbohydrate production through photosynthesis and negatively affecting energy available to C_3 plants.

■ C_4 plants continue fixing carbon and producing carbohydrates using CO_2 concentrated in the bundle sheath cells, even when stomata are closed on hot, dry days. (Once the accumulated CO_2 in bundle sheath cells is used, however, carbohydrate production ceases.)

■ C_4 plants generally have fewer stomata than C_3 plants and lose less water while CO_2 is being fixed, therefore exhibiting high water use efficiency.

Factors Affecting Photosynthesis

Light

Photosynthesis occurs only when sufficient light is available. Except for turfgrasses growing in shade, light intensity does not normally limit turf photosynthesis. The photosynthetic rate of C_3 plants increases with light intensity to a peak and then plateaus (Fig. 1-5). The level of light intensity at which photosynthesis reaches a maximum is referred to as the light saturation point (LSP). C_4 plants typically have a higher LSP than C_3 plants. Some C_4 plants do not become light saturated even in full sunlight. Very high light intensities may bleach chlorophyll and retard photosynthesis, but

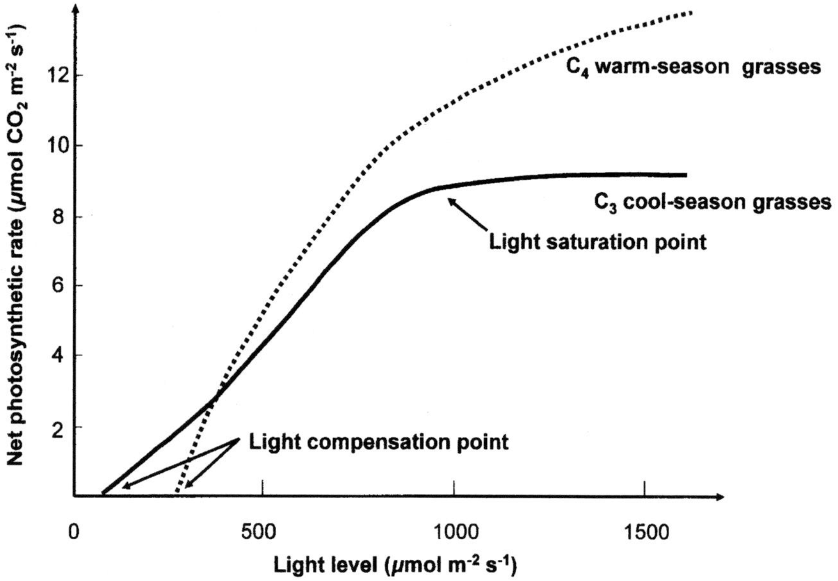

Figure 1-5
Photosynthetic responses of cool- and warm-season grasses to increasing light levels. Note the higher light compensation points for warm-season grasses and light saturation than that which occurs in cool-season grasses.

plants that typically grow under such conditions have evolved mechanisms for protection, such as thick leaf cuticles or hairy leaves to reflect light.

Plant injury resulting from high light intensity is due not to the light per se but to an excess of light energy over that utilized by photosynthesis. When light reaching the leaves is not used for photosynthesis, the excess energy triggers production of free radicals that can damage cells (oxidative damage). This often occurs when light intensity is high but photosynthesis is inhibited due to stress from temperature extremes, drought, or excessive soil water.

When light intensity is at a low level where photosynthesis and respiration reach equilibrium and the net carbon gain is zero, no plant growth will occur. This light level is the light compensation point (LCP). Leaves exposed to light levels below the LCP for an extended period of time will eventually senesce. Both LSP and LCP vary among turfgrass species and with temperature and CO_2 concentration. Under high irradiance, warm-season grasses maintain a higher rate of photosynthesis than cool-season grasses. However, cool-season grasses have a lower LCP and exhibit higher photosynthetic rates under low light levels compared to warm-season grasses. Photosynthetic rates of both warm-season and cool-season grasses exhibit a diurnal pattern on clear, sunny days, increasing from sunrise, reaching a maximum around noon, and then decreasing to the lowest levels by sunset.

Photosynthesis is affected by light duration because it occurs only during daylight. Increasing light duration may not increase the rate of carbon fixation, but the total amount of carbon fixed by photosynthesis will increase due to increased light exposure.

Sunlight has all the colors of visible light and is composed of different wavelengths. Not all wavelengths are equally effective in driving photosynthesis, however. Most photosynthetic activity is stimulated by blue and red wavelengths—chlorophylls absorb blue and red light and carotenoids absorb blue light. Green light is reflected, thus giving plants their green color. Green-yellow and far red are transmitted through the leaf. Light quality is important under artificial light (some turf managers have resorted to using supplemental artificial light) and shade. Turf in the shade of a tree receives primarily green-yellow and far-red wavelengths. Artificial lights emit a different pattern of wavelengths: fluorescent lights are highest in the blue and yellow-orange region of the spectrum but low in the red, and incandescent (tungsten) lights are poor in the blue region, moderate in the green region, and high in the red and far red region of the spectrum, with up to 50 percent of their output in the infrared region.

Temperature Many reactions in photosynthesis are controlled by temperature-sensitive enzymes; therefore photosynthesis is sensitive to temperature change (Fig. 1-6). Depending on turfgrass species, photosynthesis can occur between 32 and 104°F (0 and 40°C). The optimal temperature range for photosynthesis in cool-season grasses is 68 to 77°F (20 to 25°C), and for warm-season grasses it is 86 to 95°F (30 to 35°C). It is clear that optimal temperatures for photosynthesis in C_3 and C_4 grasses are in line with the preferred temperatures for plant growth.

As the plant's enzymes function closer to their optimal working temperature in cool-season grasses, photosynthetic rates double with increasing temperature from 50 to 68°F (10 to 20°C). When cool-season grasses are exposed to heat stress, photosynthetic rates decline because of greater photorespiration and possible enzyme denaturation. When exposed to full sunlight and high temperatures, C_4 grasses are able to produce twice the dry matter that C_3 grasses can produce.

CO₂ Concentration

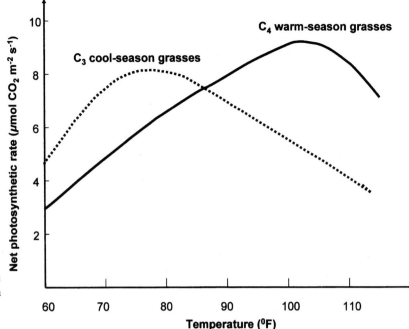

Figure 1-6
Photosynthetic responses
of cool- and warm-season
grasses to increasing
temperature.

Carbon dioxide concentration directly affects photosynthetic rates, as CO_2 is assimilated into organic compounds in photosynthesis. Photosynthetic rates increase with increasing CO_2 concentrations. The optimal short-term CO_2 concentration is about 500 ppm, but prolonged exposure to high concentrations can cause damage.

The CO_2 concentration at which carbon fixation in photosynthesis is in balance with carbon loss through respiration is called the CO_2 compensation point. Warm-season grasses are more efficient at assimilating CO_2 than cool-season grasses. The net carbon gain of C_3 grasses usually reaches zero at CO_2 concentrations of 50 to 100 ppm, whereas net CO_2 fixation for C_4 plants becomes negative only when CO_2 concentrations are as low as 5 to 15 ppm. Low CO_2 concentrations limit carbohydrate production in C_3 grasses more than in C_4 grasses due to higher levels of photorespiration in the former.

In exposed areas, wind mixes the air and brings CO_2 to turfgrass plants from the upper atmosphere. The normal atmospheric concentration of CO_2 (350 to 400 ppm) is usually not seriously limiting.

However, in wooded, enclosed areas where air movement is restricted, CO_2 concentrations may limit photosynthesis.

Water   Turfgrass leaves and roots contain about 80 percent water, and stems contain about 50 percent water. Photosynthesis is sensitive to changes in plant water status and is inhibited when water deficits or excesses occur. Inhibition of photosynthesis under water stress may be due to stomatal closure and/or metabolic limitations.

Stomata control the entry of CO_2 into the leaves for photosynthesis (Fig. 1-1 and Fig. 1-3). If the plant has too little or too much water, stomata will close and limit the entry of CO_2 into leaves, and thus chloroplasts can be deprived of CO_2 needed for photosynthesis. Stomatal closure is often thought to be the first plant response to water stress, and it can occur within seconds. Even a slight water deficit, with no visible signs of wilt, can lead to stomatal closure and a reduction in photosynthesis.

Water may also indirectly affect photosynthesis by regulating the synthesis of abscisic acid (ABA), a plant hormone. Abscisic acid production increases in roots in response to a water deficit and is then transported to leaves via the xylem and into the guard cells, inducing stomatal closure. Limitations of photosynthesis resulting from stomatal closure can easily be detected indirectly by a measured increase in leaf temperature due to reduced transpirational cooling.

Plant water status also influences photosynthesis by affecting carboxylating enzymes, electron transport, and chlorophyll content. Ultimately, it is the splitting of water molecules using solar energy during photosynthesis that generates the electrons needed to reduce NADP to NADPH, which in turn reduces CO_2 to carbohydrates, driving plant energy production. Lack of water also can directly affect electron transport, which occurs in the light reactions and through which ATP is generated from ADP. Many enzymes are involved in the conversion of solar energy to chemical energy and in carbon fixation. Water deficits and excesses limit the activity of various photosynthesizing enzymes, particularly RuBP and PEP carboxylase.

Nutrient Availability   Nutrient availability is equally important for photosynthesis in both warm- and cool-season grasses. Nitrogen and magnesium are essential constituents of the chlorophyll molecule, and iron serves as an activator for enzymes involved in chlorophyll synthesis. Sulfur is involved in photosynthetic electron transport and is a constituent of several iron-sulfur proteins that are intermediates in the process, as are manganese and copper. Chlorine is required for photosynthetic oxygen evolution. Lack of nutrients also induces stomatal closure, leading to reduced photosynthesis. Potassium acts as an osmoregulator, and its accumulation promotes the maintenance of cell turgor and stomatal opening, thus affecting photosynthesis.

Leaf
Characteristics
Leaves contain chlorophyll, which traps the sun's energy, and the photosynthetic rate typically increases with increasing chlorophyll content. Plants with greater leaf area also have higher rates of canopy photosynthesis. Damaged, senescent, or diseased leaves have lower photosynthetic rates than healthy leaves. As leaf angle increases, lower leaves become shaded and total light absorption decreases, resulting in lower photosynthetic rates. Pubescent leaves reflect more light and are less photosynthetically efficient.

RESPIRATION

Respiration is the process plants use to release the energy stored in the chemical bonds of sugars that are produced during photosynthesis (Fig. 1-7). Warm- and cool-season turfgrass species have the same respiratory pathway. Unlike photosynthesis, respiration takes place in all living parts of a plant, including leaves, stems, crowns, stolons, rhizomes, and roots. Respiration is carried out inside the numerous mitochondria of cells during the day and night. Mitochondria are membrane-enclosed organelles distributed through the cytosol of all plant cells (Fig. 1-7). Their main function is to convert energy from carbohydrates to NADH and ultimately into ATP. Respiration, like photosynthesis, involves a set of complex chemical reactions that accomplish the breaking and formation of chemical bonds. Respiratory energy is the driving force for metabolism, cell maintenance, growth, and nutrient uptake and transport processes.

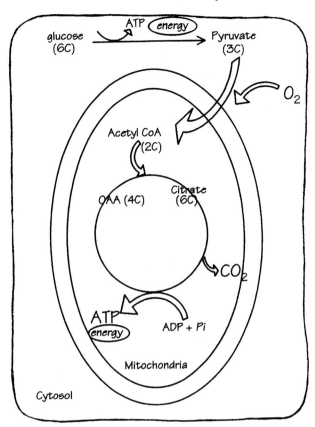

Figure 1-7
Respiration (also referred to as the Krebs cycle, citric acid cycle or ATP production cycle) as it occurs inside the mitochondria of all plant cells. (OAA = Oxaloacetic acid.)

Aerobic respiration is a biological process whereby carbohydrates (mainly glucose produced in photosynthesis or released when stored starch is hydrolyzed) are used to produce energy in the presence of oxygen. The first step in respiration is the splitting of the glucose molecule, through a process called glycolysis, to form two molecules of pyruvic acid. Energy released in glycolysis is coupled to the synthesis of ATP, the high-energy-storage molecule. For each molecule of glucose that enters glycolysis, two molecules of ADP are converted into ATP. Each molecule of pyruvic acid has the potential to generate eighteen ATP molecules. Thus the two molecules of pyruvic acid yield thirty-six ATPs, plus two from glycolysis, to yield a total of thirty-eight ATP molecules from each molecule of glucose. Chemical energy stored in ATP is essential for plant cell maintenance, growth, and development. The energy production process of respiration can be expressed using the following formula:

$$\text{Carbohydrates} + 12O_2 \xrightarrow{\text{Enzymes}} 12CO_2 + 12H_2O \; + \; \text{ATP}$$

(Sucrose)   (Chemical energy)

In some cases, such as in flooded or compacted soils, living tissues can respire in the absence of oxygen using anaerobic respiration (fermentation). This does not release as much energy as aerobic respiration, and it produces waste products, such as ethanol, that can be toxic to the plant. This respiration pathway produces only two ATP molecules from each glucose molecule. Therefore, aerobic respiration is nineteen times more efficient than anaerobic respiration. However, if oxygen is not available, anaerobic respiration replaces aerobic respiration to allow glycolysis to continue and keep plants alive, at least for a while.

Factors Affecting Respiration

Respiration rate depends on the availability of carbohydrates for enzyme function and energy production. Plants with low carbohydrate reserves cannot support high respiration rates for long. When the carbohydrate supply is exhausted, proteins can be used in respiration, but this will limit plant growth or result in no net growth.

Carbohydrate Availability

Leaves receiving full sunlight have higher respiration rates than shaded leaves, probably because there are more sugars available as a result of higher rates of photosynthesis. In fact, leaf respiration rates are much higher just after sunset, when sugar levels are high, than just before sunrise, when sugars have been consumed overnight.

Oxygen Availability

Oxygen is required for plants to carry out aerobic respiration and for efficient energy production. Ambient air contains a sufficient oxygen supply for aerobic respiration under normal conditions. The rate of oxygen penetration or diffusion into leaves, stems, and roots is usually adequate to maintain normal intracellular levels. Low ambient O_2 supplies can occur in flooded, saturated, frozen, or compacted soils. Under such conditions, aerobic respiration is inhibited, resulting in low energy production, and plants may employ anaerobic respiration. Low oxygen levels are less detrimental for respiration and growth under low temperatures (as in winter) than they are under high temperatures (as in summer) due to differences in the demand for O_2.

Temperature   There is an optimal temperature for respiration in all turfgrass species, with a higher optimum for warm-season than for cool-season grasses. Respiration ceases at temperatures near freezing and increases exponentially with temperature. Extremely high temperatures eventually result in reduced respiration as substrates become exhausted, enzymes become denatured, and tissues deteriorate. For most plant species, the respiration rate doubles for every 18°F (10°C) rise in temperature between 41 and 77°F (5 and 25°C).

Water   Respiration requires many enzymes that do not function if the plant is under stress from either too little water or too much. Lack of water restricts carbohydrate availability, in part because water acts as a solvent for carbohydrates during transport and metabolism. Excessive soil water inhibits root respiration by reducing oxygen diffusion rate and availability. Oxygen diffuses ten thousand times more slowly in water than in air. Low root respiration rates are common in waterlogged or frozen soils.

Nutrient Availability   Nitrogen stimulates respiration due to an increased demand for growth, ion transport, and nitrogen assimilation. Nitrate application can result in higher root respiration rates relative to ammonium, possibly due to the greater demands for metabolic energy required for nitrate uptake and reduction to ammonia. Phosphorus is a component of enzymes and proteins involved in respiration and a major constituent of the energy transfer molecule ATP. As such, respiration rates are lower when a phosphorus deficiency exists.

Plant Physiological Condition and Age   There is generally a positive correlation between growth rate and respiration rate. Younger tissues or plants have higher respiration rates than older ones. Root tips and shoot meristems have high respiration rates. Senescent leaves still respire for limited maintenance but have a low rate of growth respiration. Much of the respiration in mature plants occurs in young leaves and roots and in growing flowers.

Balance between Photosynthesis and Respiration

Respiration involves carbohydrate consumption and energy release, whereas photosynthesis is a carbohydrate production and energy absorption process. Between 25 and 75 percent of all the carbohydrates produced per day are respired by the plant, depending on turfgrass species and growing conditions. Plant carbohydrates that are not used for respiration will be translocated to non-photosynthesizing storage organs (such as the crown, stems, stolons, rhizomes, roots, and seeds) or stored temporarily in the photosynthesizing tissues (leaves).

Sucrose is the most common carbohydrate transported in plants. Starch and fructans, on the other hand, serve as storage carbohydrates. Fructans are the predominant storage carbohydrate in cool-season grasses, whereas starch is the most prevalent in warm-season grasses. Stored starch or fructans are broken down into more usable forms (sucrose or glucose) when carbohydrate supplies are low. Glucose, fructose, sucrose, and fructans are water-soluble carbohydrates (WSCs), and they accumulate in leaves and stems. Water-soluble carbohydrates are readily available for use in metabolism and growth. Total nonstructural carbohydrates (TNCs) are composed of WSCs and starch and are often used as a measure of total carbohydrate reserves. When plants are actively growing or producing flowers and seeds, the demands for energy are high, and stored carbohydrates are used as an energy source, resulting in a decline in the carbohydrate concentration. If growth is slow and the demand for energy is low while photosynthesis continues at a rapid rate, carbohydrates will accumulate.

Maintenance of a positive carbohydrate balance is important for plant health. This results when the net accumulation of carbohydrates from photosynthesis exceeds consumption in respiration (Fig. 1-8). A positive carbohydrate balance allows plant growth to continue after the plant's maintenance needs have been addressed. The plant demands more carbohydrates for growth than for maintenance or storage. When carbohydrate production is insufficient to meet plant needs, the stored carbohydrates are used for growth until they are exhausted. At that point, growth will decline, and the plant may die from carbohydrate starvation (Fig. 1-8), although metabolic dysfunctions will probably prove lethal before carbohydrates are exhausted.

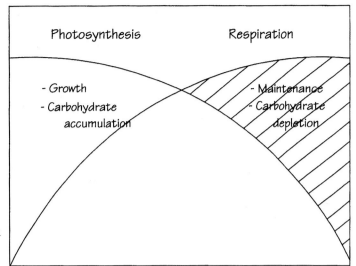

Figure 1-8
When photosynthesis exceeds respiration, growth and carbohydrate accumulation result. When respiration required for cell maintenance exceeds photosynthesis, carbohydrate depletion results, which may result in starvation (drawing by Angie Settle).

Any environmental condition or cultural practice that reduces carbohydrate production in photosynthesis or increases carbohydrate consumption in respiration to a level where carbohydrate depletion occurs can have a negative effect on plant health. For example, nitrogen fertilizer application has long been known to reduce carbohydrate levels in leaf and crown tissues. The decline in reserve carbohydrates in response to nitrogen may result from the increased shoot growth and respiration that are stimulated by its application.

Respiration has a higher optimal temperature than photosynthesis. High temperatures increase respiration rates and can lead to carbohydrate depletion, particularly when photosynthesis starts to decline (see Fig. 1-8). WSC content increases during the day, when photosynthesis takes place, and decreases during the nighttime due to respiration. Long exposure of turfgrass to shaded conditions and persistent low mowing heights reduces canopy photosynthetic capacity while maintenance respiration continues, and this can result in carbohydrate depletion.

An adequate supply of storage carbohydrates is extremely important for winter survival and spring regrowth of perennial grasses, as leaves senesce and photosynthetic capacity is much reduced in cool-season grasses and nonexistent in warm-season grasses during the winter. In warm-season grasses, carbohydrate reserves are necessary for plant respiration during winter dormancy, when photosynthesis is not possible but crowns and roots remain alive. Therefore, proper turfgrass management in the fall must maximize carbohydrate production and avoid depletion of food reserves during winter.

2

Turfgrasses

Turfgrass selection is guided most prominently by the ability of particular species and cultivars to prosper under the climatic conditions in a given area. Zones of turfgrass adaptation are broadly grouped as cool-humid, cool-arid, warm-humid, warm-arid, and the transition zone. Generally, cool-season grasses are grown as perennials in the cool-humid and cool-arid zones, and warm-season grasses are grown as perennials in the warm-humid and warm-arid zones.

There are some exceptions, however. Use of creeping bentgrass, a cool-season grass, has been extended southward into regions best suited to warm-season grasses because it provides a superior putting surface on golf greens. Cool-season grasses are used to provide green color and protection on dormant warm-season grasses growing in warm-humid and warm-arid zones. Overseeding is done in early autumn, and the cool-season species is expected to establish itself quickly, flourish until high temperatures return and impose stress, and then die and transition out smoothly so the warm-season species is not impeded by the competition.

Likewise, there are occasions when warm-season grasses, particularly bermudagrass, may be used as an annual on a sports field in a cool-humid or cool-arid zone. Sports turf managers that are in need of some type of cover when other remedies have failed may choose to seed non-hardy bermudagrass in the spring and encourage its growth through the summer. If all bermudagrass is lost due to freezing injury, the process may be repeated the following year.

The transition zone is a somewhat loosely defined region, the center of which extends from northeastern New Mexico through

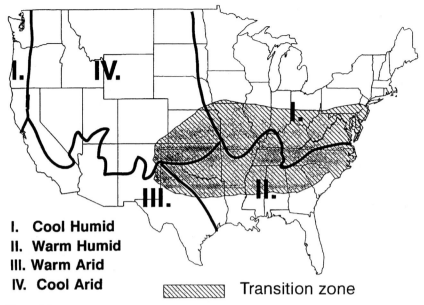

I. Cool Humid
II. Warm Humid
III. Warm Arid
IV. Cool Arid

▨▨▨▨ Transition zone

Figure 2-1
Climatic zones of turfgrass distribution in the United States. (Reprinted with
permission from Christians and Engelke, 1994. Copyright CRC Press, Boca Raton,
Florida.)

Virginia (see Fig. 2-1). This is one of the most difficult regions in the
United States to maintain turf quality, for warm-season grasses
commonly suffer low-temperature injury and cool-season grasses
suffer heat stress. As a result, there seems to be a cyclic trend in
which grasses are most popular. When a stretch of years with high
summer and moderate winter temperatures occurs, warm-season
grasses have the upper hand. When cold winters are the present
trend, cool-season grasses are back in favor.

COOL-SEASON TURFGRASSES

Preferred air temperature for shoot growth of cool-season grasses is
between 64 and 75°F (16 and 24°C), whereas root growth is most
prolific with a soil temperature between 50 and 64°F (10 and 18°C).
In northern zones of adaptation, this results in shoot and root
growth peaks in both spring and fall, with spring tending to favor
the greatest growth of each (Fig. 2-3).

Figure 2-2
This golf course in Atlanta, Georgia, employs both cool- and warm-season turfgrasses, which is typical of many in the transition zone.

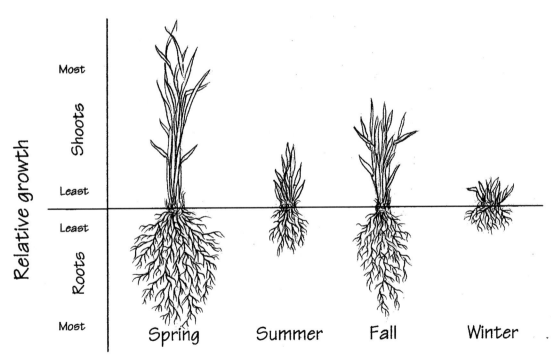

Figure 2-3
Relative shoot and root growth patterns for cool-season turfgrasses (drawing by Angie Settle).

ANNUAL BLUEGRASS
(*Poa annua* L.)

Growth habit: bunchgrass

Characteristics: Annual bluegrass is a winter annual that emerges in early autumn, grows vegetatively through the fall and early spring, and flowers in late spring before dying. *Poa annua* var. *reptans* lives as a weak, stoloniferous perennial if growing conditions are satisfactory for its survival. Both the annual and perennial types are prolific flower producers even at putting-green mowing heights. The large number of seedheads can give a whitish springtime appearance to turfs that have large populations of annual bluegrass. Annual bluegrass prefers cool, wet conditions and tolerates compacted soil. This tolerance often makes it the predominant species used for sports turfs, where compaction is excessive. Poor tolerance to heat and diseases commonly lead to the demise of annual bluegrass during summer months. Diseases of particular importance on annual bluegrass are dollar spot, summer patch, and anthracnose.

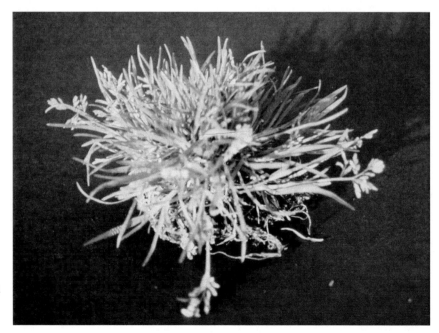

Figure 2-4
Annual bluegrass with characteristic seedheads.

Uses: On only rare occasions is annual bluegrass planted as the desired turf. In all other cases, it encroaches.

Residential Lawns	General Grounds	Sports Fields	Golf Courses			Native Areas
			Putting Greens	Tees	Fairways	
X	X	X	X	X	X	

Tolerance to environmental stresses: Although annual bluegrass is found in most locations of the world, it will perform well during only a short portion of the year in many temperate regions due to its poor tolerance to heat, drought, and cold temperatures.

Stress	Overall Resistance
Heat	Poor
Cold	Fair
Drought	Poor
Shade	Good

KENTUCKY BLUEGRASS
(*Poa pratensis* L.)

Growth habit: Rhizomatous

Characteristics: Kentucky bluegrass is recognized for its ability to create a high-quality turf. Although it is relatively slow to establish from seed, its rhizomatous growth habit and ability to knit have made it a champion of the sod industry. Kentucky bluegrass is commonly included in mixtures with turf-type fescue at levels of about 5 percent by weight to enhance knitting of sod and speed recovery of damaged areas on sports turfs. Common, recurring pest problems that may reduce turf quality include white grubs, billbugs, and the root-infecting diseases summer patch and necrotic ring spot.

Uses:

Residential Lawns	General Grounds	Sports Fields	Golf Courses			Native Areas
			Putting Greens	Tees	Fairways	
X	X	X		X	X	

Figure 2-5
Side view of a
Kentucky bluegrass.
(Photo courtesy of
Turf Producers
International.)

Tolerance to environmental stresses: Heat and drought stress can be trouble-some on Kentucky bluegrass lawns during the summer. Although non-irrigated bluegrass may go dormant, it often recovers once cool autumn temperatures and accompanying precipitation return. Kentucky bluegrass has only fair shade tolerance and is often used in mixtures with fine fescues in lawns where significant shading occurs.

Stress	Overall Resistance
Heat	Good
Cold	Excellent
Drought	Good
Shade	Fair

Cultivars: Prior to the release of Merion Kentucky bluegrass in 1945, only common-type Kentucky bluegrass cultivars were available. These included South Dakota Common, Park, and Kenblue. The primary disadvantage of these cultivars was their high susceptibility to leaf spot disease. Merion was the first cultivar released with good resistance to leaf spot. Common Kentucky bluegrasses may still be well suited for use in areas that are considered low maintenance.

Since the advent of Merion, many new Kentucky bluegrass cultivars have been released. In fact, there is a tremendous range of genetic diversity

Figure 2-6
A Kentucky bluegrass baseball field in Kansas City, Missouri.

among Kentucky bluegrass cultivars, and it is important to select cultivars that are well adapted to a particular climatic region. Researchers at Rutgers University have grouped Kentucky bluegrass cultivars into three general categories, with subgroupings under each (Bonos, Meyer, and Murphy 2000). Placement of cultivars into categories and subgroups is based upon their genetic lineage. The compact-America bluegrass cultivars, with a genetic background similar to the original America cultivar (including the cultivars Unique, Apollo, Brilliant, and Showcase), have exhibited good summer performance at golf course fairway mowing heights (Kraft 2003).

ROUGHSTALK BLUEGRASS
(*Poa trivialis* L.)

Growth habit: stoloniferous

Characteristics: Rough bluegrass produces a fine-textured turf that performs well as long as temperatures are reasonably cool and plenty of moisture is available. In recent years, it has been recognized as a significant weed problem that is unknowingly established with desired turfgrass stands when it is contained in seed lots and included in the "other crop" category on the label. Its stoloniferous growth habit leads it to segregate in circular patches in lawns of Kentucky bluegrass, tall fescue, or other grasses. Often the presence of rough bluegrass goes unnoticed until summer heat and drought take their toll and decline is evident. Declining patches of heat-intolerant rough bluegrass in lawns are often mistakenly identified as diseases.

Uses: In northern climates, rough bluegrass may be used in wet, shady areas where other grasses may not perform well. The most valuable use for rough bluegrass, however, is as a winter overseeded grass on bermudagrass turfs in warm climates. Rough bluegrass establishes fairly quickly and, most important, transitions out well in the spring when turf managers are anxious for bermudagrass to become the predominant species once again.

Residential Lawns	General Grounds	Sports Fields	Golf Courses			Native Areas
			Putting Greens	Tees	Fairways	
X	X		X			

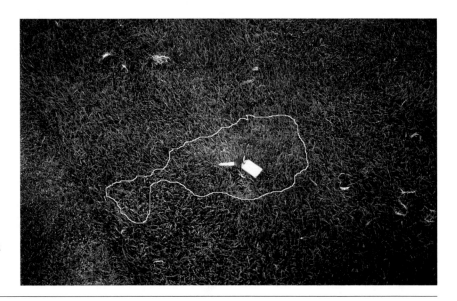

Figure 2-7
Rough bluegrass (outlined) growing in a stand of perennial ryegrass.

Tolerance to environmental stresses: Because rough bluegrass prefers wet conditions, over irrigation can promote its spread in a desirable turf.

Stress	Overall Resistance
Heat	Poor
Cold	Excellent
Drought	Poor
Shade	Fair to Good

Cultivars: Few cultivars available; Sabre is one that is commonly used.

TALL FESCUE
(*Festuca arundinacea* Schreb.)

Growth habit: Bunchgrass or weakly rhizomatous

Characteristics: Tall fescue has a medium to coarse texture, moderate density, and a deeper, more extensive root system than most other cool-season turfgrasses. Tall fescue germinates faster than Kentucky bluegrass but slightly slower than perennial ryegrass. Its bunch-type habit requires overseeding to fill in voids if significant stand loss occurs.

Uses:

Residential Lawns	General Grounds	Sports Fields	Golf Courses			Native Areas
			Putting Greens	Tees	Fairways	
X	X	X				

Tolerance to environmental stresses: Tall fescue has the best heat and drought resistance of the cool-season turfgrasses. Its exceptional drought resistance is due to an extensive root system that allows the plant to avoid drought as long as water is available deep in the soil. Tall fescue also has good shade tolerance. Greater tolerance to environmental stresses relative to Kentucky bluegrass have greatly increased the popularity of tall fescue for use in lawns in the transition zone and upper South of the United States.

Stress	Overall Resistance
Heat	Very good
Cold	Very good
Drought	Very good
Shade	Very good

Figure 2-8
A tall fescue sod production field in California. Notice the netting that is used to help hold the sod together and speed the time required before harvest.

Figure 2-9
A tall fescue home lawn in Lawrence, Kansas.

Figures 2-10 and 2-11
Side views of a coarse-textured, pasture-type tall fescue (top) and a turf-type tall fescue (bottom). (Photo courtesy of Turf Producers International.)

Cultivars: Tall fescue cultivars can be broadly categorized into two groups: pasture types and turf types. The pasture-type cultivars were the first to be used as turfgrasses, and include Kentucky-31, Alta, and Fawn. Although better cultivars are available, these are still used extensively in some parts of the United States.

Turf-type cultivars have a finer texture and better density than the pasture-types and are preferred for home lawns. There are over one hundred turf-type cultivars presently on the market. Some of the turf-type cultivars are referred to as dwarf types in recognition of their slower vertical growth habit. The list of dwarf-type cultivars includes Bonsai II, Rebel Jr., Short-stop, Trailblazer, Pixie, and Mini-Mustang. Although the slower growth rate may result in less mowing, these cultivars have also exhibited poorer drought resistance and poorer recovery from brown patch infestations.

FINE FESCUES
(*Festuca* spp.)

Growth habit: Rhizomatous or bunchgrass

Characteristics: Fine fescue is a broad term that refers to species whose aboveground appearance is somewhat similar. These species include creeping red fescue (*F. rubra* L.), Chewings fescue (*F. rubra* ssp. *commutata* Gaud.), hard fescue (*F. longifolia* Thuill.), and sheep fescue (*F. ovina* L.). Growth habits differ among the species, with creeping red fescue being rhizomatous and Chewings, hard, and sheep fescues being bunchgrasses.

Uses: Fine fescues are often included in mixtures with other grasses, such as Kentucky bluegrass and perennial ryegrass, where a good portion of the lawn may be shaded. Fine fescues also may be used as low-maintenance grasses in nonirrigated or unmowed areas. Where well adapted, un-mowed fine fescues create a unique landscape appeal on steep banks.

Residential Lawns	General Grounds	Sports Fields	Golf Courses			Native Areas
			Putting Greens	Tees	Fairways	
X	X					

Tolerance to environmental stresses: Fine fescues are revered for their ability to tolerate moderate to heavy shade where soil remains relatively dry. Although full-sun plantings may be successful in some regions of the country, heat and drought stress take their toll on these species in the transition zone, and turf quality declines quickly.

Stress	Overall Resistance
Heat	Fair
Cold	Excellent
Drought	Very good
Shade	Very good to Excellent

Cultivars: Several cultivars of each of the fine fescue species are available.

Figure 2-12
Side view of a fine fescue turf. (Photo courtesy of Turf Producers International.)

PERENNIAL RYEGRASS
(*Lolium perenne* L.)

Growth habit: Bunchgrass

Characteristics: Perennial ryegrass produces a dense, fine-textured turf. Probably the most desirable characteristic of perennial ryegrass is its fast germination and establishment rate. It is not unusual for germination to occur in four days during good conditions, and a good stand of turf can be achieved within just a few weeks. Maintaining perennial ryegrass quality through hot summer months can require a significant investment in fungicides. Susceptibility to brown patch, Pythium blight, and gray leaf spot has

Figure 2-13
Side view of a perennial ryegrass turf. (Photo courtesy of Turf Producers International.)

led many turf managers to seek other grasses that are less costly to maintain.

Uses: Although perennial ryegrass may be used alone on sports turfs, such as golf course fairways, it is seldom seeded alone in lawn mixtures. It is commonly mixed with Kentucky bluegrass, although including ryegrass as more than about 20 percent of the mixture by weight will result in a stand that is predominantly ryegrass. Perennial ryegrass is also commonly used in the southern United States for winter overseeding of warm-season grasses.

Residential Lawns	General Grounds	Sports Fields	Golf Courses			Native Areas
			Putting Greens	Tees	Fairways	
X	X	X	X	X	X	

Tolerance to environmental stresses: Perennial ryegrass has only fair heat tolerance, which is a disadvantage for those managing it as a perennial turf but a positive attribute that speeds spring transition when it is used for winter overseeding in southern climates. It generally has good cold tolerance, although extremely low temperatures, particularly in combination with ice cover, can result in significant loss of turf.

Stress	Overall Resistance
Heat	Fair
Cold	Good
Drought	Fair
Shade	Poor

Figure 2-14
The ability to germinate and establish rapidly is a favorite characteristic of perennial ryegrass. Here, three weeks after seeding, perennial ryegrass is much further along in development than the Kentucky bluegrasses and bentgrasses with which it was seeded.

Figure 2-15
The bunch-type habit of perennial ryegrass (left) relative to Kentucky bluegrass is evident in Colorado where turf received only natural rainfall for five years.

Figure 2-16
A perennial ryegrass golf course tee and fairway at Prarie Dunes Country Club, Hutchinson, Kansas.

Cultivars: Perennial ryegrass was originally used on pastures, and the first cultivars employed for turf had high lignin contents and would not cut cleanly. Linn, one of these cultivars, is still marketed today. Many new ryegrass cultivars are available for use, and selection often depends upon the purpose for which it used. For example, turf managers growing perennial ryegrass in the Midwest are interested in disease- and stress-resistant cultivars that reduce cultural inputs. Southern turf managers using perennial ryegrass for overseeding prefer cultivars that are sensitive to heat and warm-weather diseases and transition out quickly when temperatures begin to encourage growth of the underlying warm-season turf.

CREEPING BENTGRASS
(*Agrostis palustris* L.)

Growth habit: Stoloniferous

Characteristics: Creeping bentgrass produces a dense turf with a very fine texture. Its aggressive, stoloniferous habit makes it a candidate for rapid thatch accumulation. As such, a routine cultivation program that includes aerification, vertical mowing, and topdressing is necessary to maintain quality. Intensive maintenance that includes frequent mowing, irrigation, fertilization, and pesticide applications makes creeping bentgrass an illogical choice for homeowners.

Uses: Creeping bentgrass can be mowed at heights as low as 0.125 inches (3.2 mm). It produces the finest golf putting surface in the world, and until fairly recently it was used almost exclusively for putting greens or lawn bowling and tennis courts. The use of bentgrass has been expanded to include golf course tees and fairways, in part because of the expense involved in maintaining perennial ryegrass.

Residential Lawns	General Grounds	Sports Fields	Golf Courses			Native Areas
			Putting Greens	Tees	Fairways	
			X	X	X	

Figure 2-17
A creeping bentgrass putting green.

Tolerance to environmental stresses: Although creeping bentgrass has excellent cold resistance, it is susceptible to heat injury, particularly at putting-green mowing heights. Winter and summer desiccation is a concern when thatch accumulates and crowns and roots are elevated above the soil surface.

Stress	Overall Resistance
Heat	Fair
Cold	Excellent
Drought	Fair
Shade	Fair

Cultivars: Early creeping bentgrass cultivars were vegetative selections that arose from mixed stands of bentgrass species that were commonly referred to as South German bentgrass. Some of these vegetative types included Cohansey, Toronto, and Washington. From these vegetative types, seeded selections were developed. The most familiar seeded creeping bentgrass cultivar is Penncross, which can be found on putting greens throughout the world. Over the past ten to fifteen years, new varieties of creeping bentgrass have been released that are finer in texture and produce a denser canopy than Penncross at ultra low mowing heights. These cultivars include A-4, G-2, L-93, Cobra, Putter, and others. Management requirements for the new creeping bentgrass cultivars have not been well defined. However, it is clear that with greater density, there is a tendency to produce an organic layer on the surface, which necessitates frequent vertical mowing and topdressing.

COLONIAL BENTGRASS
(*Agrostis tenuis* L.)

Growth habit: Weakly rhizomatous and stoloniferous

Characteristics: Colonial bentgrass does not have the aggressive lateral spreading ability that creeping bentgrass does. It is quite susceptible to brown patch.

Uses: Colonial bentgrass is found in home lawns in the Pacific Northwest and other cool, wet regions. It does not tolerate the low mowing heights that creeping bentgrass does and is therefore better suited to use on golf course fairways and tees.

Residential Lawns	General Grounds	Sports Fields	Golf Courses			Native Areas
			Putting Greens	Tees	Fairways	
X	X			X	X	

Tolerance to environmental stresses:

Stress	Overall Resistance
Heat	Fair
Cold	Excellent
Drought	Fair
Shade	Fair

Cultivars: Highland and Exeter are two commonly used cultivars. Additional breeding work is being done with this species.

Figure 2-18
Side view of colonial bentgrass. (Photo courtesy of Turf Producers International.)

VELVET BENTGRASS
(*Agrostis canina* L.)

Growth habit: Stoloniferous

Characteristics: Velvet bentgrass has a finer texture and produces a better putting surface than creeping bentgrass, yet its supposed lack of environmental tolerances and lack of research have limited the use of this species. Like creeping bentgrass, its strong stoloniferous habit makes it a heavy thatch producer.

Uses:

Residential Lawns	General Grounds	Sports Fields	Golf Courses			Native Areas
			Putting Greens	**Tees**	**Fairways**	
			X	X	X	

Tolerance to environmental stresses: Because velvet bentgrass has not been widely used in the United States, it was assumed that it was adapted only to cool, moist regions of the Northeast and Northwest. However, there is evidence to suggest that velvet bentgrass may have superior heat and drought tolerance compared to creeping bentgrass (Brilman and Meyer 2000).

Stress	Overall Resistance
Heat	Fair
Cold	Excellent
Drought	Fair
Shade	Fair

Cultivars: Vegetative selections were used early. The seeded cultivar Kingstown was developed through the University of Rhode Island. There is increasing interest in this species, and research to identify improved cultivars is ongoing at Rutgers University and the University of Rhode Island.

WARM-SEASON TURFGRASSES

The optimal range of air temperatures for shoot growth of warm-season grasses is 80 to 95°F (27 to 35°C), whereas the optimal range of soil temperatures for root growth is 75 to 85°F (24 to 29°C). As such, shoot and root growth exhibit one peak in midsummer where warm-season grasses are grown.

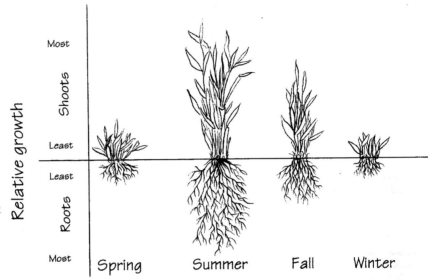

Figure 2-19
Relative shoot and root growth patterns for warm-season turfgrasses (drawing by Angie Settle).

Grasses Adapted to Southern Climates and the Transition Zone

BERMUDAGRASS
(*Cynodon* spp.)

Growth habit: Rhizomatous and stoloniferous

Characteristics: Bermudagrass is revered for its heat and drought tolerance and for its ability to produce an excellent turf at low mowing heights. Its exceptional recuperative ability under good growing conditions makes it a preferred species for many sports turf managers.

Uses:

Residential Lawns	General Grounds	Sports Fields	Golf Courses			Native Areas
			Putting Greens	Tees	Fairways	
X	X	X	X	X	X	

Tolerance to environmental stresses: Bermudagrass is sensitive to freezing temperatures and shade. Some cultivars have been selected for use in climates that experience very cold weather; use of cultivars other than these will likely result in winterkill

Stress	Overall Resistance
Heat	Excellent
Cold	Poor to Good
Drought	Excellent
Shade	Poor

Cultivars: Common bermudagrass (*C. dactylon*) is a coarse-textured grass with a gray-green color. Much variability exists among the common bermudagrasses. In and north of the transition zone, common bermudagrass may be present as a very coarse-textured weed with large,

Figure 2-20
Side view of hybrid bermudagrass. (Photo courtesy of Turf Producers International.)

aggressive rhizomes. Improved types of *C. dactylon* have also been developed that are finer in texture, denser, and somewhat less aggressive. Most *C. dactylon* cultivars are established by seed; as a general group, these seeded cultivars have poor to average cold hardiness. Exceptions include Yukon and Riviera, cultivars developed at Oklahoma State University. Quickstand is a *C. dactylon* cultivar with good cold hardiness that must be established vegetatively.

The highest-quality bermudagrass cultivars were developed by crossing *C. dactylon* with *C. transvaalensis*, African bermudagrass. African bermudagrass is a slow-growing species with a fine texture. Crossing these species produces a plant with quality features that combine the aggressiveness of *C. dactylon* and the high quality of *C. transvaalensis*. Genotypes developed from this cross are sterile and must be established vegetatively. The first vegetative bermudagrasses produced from this

Figure 2-21
A bermudagrass
lawn in southern
Florida.

cross included Tifway (sometimes referred to as 419), Tifgreen (328), and Tifdwarf, all of which were developed by Dr. Glen Burton, a forage and turf breeder based in Tifton, Georgia. These cultivars are still widely used, particularly Tifway. Some new vegetative bermudagrasses that are used on putting greens include Floradwarf, Mini-verde, Champion, and Tifeagle. These grasses perform well at very low mowing heights but require intensive cultivation to minimize thatch production.

Bermudagrass is also popular for use on golf courses and athletic fields in the Midwest, but winter injury is a primary concern. Cold-hardy vegetative bermudagrasses include Midlawn, Tifsport, Quickstand, and Patriot.

ZOYSIAGRASS
(*Zoysia* spp.)

Growth habit: Rhizomatous and stoloniferous

Characteristics: Zoysiagrass produces a dense, fine- to medium-textured turf that is medium to dark green in color. Density and turf quality can be maintained with relatively low inputs of fertilizer and pesticides. Leaves and stems contain silica and lignin, which make them very tough, stiff, and somewhat difficult to mow. Tissue is also slow to break down, which may lead to thatch accumulation.

Uses: Zoysiagrass is used extensively on golf courses in the transition zone. Slow recuperative potential and poor tolerance to soil compaction preclude its use on athletic fields.

Residential Lawns	General Grounds	Sports Fields	Golf Courses			Native Areas
			Putting Greens	Tees	Fairways	
X	X			X	X	

Tolerance to environmental stresses: Resistance to freezing temperatures and shade vary with cultivar. Freezing injury on Meyer zoysiagrass usually occurs where turf has been mismanaged with overapplication of nitrogen fertilizer and thatch becomes excessive. Emerald zoysiagrass has moderate shade tolerance and is used the southern United States for this purpose; it has poor freezing resistance.

Figure 2-22
Side view of a
Z. japonica turf.
(Photo courtesy of Turf
Producers International.)

Stress	Overall Resistance
Heat	Excellent
Cold	Poor to Good
Drought	Very good
Shade	Fair to Good

Cultivars: Highest-quality zoysiagrasses have traditionally arisen from vegetative cultivars, including Meyer, a *Zoysia japonica* cultivar that has good freezing resistance and is used throughout the transition zone of the United States. Another *Z. japonica* cultivar that is best suited for climates warmer than that of the transition zone is Emerald, a dense, dark green cultivar adapted to the southern United States that results from a cross between *Z. japonica* and *Z. tenuifolia*, a very fine textured, slow-growing species.

Texas A and M University released several zoysiagrass cultivars in the mid-1990s, including Cavalier, a stoloniferous *Z. matrella* with moderate shade tolerance; Crowne, a *Z. japonica* with good cold tolerance and aggressive growth; Diamond, a very fine-textured *Z. matrella* that tolerates low mowing and has good shade tolerance; and Palisades, a *Z. japonica* that has good quality for golf course fairways. Although all of these zoysiagrasses have a niche for use in warm, southern climates, their cold

Figure 2-23
A Meyer zoysiagrass golf course fairway in Kansas.

hardiness is not as good as Meyer; therefore, their use through the transition zone has been limited.

Some *Z. japonica* cultivars can be seeded, but a thick seed coat requires that the seed be treated before it is marketed. Unlike seeded bermudagrasses, most seeded zoysiagrasses are cold hardy. Zoysiagrass seed can require up to two weeks to germinate. Zenith is one popular seeded cultivar.

BUFFALOGRASS
(*Buchloe dactyloides* [Nutt.] Engelm.)

Growth habit: Stoloniferous

Characteristics: Buffalograss is the only turfgrass commonly used in the United States that is native to North America. Native buffalograss can be found growing from southern Texas up into Canada. It has a light green color and is most often used in low-maintenance areas. Buffalograss is dioecious, meaning there are male and female plants within a single stand of turf. Seeded stands contain both male and female plants, whereas new vegetative selections are composed of primarily female plants.

Figure 2-24
Side view of a
buffalograss turf.
(Photo courtesy of Turf
Producers International.)

Uses:

Residential Lawns	General Grounds	Sports Fields	Golf Courses			Native Areas
			Putting Greens	Tees	Fairways	
X	X				X	X

Figures 2-25 and 2-26. Close-ups of female (left) and male (right) buffalograss flowers.

Tolerance to environmental stresses: Buffalograss has good tolerance to all stresses except shade. Some of the newer vegetative selections that originated in warmer climates, such as the cultivar 609, may experience winter injury.

Stress	Overall Resistance
Heat	Excellent
Cold	Very good
Drought	Excellent
Shade	Poor

Cultivars: Seeded buffalograss cultivars include Sharp's Improved, Sharpshooter, Cody, Tatanka, and Bowie. High-quality vegetative buffalograss cultivars have been selected from female clones. Some of these include 609, 315, Legacy, and Prairie.

Figure 2-27. An improved, vegetative buffalograss turf used on a roadside median.

Grasses Adapted to Tropical Climates Only

ST. AUGUSTINEGRASS
(*Stenotaphrum secundatum* [Walt.] Kuntze)

Growth habit: Stoloniferous

Characteristics: St. Augustinegrass is a coarse-textured grass of light to medium green color. It forms a dense, prostrate turf that is virtually weed free, but thatch is a severe problem. It grows fast and has thick, fleshy stolons; thus establishment is quick and it has good recuperative potential. St. Augustinegrass is vegetatively propagated.

Uses: St. Augustinegrass has relatively poor tolerance to traffic and is used primarily in home lawns.

Residential Lawns	General Grounds	Sports Fields	Golf Courses			Native Areas
			Putting Greens	Tees	Fairways	
X	X					

Figure 2-28
Side view of
St. Augustinegrass.
(Photo courtesy of Turf
Producers International.)

Figure 2-29
A St. Augustinegrass lawn in
West Palm Beach, Florida.

Tolerance to environmental stresses: St. Augustinegrass is recognized for its relatively good shade tolerance and poor cold tolerance. Some cultivars, such as Floratam, have no capacity to acclimate to freezing temperatures.

Stress	Overall Resistance
Heat	Excellent
Cold	Poor
Drought	Good
Shade	Very good

Cultivars: Raleigh is a popular cultivar that has better freezing resistance than some. Floratam is recognized for its resistance to chinch bugs, although some strains of chinch bugs have overcome this resistance.

CENTIPEDEGRASS
(*Eremochloa ophiuroides* [Munro] Hack.)

Growth habit: Stoloniferous

Characteristics: Centipedegrass has a medium texture and medium to dark green leaves. It is usually established vegetatively but can be seeded. Centipedegrass has poor tolerance to traffic and is slow to recover from injury. Centipedegrass prefers a low pH (4.5 to 6) and is well adapted to growth on fine-textured soils in the Gulf coast region of the United States. Tissue is slow to degrade, and thatch accumulation is common when it is overfertilized with nitrogen.

Uses:

Residential Lawns	General Grounds	Sports Fields	Golf Courses			Native Areas
			Putting Greens	Tees	Fairways	
X	X					

Figure 2-30
Side view of centipedegrass. (Photo courtesy of Turf Producers International.)

Tolerance to environmental stresses: Centipedegrass has poor cold tolerance but is more resistant than St. Augustinegrass. Its shade tolerance is similar to that of St. Augustinegrass, but it does not perform as well on sandy soils, where nematodes are a potential pest problem.

Stress	Overall Resistance
Heat	Excellent
Cold	Poor
Drought	Good
Shade	Very good

Cultivars: Although there are cultivars, such as Oklawn and Centennial, common centipedegrass is most widely used.

BAHIAGRASS
(*Paspalum notatum* Flugge)

Growth habit: Rhizomatous

Characteristics: A fast-growing tropical grass that is coarse-textured and lacks density. Rhizomes are thick and fleshy. Bahiagrass produces a tall,

Figure 2-31
Side view of bahiagrass. (Photo courtesy of Turf Producers International.)

fibrous seed stalk that is difficult to mow. It is commonly used on roadsides in the southern United States, where it performs well due to its low maintenance requirement.

Uses: Bahiagrass can be found on many lawns in Florida and other states in the deep South. Best fit is as a low-maintenance turf for roadsides and other similar uses.

Residential Lawns	General Grounds	Sports Fields	Golf Courses			Native Areas
			Putting Greens	Tees	Fairways	
X	X					

Tolerance to environmental stresses:

Stress	Overall Resistance
Heat	Excellent
Cold	Poor
Drought	Very good
Shade	Fair

Cultivars: Pensacola is commonly used for roadsides, whereas Argentine is used on home lawns.

Figure 2-33
Bahiagrass with its characteristic seed stalk.

SEASHORE PASPALUM
(*Paspalum vaginatum* Swarz.)

Growth habit: Stoloniferous

Characteristics: Texture is generally coarser than bermudagrass but finer than centipedegrass. Characterized for its exceptional tolerance to saline conditions, this grass is seeing increased interest in warm, humid areas where effluent irrigation is employed.

Uses:

Residential Lawns	General Grounds	Sports Fields	Golf Courses			Native Areas
			Putting Greens	Tees	Fairways	
X	X	X	X	X	X	

Tolerance to environmental stresses:

Stress	Overall Resistance
Heat	Excellent
Cold	Poor
Drought	Good
Shade	Good

Cultivars: Intensive breeding of seashore paspalum by Dr. Ronnie Duncan at the University of Georgia has resulted in the release of Sea Isle I and Sea Isle 2000, among others.

REFERENCES

Bonos, S. A., W. A. Meyer, and J. A. Murphy. 2000. Kentucky bluegrasses make comeback on fairways, roughs. *Golf Course Management* 68 (10):59–64.

Brilman, L. A., and W. A. Meyer. 2000. Velvet bentgrass: Rediscovering a misunderstood turfgrass. *Golf Course Management* 68 (10):70–75.

Christians, N. E., and M. C. Engelke. 1994. Choosing the right grass to fit the environment. Pp. 99–113 in A. R. Leslie, ed., *Integrated Pest Management for Turf and Ornamentals*. Boca Raton, FL: CRC Press.

Kraft, R. 2002. Improved Kentucky bluegrass cultivars for upper transition zone golf course fairway use. M.S. thesis, Kansas State University.

Levitt, J. 1980. *Responses of plants to environmental stresses*. New York: Academic Press.

Waddington, D. V., R. N. Carrow, and R. C. Shearman, eds. 1992. *Turfgrass*. Madison, WI: ASA, CSSA, SSSA.

PART II

Environmental Stresses and Pests

Turfgrasses growing in temperate climates are constantly subjected to changing environments. Changes may occur diurnally or seasonally, particularly for temperature, light levels, and rainfall. A change in environmental conditions that may reduce or adversely change a plant's growth or development is defined as environmental stress. The primary environmental stresses influencing turfgrass growth include drought (Chapter 3), temperature extremes (Chapter 4), and shade (Chapter 5). In each section the physiology of each stress is defined, and inter- and intra-specific differences among turfgrasses are discussed. These stresses may occur individually or simultaneously. A combination of stresses may result in different plant responses compared to one stress alone. Plant response to environmental stresses is also affected by cultural practices, the focus of the third section of this text.

Myriad pests affect turfgrass swards. In Chapter 6, we provide an overview of the pest problems that have been shown to be affected by turfgrass culture.

3

Drought

The demand on water for agricultural, residential, and industrial use is increasing, while water availability is becoming limited in many regions of the world. Drought occurs when soil water content is reduced to a point that causes negative effects on plant growth. Water is the major factor limiting growth of both warm-season and cool-season grasses in semiarid and arid regions. Plants can experience periodic or seasonal droughts, even in regions that have reasonably wet climates. Therefore, one of the most important challenges facing the turfgrass industry is dealing with drought stress and water conservation. Knowledge of the physiological effects of drought stress on turfgrass plants and of the mechanisms by which plants deal with drought is essential for producing and maintaining quality turf with limited water resources.

Turfgrass Drought Stress Is Affected By:	See Information Beginning on Page:
Irrigation	153
Mowing	193
Fertilization	217
Cultivation	249
Thatch	264
Topdressing	270
Plant growth regulators	277

PLANT–WATER RELATIONS

Water is absorbed in far greater quantities than any other substance required for turfgrass growth. However, only 1 to 3 percent of the absorbed water is actually utilized in plant metabolism. Most of the water absorbed is transported to shoots and transpired through leaves. The interrelated effects of water absorption and transpiration influence the internal plant water balance.

Water Absorption

The turfgrass plant's ability to absorb water is affected by the depth, number, extension rate, length, and viability of roots, and by root hair formation. A viable, extensive root system can exploit a large soil volume for water uptake. Any environmental factors or cultural practices that favor root growth help to facilitate water uptake. Conversely, the following factors may limit root growth and water absorption capability:

- *Heavy soils.* Rooting is generally better on sandy soils due to greater oxygen availability and less resistance to root penetration.
- *Soil compaction.* Compacted soils have less oxygen available for root respiration, and a high impedance strength that makes it difficult for roots to penetrate, ultimately restricting growth and water uptake.

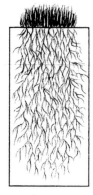

Clay Loam Sand

Figure 3-1
Turfgrass is able to root more extensively in sandy compared to heavy soils (drawing by Angie Settle).

■ *Overwatering of poorly drained soil.* Excessive water in the soil limits oxygen supply to roots and inhibits root respiration and water uptake.

■ *Low soil water availability.* Moderate soil surface drying encourages deep rooting and increases water use from the deeper soil profile. Severe drought stress restricts root proliferation and elongation and can cause desiccation of roots, reducing their ability to absorb water. (See discussion on page 170.)

■ *Low or high soil temperatures.* Either can reduce root growth or cause death in severe cases, reducing water uptake capacity. (See Chapter 4 for more discussion.)

■ *Excessive nitrogen fertilization.* Excessive nitrogen stimulates shoot growth at the expense of roots and thus reduces the root-to-shoot ratio. (See page 218 for additional discussion.)

■ *Low mowing.* Low mowing produces shallow root systems that restrict water uptake from the deeper soil profile. (See page 198 for additional discussion.)

Transpiration

Definition and Physics

Transpiration is a process during which water is lost from the leaf into the atmosphere as water vapor, mainly through microscopic pores, called stomata, on the leaf's adaxial (top) and abaxial (bottom) surfaces. The vaporization of water is a heat-releasing process that cools the surface on which it occurs. During transpiration, heat is transferred from the leaves to the atmosphere. Without transpiration, grasses would not be able to release heat resulting from radiation and would suffer from internal heat stress. Humans experience the same cooling effect after stepping out of the shower, when water evaporates from the surface of the skin.

Transpiration is also the driving force for the water stream that flows through the plant's vascular system. It serves to carry nutrients and hormones up from the roots to the crown, stem tissues, and leaves. When grasses transpire water faster than it can be absorbed, which might occur due to various reasons, leaf wilt results. Grasses differ in transpiration rates, which are influenced by internal leaf diffusion resistance, external boundary layer resistance, and the vapor pressure gradient between the leaf and the air.

Internal leaf diffusion resistance is controlled by the opening and closing of the stomata, the thickness of the wax layer (cuticle) on leaf

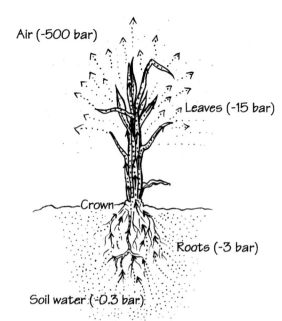

Air (-500 bar)

Leaves (-15 bar)

Crown

Roots (-3 bar)

Soil water (-0.3 bar)

Figure 3-2
Water moves from the area of
highest potential (soil) to that
of lowest potential (air)
(drawing by Angie Settle).

surface, and the compactness of mesophyll cells. Stomata facilitate
the exchange of gases and water vapor between the leaf and the
atmosphere. Stomatal densities in ten species and cultivars of
warm-season grasses ranged from 96 to 468 per mm² on the adaxial
side and 84 to 348 per mm² on the abaxial side (Casnoff, Green, and
Beard 1989). In many cases, stomata in warm-season grasses are
present in rows between veins on either surface of the leaf blade
(Green, Casnoff, and Beard 1993). Cool-season grasses have a pre-
ponderance of stomata on the adaxial side of the leaf. Among
twelve cool-season grasses, stomatal numbers ranged from 68 to
203 per mm² and 0 to 100 per mm² on the adaxial and abaxial sides
of the leaf, respectively (Green, Beard, and Casnoff 1990).

The opening and closing of a stoma are governed by the influx or
efflux of potassium ions into or out of two thin-walled guard cells
surrounding the stoma (Salisbury and Ross 1978). A stoma opens
when an influx of potassium occurs, the osmotic potential drops,
and water moves into the cell, increasing turgor. The stoma closes
when potassium exits the cell, osmotic potential increases, and less
water is retained in leaves, creating a less turgid cell. Approximately 90 to 95 percent of the water loss from the leaf occurs
through stomata; the remainder escapes through the leaf cuticle.

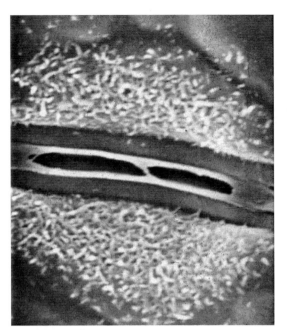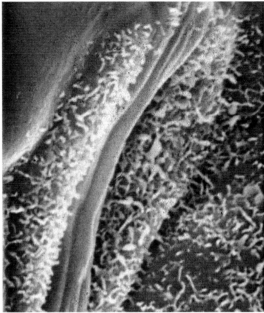

Figures 3-3 and 3-4
A bahiagrass stoma under nonstressed conditions (Fig. 3-3, left) and eight days into a dry down (Fig. 3-4, right). Note how the stoma is open before stress begins, and closed after stress is prolonged. (Photos courtesy of Dr. Robert Green.)

The boundary layer, also referred to as the "unstirred layer," is a thin transfer zone of water vapor directly above the leaf's surface (Salisbury and Ross 1978). The thinner the boundary layer, the greater the ability of a plant to transfer heat through transpiration. A thicker boundary layer creates greater resistance to transpiration. Larger leaves have thicker boundary layers, whereas smaller leaves have thinner boundary layers. The boundary layer is easily disturbed by wind, which promulgates a greater vapor pressure gradient between the leaf and atmosphere. This is in part why turfgrass water demands are higher on windy days compared to when it is calm. Another factor is canopy resistance, a layer of higher humidity that retards water vapor loss; this depends on leaf orientation, shoot density, and mowing height.

The driving force for transpiration is the difference in the vapor pressure gradient between the leaf and the air. Vapor pressure and relative humidity are analogous for the purposes of this discussion. (Technically, the vapor pressure above pure water in a closed con-

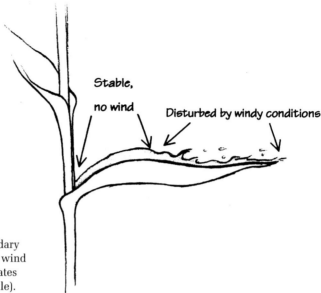

Stable,

no wind

Disturbed by windy conditions

Figure 3-5
Under calm conditions, the boundary
layer remains undisturbed; when wind
disturbs the boundary layer, ET rates
are higher (drawing by Angie Settle).

tainer is equal to 100 percent relative humidity.) The relative humidity inside the stoma is almost always 100 percent. Hence, the gradient between the relative humidity in the stoma and the atmosphere is greater on days when atmospheric relative humidity is lower. As such, transpirational cooling is more effective in environments where a low relative humidity is present.

Plant Factors Affecting Transpiration

The characteristics of the turfgrass plant's leaves and their orientation also influence transpiration. These include:

- *Leaf area.* Grasses that have less leaf area exposed to the atmosphere transpire less. Many grasses will roll or fold their leaves at the onset of drought stress. Although this is largely a result of loss of turgor, it also serves to reduce leaf area and create protective cavities with greater boundary layer resistance, resulting in a concomitant reduction in water loss.
- *Leaf orientation.* Horizontally oriented leaves have higher boundary layer resistance and lower transpiration rates.
- *Leaf surface characteristics.* Some grasses have leaf surface characteristics that may serve to reduce transpiration. For example,

Figure 3-6
Some grasses, such as buffalograss, have prominent hairs on the leaf surface that may help to reflect sunlight and lessen wind effects on the boundary layer, thereby reducing ET.

buffalograss has hairy leaves, which may help reflect radiation and increase boundary layer resistance by impeding airflow over the leaf. Perennial ryegrass, among others, has a waxy cuticle, which may also serve to reflect radiation and to minimize cuticular transpiration.

Stomata. It would seem logical that grasses with higher densities of stomata would also transpire more rapidly. However, researchers have shown that there is little correlation between stomatal density and transpiration. For example, Waldina tall fescue had a stomatal density of 203 per mm^2 on the adaxial leaf side and a corresponding ET rate of 0.29 inches (7.4 mm) per day (Green, Beard, and Casnoff 1990). In the same test, Merion Kentucky bluegrass had an adaxial stomatal density of 73 per mm^2 and an ET rate of 0.49 inches (12.4 mm) per day. It is likely that stomatal control has a significant effect on transpiration, but this is very difficult to measure. Stomatal control seems to differ among grass species and cultivars within a species. Bermudagrass, for example, seems to possess more stomatal control even under very moist conditions and exhibits lower transpiration rates than some other species.

EFFECTS OF DROUGHT ON GROWTH AND PHYSIOLOGY

Drought in turfgrass is manifested by leaf wilting, desiccation, slow shoot growth, and loss of turf quality. A typical visual symptom of drought stress is the presence of footprints following foot traffic on the turf area. This is due to the lack of leaf elasticity during water deficits.

Cellular growth appears to be one of the plant processes most sensitive to drought stress and is usually reduced long before photosynthesis or stomatal conductance is affected (Hsiao 1973). Cell expansion is dependent on cell turgor (hydrostatic pressure) being above a critical threshold, as well as the cell wall being expandable. For most plants this critical threshold is around 15 to 50 percent of the turgor pressure under normal (non-stressed) conditions (Lambers, Chapin, and Pons 1998). Therefore, during drought, when water potentials are lower, cell expansion is limited and growth can be greatly reduced. In drought-stressed plants, cell walls become inflexible and membranes shrink and pull away from the wall. A reduction in cell wall elasticity also contributes to the decrease in cell expansion during drought stress.

Severe drought stress reduces total root length and mass and increases root mortality. Root distribution throughout the soil profile may be altered as water deficits develop. Surface soil drying reduces root growth in the surface profile but increases the proportion of roots deeper in the soil profile, where water is adequate. This phenomenon has been observed in several turfgrass species, including seashore paspalum, zoysiagrass, buffalograss, tall fescue, and Kentucky bluegrass (Huang et al. 1997; Huang 1999; Huang and Fu 2001). The ratio of root mass to shoot mass typically increases under drought stress (Carrow 1996a), which may be due to the greater reduction in shoot growth than root growth.

Shoot growth is usually more sensitive to drought stress than root growth. Roots have a greater ability to maintain turgor through osmotic adjustment than leaves. The differences in sensitivity between shoots and roots to drought stress may also be related to the effects of abscisic acid (ABA), which serves to inhibit shoot growth while maintaining root growth (Hsiao and Xu 2000). During drought stress, there is increased carbon allocation to roots relative to shoots (Lambers, Chapin, and Pons 1998; Huang and Fu 2000), which assists with root survival as soil dries.

Many physiological processes in the turfgrass plant are interrupted during drought stress, including photosynthesis, respiration, hormone synthesis, and water and nutrient uptake (Huang and Gao 1999). The maintenance of high leaf water potential, stomatal conductance, transpiration, and photosynthesis, along with minimization of electrolyte leakage (an indicator of cell membrane stability), contribute positively to drought resistance (Huang and Gao 1999; Jiang and Huang 2001; Lehman, Engelke, and White 1993). Photosynthesis is a drought-sensitive plant metabolic process. Reductions in photosynthesis during drought may be due to stomatal closure and/or metabolic limitations. Stomata are constantly reacting to environmental stimuli, with responses that can occur in a matter of seconds. The primary environmental factors that influence stomatal conductance are similar to those that affect photosynthesis: light, temperature, humidity, and internal CO_2 concentration.

Stomatal regulation is often thought to be the first line of defense against drought stress, for it controls transpiration and carbon fixation in photosynthesis. Water deficits, as manifested by the decrease in leaf water status, can directly limit growth and cause stomatal closure (Kramer and Boyer 1995). However, in some cases stomatal conductance does not correspond with changes in leaf water status, particularly during mild drought stress. Reductions in stomatal conductance can occur without water deficits in leaves (non-hydraulic limitation). Non-hydraulic control of stomatal closure may be chemically regulated. It has been proposed that a chemical signal moving from roots to shoots in response to localized soil drying may induce stomatal closure and reduce water loss (Blackman and Davies 1985; Davies, Wilkinson, and Loveys 2002; Zhang and Davies 1989). This hypothesis has been tested in experiments utilizing split-root systems in which part of the root system is exposed to drying soil while the remaining roots are maintained in moist soil (Gowing, Davies, and Jones 1990; Zhang and Davies 1989). The split-root technique has demonstrated that restrictions in stomatal conductance and growth occur even though roots in the well-watered soil provide sufficient moisture to maintain favorable leaf water status.

Abscisic acid is believed to be the primary chemical signal controlling stomatal response to drying soil (Wilkinson and Davies 2002). Stomatal conductance is negatively related to ABA accumulation in various plant species, including Kentucky bluegrass (Wang and Huang 2003), suggesting that chemical signaling is an important factor regulating physiological response to drought, particularly mild to moderate stress. Abscisic acid is synthesized in roots exposed to dry soil and transported to shoots, where it triggers a signal transduction cascade eventually leading to a reduction in guard cell turgor and stomatal closure (Assmann and Shimazaki 1999; McAinsh, Brownlee, and Hetherington 1997; Wilkinson and Davies 2002). Abscisic acid is additionally involved in reduction of water loss by inhibiting leaf growth, which reduces leaf area and thus water loss (Alves and Setter 2000; Bacon, Wilkinson, and Davies 1998).

The inhibitory effects of drought on turfgrass photosynthesis have also been attributed to metabolic limitations associated with reductions in enzyme activity, electron transport efficiency, and chlorophyll content. Loss of chlorophyll due to degradation is often observed early during drought stress. Electron transport and rubisco activity (carboxylation) are both considered to be fairly resistant to drought stress. Depending on the species and the severity of the drought, the largest reductions in photosynthesis may actually be due to leaf area reductions arising from senescence or delayed leaf growth and development.

Drought Survival Strategies The ability of turfgrasses to survive drought stress involves morphological and physiological adaptations. The primary drought resistance mechanisms turfgrasses employ are avoidance and tolerance. Some weedy annual grasses also use drought escape.

Avoidance Drought avoidance is the ability of plants to postpone tissue dehydration by reducing transpiration and/or increasing water uptake. Plant water loss can be reduced by modification of shoot characteristics such as leaf shedding or folding, or the development of a thick cuticle and sensitive stomatal responses. Better tall fescue performance during drought stress was positively related to leaf thickness, epicuticular wax content, and tissue density but negatively related to stomatal density and leaf width (Fu and Huang 2004). Beard and Sifers (1997) reported that better dehydration avoidance among *Cynodon* species compared to *Zoysia* species was attributed to lower evapotranspiration (ET) rates due to a faster rate of wax formation over the stomata during progressive drought stress.

Roots have the responsibility of meeting transpirational water demand and play an important role in controlling plant water status to avoid drought injury. Water uptake is controlled by extent of rooting, root size, spatial distribution, and viability. Development of long roots facilitates the extraction of water from deep in the soil profile. The development of lateral roots at very shallow soil depths may serve a role in capturing small amounts of water resulting from intermittent rainfall.

Differences in drought resistance among species and cultivars of turfgrasses have been attributed to variability in rooting depth. Huang and Gao (2000) reported that drought-resistant tall fescue cultivars had deeper root systems than sensitive cultivars. White, Bruneau, and Cowett (1993) and Carrow (1996b) suggested that good drought resistance of tall fescue cultivars was related to greater total root length and root length density compared to cultivars with inferior drought resistance. Deep and extensive root systems contribute positively to water uptake (Sheffer, Dunn, and Minner 1987; Huang, Duncan, and Carrow 1997; Huang and Fry 1998; Bonos and Murphy 1999) and alleviation of leaf wilting (Qian, Fry, and Upham 1997). Carrow (1996b) also suggested that high root length density in the deeper soil root zone and the ability to maintain ET as the soil dries are important for drought resistance of tall fescues. Marcum and colleagues (1995) indicated that rooting depth, weight, and branching at lower depths were important drought resistance mechanisms in zoysiagrasses. Root distribution is associated with drought avoidance more consistently than root mass in Kentucky bluegrass (Keeley and Koski 2001).

Deep, extensive rooting allows plants to exploit a larger soil volume and increase water absorption. However, plants must invest significant amounts of carbon in developing and maintaining large root systems. Among all root characteristics, root viability is the most important factor for efficient water uptake, and drought resistance of tall fescue was more closely related to root viability than to total root mass or length (Huang, Duncan, and Carrow 1997).

Some grasses avoid drought stress by transporting water from deeper soil depths, via roots, to surface soil zones. This phenomenon is referred to as hydraulic lift. In buffalograss, water absorbed by deep roots in moist soil moves upward and leaks into the dry surface soil at night (Huang 1999). Hydraulic lift may serve to sustain root growth and nutrient uptake in the drying surface soil layer during short-term drought stress. Nitrogen uptake by buffalograss roots in the drying surface soil layer was enhanced when the lower soil layer was well watered compared to drying the entire soil profile (Huang 1999).

During drought, turfgrass root metabolism and carbohydrate allocation levels change in response to the plant's effort to cope with the stress. As discussed above, drought increases carbon allocation to roots, which can have tremendous positive effects on whole plant growth, sometimes even more so than the photosynthesis rate. Increasing root carbon allocation ultimately benefits leaf tissues and allows maintenance of photosynthesis during periodic water shortages. It is unknown exactly how a carbon balance is reached between roots and shoots, particularly during drought stress.

Huang and Fu (2000) reported that respiration rate and carbon allocation to roots in the drying surface profile decreased during drought, but both increased for roots in the wetter soil deeper in the soil profile. This adjustment may help sustain roots and prolong turfgrass growth under localized drying conditions, especially for deep-rooted plants.

As discussed earlier, roots are important sites for the synthesis of ABA, which is transported to shoots and initiates a signal cascade in guard cells that alters the membrane transport of several ions, causing guard cells to lose their turgor and stomata to close. This results in changes in stomatal conductance, transpiration rate, and photosynthesis. The importance of ABA as a metabolic factor in the regulation of plant tolerance to stresses has received great attention in recent years in other plant species. However, limited information is available on the association of ABA signaling and drought tolerance in turfgrass. Wang, Huang, Bonos, and Meyer (2003) reported that drought-resistant Kentucky bluegrass cultivars exhibited slower ABA accumulation rates than drought-sensitive cultivars during short-term stress, suggesting that low accumulation rates of ABA in leaves would be beneficial for the maintenance of photosynthesis under these conditions. Drought-resistant cultivars of Kentucky bluegrass were characterized by lower ABA accumulation and less severe decline in leaf water potential, photosynthetic rate, transpiration rate, and turf quality during drought stress. The stomata of drought-resistant cultivars responded more readily to changes in ABA levels in leaves than drought-sensitive cultivars (Wang and Huang 2003).

Exogenous ABA application to tall fescue and Kentucky bluegrass leaves improved drought resistance in tall fescue and Kentucky bluegrass under controlled environmental conditions (Jiang and Huang 2001; Wang and Huang 2003). In addition to ABA effects on shoot growth and stomata, it may also facilitate osmotic adjustment and expression of specific proteins.

Tall fescue is an excellent example of a drought avoider. However, once soil water is depleted and tall fescue is subjected to extended drought, it does not recover well. Tall fescue mowed at 2.5 inches (6.5 cm) exhibited maximum root extension 33 to 60 percent greater than buffalograss, zoysiagrass, or bermudagrass mowed at 1.75 inches (4.5 cm) in the greenhouse (Qian, Fry, and Upham 1996). Furthermore, in the field, tall fescue extracted over 50 percent more water at a 36-inch (90 cm) depth than tall fescue or zoysiagrass. If one considers tall fescue's relatively high ET rate (Qian, Fry, and Upham 1996) and its ability to extract water deep in the soil, tall fescue could be considered a water "harvester." Drought avoiders such as tall fescue perform well on good soils in areas where periodic rainfalls replenish water levels deep in the soil.

Tolerance Turfgrasses that tolerate drought experience the stress but survive. In many cases, these grasses go dormant and leaves may desiccate and die, but the crowns survive and the plant recovers when adequate rainfall and good growing conditions return. In general, grasses best suited to tolerate an extended period without rainfall are those that have low ET rates, deep root systems, the physiological ability to adjust osmotically to the stress, and the potential to recover and spread when the drought is over. Plants with sufficient drought avoidance traits do best during drought stress when they go into stress rather slowly. When water deficits develop, various organic solutes such as sucrose, proline, sugar alcohol, and glycinebetaine and inorganic solutes such as potassium accumulate in cells. The increased accumulation of solutes results in a reduction in tissue osmotic potential, which is defined as osmotic adjustment. Osmotic adjustment helps to retain water in cells and maintain cellular turgor at a given leaf water potential, thus delaying leaf wilt and allowing growth to continue at a lower plant water status. The accumulated solutes protect cellular proteins, various enzymes, and cellular organelles and membranes against desiccation injury. Osmotic adjustment is crucial for maintaining meristem viability during desiccation and for recovery of function upon rehydration. Upon rehydration the various solutes are recycled and metabolized, and the accumulated sugars are an important energy resource for recovery growth.

Qian and Fry (1997) reported that turfgrass drought tolerance varied with the magnitude of osmotic adjustment, with buffalograss and zoysiagrass equally tolerant, both more tolerant than bermudagrass, and all three more tolerant than tall fescue. They found that turf recuperative ability following rewatering correlated positively with the magnitude of osmotic adjustment. Buffalograss is a species that has evolved to perform well under conditions of very little rainfall. It exhibits good drought resistance in part because it has a deep root system that allows it to avoid drought (Qian, Fry, and Upham 1996). However, it also has a low ET rate (Qian, Fry, and Upham 1996) and excellent ability to tolerate drought and then recover (Qian and Fry 1997). White and colleagues (2001) reported that zoysiagrass genotypes with high relative water content at zero turgor and tissue elasticity demonstrated better recovery from stress and required less supplemental irrigation, suggesting that the improvement in biophysical properties is also an important factor contributing to drought tolerance.

Altered protein synthesis or degradation is one of the fundamental metabolic processes that may influence drought tolerance.

Table 3-1

Recovery of turfgrasses after exposure to prolonged soil drought under greenhouse conditions (after Qian and Fry 1997)

Grass	Green Shoot Recovery (%)[1]	Osmotic Adjustment (%)[2]
Midlawn bermudagrass	14	54
Meyer zoysiagrass	22	67
Prairie buffalograss	50	78
Mustang tall fescue	4	26

[1] Soil was dried to 8 percent water by volume before rewatering.

[2] Osmotic adjustment is an indication of the plant's accumulation of solutes in cells during the drought period. Higher levels of adjustment indicate better drought tolerance.

Accumulation of certain drought-induced proteins enhances physiological adaptation to water deficits. One family of proteins that accumulates in a wide range of plant species during drought stress is the dehydrins, which are abundant in drying seeds during late embryogenesis. Dehydrins are hydrophilic and heat stable, and they may protect other proteins and help maintain cell physiological integrity. Although dehydrin proteins have been investigated widely in many plant species, information on stress-related proteins in turfgrasses is limited. Accumulation of dehydrin-like proteins was induced during a progressive water deficit in tall fescue (Jiang and Huang 2002).

Escape   Some grasses escape drought by completing their life cycle before drought typically occurs. For example, annual bluegrass is a winter annual that germinates in autumn and grows vegetatively until late spring, when seeds are produced and the mother plants die. Although efficient in nature, grasses that escape drought are not reliable selections for perennial stands.

GENETIC VARIABILITY IN TURFGRASS DROUGHT RESISTANCE

There are large differences among and within turfgrass species in their ability to resist drought. To most turfgrass managers, overall drought resistance is most important, and how the plant achieves this may be of little interest. Table 3-2 addresses the overall drought resistance of commonly used turfgrasses and indicates how well each avoids or tolerates drought. It is interesting to note that some grasses have evolved utilizing primarily one mode of drought resistance, such as drought avoidance in tall fescue. Other grasses, such as buffalograss, have good drought avoidance and tolerance characteristics.

Cool-Season Grasses

Creeping Bentgrass   Creeping bentgrass cultivars vary in drought avoidance characteristics, including low ET rates and deep rooting (Salaiz et al. 1991). The cultivars Cobra, Penncross, Pennlinks, Providence, and SR-1020 had root lengths from 24 to 30 inches (600 to 750 mm) under hydroponic conditions in the greenhouse. Root lengths of the

73

Table 3-2

Relative drought resistance, avoidance, and tolerance of commonly used turfgrass species

Turfgrass	Overall Resistance[1]	Drought Avoidance[2]	Drought Tolerance[3]
Kentucky bluegrass	Good	Fair	Good
Annual bluegrass	Poor	Poor	Poor
Tall fescue	Very good	Excellent	Fair
Fine fescues	Very good	Fair	Excellent
Perennial ryegrass	Fair	Good	Poor
Creeping bentgrass	Fair	Fair	Poor
Zoysiagrass	Very good	Good	Excellent
Bermudagrass	Excellent	Excellent	Very good
Buffalograss	Excellent	Excellent	Excellent
St. Augustinegrass	Good	Very good	Fair
Centipedegrass	Good	Good	Fair
Bahiagrass	Very good	Excellent	Good
Seashore paspalum	Good	Very good	Fair

[1] Resistance is the ability to avoid and tolerate drought.

[2] Avoidance is the ability to maintain quality during drought stress, primarily by deep rooting.

[3] Tolerance is the ability to recover after experiencing symptoms of drought stress.

cultivars Emerald and Penneagle did not exceed 18 inches (450 mm). National was a cultivar that had relatively deep roots and a low ET rate.

Kentucky Bluegrass Studies comparing drought responses of Kentucky bluegrass cultivars suggested that common-type cultivars had superior drought resistance and were well suited to low-maintenance sites (Dernoeden and Butler 1978; Burt and Christians 1990) (Table 3-3). Since 1990, there have been some new cultivars developed that have exhibited drought resistance superior to the common-type cultivars (Keeley and Koski 2001).

Table 3-3

Intra-specific differences in Kentucky bluegrass drought resistance

Number of Cultivars Evaluated	Description of Study	Best-Performing Cultivars	Comments	Reference
25 plus 5 blends	Field evaluation	Common types, including Kenblue and South Dakota Common	Evaluated common types and early improved cultivars	Dernoeden and Butler 1978
10 (5 common types that exhibited good low-maintenance field performance, and 5 improved cultivars that did not perform well in the field)	Greenhouse evaluation	Common types, which produced deeper roots and more root mass than other cultivars, had less leaf tissue moisture, and fewer leaves per shoot	Test was done to identify characteristics of common types that resulted in improved performance during drought	Burt and Christians 1990
15	Field evaluation, dehydration avoidance	Mid-Atlantic types were better than Bellevue types, which were better than Baron, Victa, Merit, Gnome-types, which in turn were superior to Common types	Livingston, Monopoly, and SR2000, mid-Atlantic types, performed well	Keeley and Koski 2001

Tall Fescue   Most of the work done to compare the drought resistance of tall fescue cultivars has focused on those selections with varying growth rates, such as the pasture-type Kentucky-31 versus turf-type cultivars or dwarf cultivars such as Bonsai (Table 3-4). In general, the slower-growing cultivars have been shown to have inferior rooting ability and poorer drought resistance than pasture-type or non-dwarf turf-type cultivars (White, Bruneau, and Cowett 1993; Huang, Fry, and Wang 1998; Carrow 1996b). Because of this, breeders are attempting to select deeper-rooted cultivars with improved turf-type characteristics (Bonos et al. 2004).

Tissue-level measurements have also supported the stance that dwarf-type cultivars have inferior drought resistance. Reductions in relative leaf water content, leaf water potential, canopy green leaf

Table 3-4

Intra-specific differences in tall fescue drought resistance

Number of Cultivars Evaluated	Description of Study	Best-Performing Cultivars	Comments	Reference
4	Greenhouse evaluation	Arid was superior to Bonsai in rooting, while Rebel Jr. and Kentucky-31 were intermediate; in ability to recover from severe drought, Arid had the best ability and Bonsai the least		White, Bruneau, and Cowett 1993
3	Field and growth chamber tests	Kentucky-31 (pasture-type) = Mustang (turf-type) > MIC18 (dwarf turf-type)	MIC18 had a shorter, less extensive root system than other cultivars under well-watered conditions; shoots and root physiological measurements showed that the dwarf cultivar was inferior to the other two during drought	Huang, Fry, and Wang 1998; Huang and Fry 1998
6	Field study	Rebel II was better than Rebel Jr., Kentucky-31, and GA-5-EF (endophyte-infected or -free); all of these were better than Bonsai	High root length density at deeper soil depths enhanced drought resistance, but extensive rooting near the surface reduced resistance	Carrow 1996b

biomass, and leaf area index were more severe during dry-down in the greenhouse for MIC18, a dwarf cultivar, than for Kentucky-31, a pasture-type selection (Huang et al. 1998). Roots of Kentucky-31 also exhibited less turgor loss than those of MIC18 during dry-down (Huang and Fry 1998). After a twenty-one-day dry-down in the greenhouse, less electrolyte leakage occurred from Kentucky-31 than MIC18 roots. Hence, not only do dwarf cultivars appear to root less extensively, their roots also do not tolerate soil drying as well as non-dwarf selections.

Warm-Season Grasses

Bermudagrass

A greenhouse evaluation of seven experimental bermudagrass lines and the cultivars U-3, Midiron, and Tifgreen indicated that there was variability in their vertical root distribution (Hays et al. 1991). Among the genotypes, root mass at depths of 12, 24, 36, and 60 inches (30, 60, 90, and 150 cm) was most highly correlated with turf quality during drought stress. Root carbohydrate distribution was not correlated with drought performance.

Centipedegrass

Genetic variability in centipedegrass has been demonstrated under a rainout shelter in Georgia (Hook and Hanna 1994). Two experimental selections were compared to common centipedegrass under no stress, moderate drought, and severe drought conditions. The visual ratings for the experimental lines were 18 percent higher than those of common centipedegrass under moderate stress and 24 percent higher under severe stress. The researchers concluded that there are superior lines of centipedegrass that have the potential to perform better than common types during periods of drought.

St. Augustinegrass

Polyploid St. Augustinegrass cultivars, including FX-10, exhibited less wilt in the field in Florida than diploid selections, including Jade (Busey 1996). FX-10 and Floratam also experienced less severe turf quality decline following an extended drought. A relatively shallow water table may have been accessible to some of the cultivars, resulting in drought avoidance.

When Palmetto, FX-10, and Floratam St. Augustinegrass were evaluated in 26-inch- (65-cm-) deep lysimeters for drought responses, few differences were observed (Miller and McCarty 2001). FX-10 and Floratam were similar in the number of days before leaf wilt was observed; Palmetto wilted sooner than FX-10 but was statistically similar to Floratam. Measurements of leaf water potential during dry-down did not reveal consistent differences among the cultivars and was not considered a reliable method for determining dehydration avoidance.

Zoysiagrass

As part of the zoysiagrass breeding efforts at Texas A and M University, researchers have evaluated the variability in drought resistance among experimental selections. Marcum and colleagues (1995) found that grasses with superior maximum rooting depth, total root weight, and root numbers at 12 to 20 inches (30 to 50 cm) in the greenhouse were QT2047, El Toro, DALZ 8512, TC5018,

Meyer, DALZ 8514, and DALZ 8516. Drought performance of zoysiagrass selections in the field was positively correlated with rooting ability in the greenhouse.

Crowne, El Toro, and Palisades zoysiagrasses exhibited the greatest recovery from drought stress in the greenhouse and also had the lowest irrigation requirements, more negative leaf water potentials at zero turgor and osmotic potentials at full turgor, and more positive relative water content at zero turgor (White et al. 2001). The authors concluded that a lot of variability exists among zoysiagrass germplasm in drought resistance.

REFERENCES

Alves, A. A. C., and T. L. Setter. 2000. Response of cassava to water deficit: Leaf area growth and abscisic acid. *Crop Sci.* 40:131–37.

Assmann, S. M., and K. L. Shimazaki. 1999. The multisensory guard cell, stomatal responses to blue light and abscisic acid. *Plant Physiol.* 119:809–16.

Bacon, M. A., S. Wilkinson, and W. J. Davies. 1998. pH-regulated leaf cell expansion in droughted plants is abscisic acid dependent. *Plant Physiol.* 118:1507–15.

Beard, J. B., and S. I. Sifers. 1997. Genetic diversity in dehydration avoidance and drought resistance within the *Cynodon* and *Zoysia* species. *Int. Turfgrass Soc. Res. J.* 8:603–10.

Blackman, P. G., and W. J. Davies. 1985. Root to shoot communication in maize plants of the effects of soil drying. *J. Exp. Botany* 36:39–48.

Bonos, S. A., K. Hignight, D. Rush, and W. A. Meyer. 2004. Selection for deep root production in tall fescue and perennial ryegrass. *Crop Sci.*, in press.

Bonos, S. A., and J. A. Murphy. 1999. Growth responses and performance of Kentucky bluegrass under summer stress. *Crop Sci.* 39:770–74.

Burt, M. G., and N. E. Christians. 1990. Morphological and growth characteristics of low- and high-maintenance Kentucky bluegrass cultivars. *Crop Sci.* 30:1239–43.

Busey, P. 1996. Wilt avoidance in St. Augustinegrass germplasm. *HortScience* 31:1135–38.

Carrow, R. N. 1996a. Drought resistance aspects of turfgrasses in the southeast: Root-shoot responses. *Crop Sci.* 36:687–94.

———. 1996b. Drought avoidance characteristics of diverse tall fescue cultivars. *Crop Sci.* 36:371–77.

Casnoff, D. M., R. L. Green, and J. B. Beard. 1989. Leaf blade stomatal densities of ten warm-season perennial grasses and their evapotranspiration rates. Pp. 129–31 in H. Takatoh, ed., *Proceedings of the Sixth International Turfgrass Research Conference.* Tokyo: International Turfgrass Society and Japanese Society of Turfgrass Science.

Davies, W. J., S. Wilkinson, and B. Loveys. 2002. Stomatal control by chemical signaling and the exploitation of this mechanism to increase water use efficiency in agriculture. *New Phytologist* 153:449–60.

Dernoeden, P. H., and J. D. Butler. 1978. Drought resistance of Kentucky bluegrass cultivars. *HortScience* 13:667–68.

Fu, J., and B. Huang. 2004. Leaf characteristics associated with drought resistance in tall fescue cultivars. *Acta Horticulturae,* in press.

Gowing, D. J. G., W. J. Davies, and H. G. Jones. 1990. A positive root-sourced signal as an indicator of soil drying in apple, *Malus x domestica* Borkh. *J. Exp. Botany* 41:1535–40.

Green, R. L., J. B. Beard, and D. M. Casnoff. 1990. Leaf blade stomatal characterizations and evapotranspiration rates of 12 cool-season perennial grasses. *HortScience* 25:760–61.

Green, R. L., D. M. Casnoff, and J. B. Beard. 1993. Stomatal-row patterns among warm-season turfgrasses with a discussion of water conservation via stomatal anatomy. *Int. Turfgrass Society Res. J.* 7:614–20.

Hays, K. L., J. F. Barber, M. P. Kenna, and T. G. McCollum. 1991. Drought avoidance mechanisms of selected bermudagrass genotypes. *HortScience* 26:180–82.

Hook, J. E., and W. W. Hanna. 1994. Drought resistance in centipedegrass cultivars. *HortScience* 29:1528–31.

Hsiao, T. C. 1973. Plant responses to water stress. *Ann. Rev. Plant Physiol.* 24:519–70.

Hsiao, T. C., and L.-K. Xu. 2000. Sensitivity of growth of roots versus leaves to water stress: biophysical analysis and relation to water transport. *J. Exp. Botany* 51:1595–616.

Huang, B. 1999. Water relations and root activities of *Buchloe dactyloides* and *Zoysia japonica* in response to localized soil drying. *Plant and Soil* 208:179–86.

Huang, B., R. R. Duncan, and R. N. Carrow. 1997. Drought-resistance mechanisms of seven warm-season turfgrasses under surface soil drying: II. Root aspects. *Crop Sci.* 37:1863–9.

Huang, B., and J. Fry. 1998. Root anatomical, physiological, and morphological responses to drought stress for tall fescue cultivars. *Crop Sci.* 38:1017–22.

Huang, B., J. Fry, and B. Wang. 1998. Water relations and canopy characteristics of tall fescue cultivars during and after drought stress. *HortScience* 33:837–40.

Huang, B., and J. Fu. 2000. Photosynthesis, respiration, and carbon allocation in two cool-season perennial grasses in response to surface soil drying. *Plant and Soil* 227:17–26.

_____. 2001. Growth and physiological responses of tall fescue to surface soil drying. *Int. Turfgrass Soc. Res. J.* 9:291–96.

Huang, B., and H. Gao. 1999. Gas exchange and water relations of diverse tall fescue cultivars in response to drought stress. *HortScience* 34:490.

_____. 2000. Root physiological characteristics associated with drought resistance in tall fescue cultivars. *Crop Sci.* 40:196–203.

Jiang, Y., and B. Huang. 2001. Drought and heat stress injury to two cool-season turfgrasses in relation to antioxidant metabolism and lipid peroxidation. *Crop Sci.* 41:436–42.

_____. 2002. Protein alterations in tall fescue in response to drought stress and abscisic acid. *Crop Sci.* 42:202–7.

Keeley, S. J., and A. J. Koski. 2001. Dehydration avoidance of diverse *Poa pratensis* cultivars and cultivar groups in a semi-arid climate. *Int. Turfgrass Soc. Res. J.* 9:311–16.

Kramer, P. J., and J. S. Boyer. 1995. *Water relations of plants and soils*. San Diego: Academic Press.

Lambers, H., F. S. Chapin, and T. Pons. 1998. *Plant physiological ecology*. New York: Springer-Verlag.

Lehman, V. G., M. C. Engelke, and R. H. White. 1993. Leaf water potential and relative water content variation in creeping bentgrass clones. *Crop Sci.* 33:1350–3.

Marcum, K. B., M. C. Engelke, S. J. Morton, and R. H. White. 1995. Rooting characteristics and associated drought resistance of zoysiagrasses. *Agron. J.* 87:534–38.

McAinsh, M. R., C. Brownlee, and A. M. Hetherington. 1997. Calcium ions as second messengers in guard cell signal transduction. *Physiologia Plantarum* 100:16–29.

Miller, G. L., and L. B. McCarty. 2001. Water relations and rooting characteristics of three *Stenotaphrum secundatum* turf cultivars grown under water deficit conditions. *Int. Turfgrass Soc. Res. J.* 9:323–27.

Qian, Y., and J. D. Fry. 1997. Water relations and drought tolerance of four turfgrasses. *J. Am. Soc. Hort. Sci.*122:129–33.

Qian, Y. L., J. D. Fry, and W. S. Upham. 1996. Rooting and drought avoidance of warm-season turfgrasses and tall fescue in Kansas. *Crop Sci.* 37:905–10.

Salaiz, T. A., E. J. Kinbacher, T. P. Riordan, and R. C. Shearman. 1991. Creeping bentgrass cultivar water use and rooting responses. *Crop Sci.* 31:1331–34.

Salisbury, F. B., and C. Ross. 1992. *Plant physiology,* 4th ed. Belmont, CA: Wadsworth.

Sheffer, K. M., J. H. Dunn, and D. D. Minner. 1987. Summer drought response and rooting depth of three cool-season turfgrasses. *HortScience* 22:296–97.

Wang, Z., and B. Huang. 2003. Genotypic variation in abscisic acid accumulation, water relations, and gas exchange for Kentucky bluegrass exposed to drought stress. *J. Am. Soc. Hort. Sci.*128:349–55.

Wang, Z., B. Huang, S. Bonos, and W. Meyer. 2003. Abscisic acid accumulation in relation to drought tolerance in Kentucky bluegrass. *HortScience* 39 (in press).

Wang, Z., B. Huang, and Q. Xu. 2003. Effects of abscisic acid on drought responses of Kentucky bluegrass. *J. Am. Soc. Hort. Sci.*128:36–41.

White, R. H., A. H. Bruneau, and T. J. Cowett. 1993. Drought resistance of diverse tall fescue cultivars. *Int. Turfgrass Soc. Research J.* 7:607–13.

White, R. H., M. C. Engelke, S. J. Anderson, B. A. Ruemmele, K. B. Marcum, and G. R. Taylor. 2001. Zoysiagrass water relations. *Crop Sci.* 41:133–38.

Wilkinson, S., and W. J. Davies. 2002. ABA-based chemical signaling: The coordination of responses to stress in plants. *Plant, Cell and Environment* 25:195–210.

Zhang, J., and W. J. Davies. 1989. Abscisic acid produced in dehydrating roots may enable the plant to measure the water status of the soil. *Plant, Cell and Environment* 12:73–81.

4

Temperature Stresses

Depending on the species, plants grow at temperatures between 32 and 120°F (0 and 50°C) but have an optimal temperature for growth and metabolism (Levitt 1980). Optimal temperature requirements vary among species and between shoots and roots. In cool-season grasses, optimal temperatures are 64 to 75°F (18 and 24°C) for shoot growth and 50 to 64°F (10 and 18°C) for root growth. In warm-season grasses, optimal temperatures are 80 to 95°F (27 to 35°C) for shoot growth and 75 to 85°F (24 to 29°C) for root growth (Beard 1973).

When temperatures fall well outside the optimal range, high or low temperature injury occurs. Temperatures that result in stress injury vary with turfgrass species, cultivar, plant growth stage, and cultural practices employed. The severity of the injury, whether due to high or low temperature exposure, is positively associated with the duration of the stress.

Temperature Stresses Are Affected By:	See Information Beginning on Page:
Irrigation	153
Mowing	193
Fertilization	217
Cultivation	249
Thatch	264
Topdressing	270
Plant growth regulators	277
Biostimulants	292

FREEZING STRESS

Freezing stress occurs when temperatures fall below 32°F (0°C) and is a primary factor limiting growth of warm-season grasses in the upper South and transition zone in the United States. Some cool-season grasses are also susceptible to freezing injury, including annual bluegrass and perennial ryegrass. In order to develop management practices to effectively alleviate or prevent freezing injury in turfgrass, it is important to understand the physiological processes that result in freezing injury.

Types of Freezing Stress

Freezing injury is caused by ice formation, not low temperatures per se. In the event of a rapid, extreme drop in temperature, ice forms inside cells. This is referred to as intracellular freezing. Freezing of water inside the plant cell is lethal, for ice crystals rupture membranes. Intracellular freezing is most common in low, poorly drained areas where turfgrass plants absorb water and have well-hydrated cells. This type of freezing injury is common in spring, when plants are becoming de-acclimated.

When temperatures drop slowly below 32°F (0°C), ice can also form between cells, which results in extra-cellular freezing. Extra-cellular freezing is not normally lethal, but it can cause metabolic injury and kill plants if temperatures are low enough for an extended period of time. After ice crystals form in the intercellular spaces, water moves from the interior of cells to the exterior, because of the reduction in the water potential outside the cell (i.e., water moves from a region of higher potential to lower potential). If temperatures stay cold for a long period of time, cells will become dehydrated to a point where injury or death results. Severe tissue desiccation can occur with prolonged extra-cellular freezing, especially if dry and/or windy conditions prevail. Extra-cellular freezing is most common during dry, cold weather on exposed sites. Turfgrass growing on sandy soils and cut at a low mowing height is more susceptible to extra-cellular freezing stress.

Freezing injury often occurs in early spring, when plants are beginning to grow, and a cold front passes through and drops temperatures well below freezing. The presence of snow cover serves as an effective insulator to both cold temperatures and desiccating winds. Snow creates a physical barrier to heat loss, and tempera-

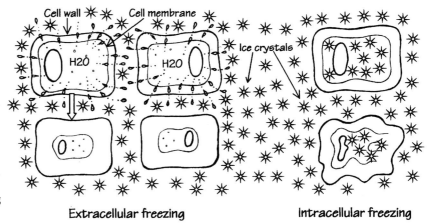

Figure 4-1
Extracellular freezing (left) results in water exiting the cell as it moves from a higher (inside) to lower (outside) water potential. Intracellular freezing (right) is lethal as ice crystals form inside the cell (drawing by Angie Settle).

Extracellular freezing   Intracellular freezing

tures can actually remain above freezing under the snow due to soil heat and possibly turfgrass metabolic activity.

Symptoms and Location of Freezing Injury

Leaf discoloration, a water-soaked appearance, and tissue death are typical symptoms of freezing injury. However, in perennial ryegrass and supina bluegrass (*Poa supina* Schrad.), freezing originates in roots, and ice crystals develop both upward and downward throughout connecting root tissues until they come into contact with the crown (Stier et al. 2003). Freezing is slow in the crown and then spreads rapidly upward into shoots and leaves. Pomeroy and colleagues (1985) reported that damage to the region where roots meet the crown in winter wheat affects crown survival. When tissue in this region is severely injured, the crown fails to recover. Protecting the turfgrass crown from freezing injury is essential for plant survival because leaves, roots, and lateral shoots are regenerated from the crown. Generally, as long as the crown is protected and survives, the whole plant is able to resume growth following freezing stress.

The extent of freezing injury increases with freezing and thawing rate and duration of exposure. Anderson, Taliaferro, and Martin (2003) concluded that bermudagrass freezing injury increased as exposure duration increased, although the minimum exposure temperature was the primary determinant of survival.

Physiological Responses to Freezing and Mechanisms of Resistance

Plants exposed to cold, nonfreezing temperatures may become hardened, or acclimated, allowing greater resistance to freezing stress. During acclimation, the properties of cell membranes are altered and cell water content is reduced. Freezing injury usually occurs in turfgrasses that are not acclimated or are unable to acclimate to low temperatures and thus are sensitive to ice formation. Hydrated, nonhardy cells are more susceptible to freezing stress than dehydrated, acclimated cells. Ice crystals form readily when cells are hydrated, and thus plants may suffer intracellular freezing when temperatures drop rapidly. Non-acclimated seashore paspalum plants were killed at 19°F (–7°C), whereas acclimated plants survived until temperatures dropped to about 16°F (–9°C) (Cardona, Duncan, and Lindstrom 1997). Acclimated centipedegrass stolons exhibited about 69 percent better survival at 25°F (–4°C) than non-acclimated stolons (Fry et al. 1993). For warm-season grasses that are sensitive to freezing temperatures, it is critical to develop cultural strategies that maximize acclimation as winter approaches.

Water expands when it becomes ice, and when this occurs inside cells it causes membranes and cell walls to burst. The water content of tissue is inversely related to freezing tolerance, and cold acclimation promotes water loss from the tissue. The loss of water has obvious adaptive advantages because there is less free water to freeze, less ice to accommodate, and less expansion in the intercellular spaces. Maier, Lang, and Fry (1994) reported that stolons of cold-acclimated Raleigh St. Augustinegrass had lower water content than non-acclimated plants, suggesting that reduced water content during winter months may contribute to cold acclimation.

Freezing-resistant turfgrasses will harden as winter approaches, undergoing numerous metabolic changes necessary for preventing ice formation outside or within the cells. As a consequence, metabolite levels and enzyme activities change (Levitt 1980). Physiological mechanisms that contribute to freezing tolerance are not well understood. During acclimation, there is an increase in cytoplasmic solutes that act as cryoprotectants and buffer any freezing-induced concentration of other solutes that could become toxic at high levels. Cold hardening also induces accumulation of soluble proteins, amino acids, carbohydrates, and inorganic solutes in plant tissues. Solute accumulation depresses the freezing point or ice nucleation point of cells and thus increases cell resistance to ice formation and regulates dehydration. Although intercellular water freezes at 14 to 23°F (–10 to –5°C), the concentrated solution inside plant cells freezes at –4 to –40°F (–20 to –40°C), depending on the amount and type of solutes present. If a plant has time to prepare and adjust water and solute content, it can withstand quite cold temperatures.

During cold acclimation, amino acid content increased in stolons of three annual bluegrass ecotypes of contrasting freezing tolerance (Dionne et al. 2001a). The greatest contributors to total amino acid accumulation at subfreezing temperatures were proline, glutamine, and glutamic acid; however, amino acid levels were not related to differential freezing tolerance among the three annual bluegrass ecotypes tested in this study.

Protein synthesis is also altered during cold acclimation. Increased synthesis of some proteins associated with cold acclimation in Midiron bermudagrass crowns was correlated with its superior freezing tolerance compared to Tifgreen (Gatschet et al. 1996). The peak accumulation of some soluble polypeptides and thermostable proteins coincided with maximum freezing tolerance in annual bluegrass (Dionne et al. 2001a). Some proteins induced under low temperatures may serve as antifreeze agents that help to prevent growth of ice crystals and reduce freezing damage.

Tissue survival during freezing and its regrowth following freezing depends upon carbohydrate reserves. Starch, fructans, and sucrose are the primary storage carbohydrates in crowns and stolons in overwintering turfgrasses, and they serve to provide energy for respiration. Soluble sugars, such as sucrose, also act as cryoprotectants that reduce cell water potential, thereby reducing the total amount of water lost due to extracellular freezing (Fig. 4-2). Cold-acclimated centipedegrass stolons had higher sucrose concentrations than non-acclimated stolons (Fry et al. 1993). Maximum sucrose concentration coincided with maximum freezing tolerance of annual bluegrass; however, variations in fructan and sucrose levels were not related to differential freezing tolerance among three ecotypes of annual bluegrass differing in freezing tolerance (Dionne et al. 2001b). The inferior freezing tolerance of one perennial ryegrass cultivar was associated with significantly lower levels of sugars compared to hardy cultivars (Bredemeijer and Esselink 1995). In contrast, no relationship between nonstructural carbohydrate accumulation and low-temperature tolerance was found in

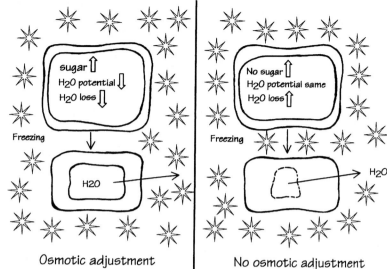

Figure 4-2
During acclimation, increases in soluble sugars, or inorganic solutes, may occur, and is referred to as osmotic adjustment. Osmotic adjustment reduces the water potential of the cell, minimizes water loss that occurs during extracellular ice formation, and may enhance survival (drawing by Angie Settle).

other studies (Maier, Lang, and Fry 1994; Bush et al. 2000; Pollock, Eagle, and Sims 1988).

Inorganic solutes such as potassium also serve as cellular antifreeze. Potassium reduces the amount of free water in the plant cells and actually acts as antifreeze, lowering the freezing point of the cell. In autumn, plants accumulate solutes to lessen the chance of ice crystal formation. The potential role of potassium fertilization in reducing winter injury is discussed in greater detail in Chapter 9.

Cell membranes are key sites of injury during freezing stress. Membranes are composed of two layers of lipids with proteins embedded within. Freezing can cause a membrane to change from a liquid to a gel phase, which reduces the membrane's fluidity, leading to "leaks" after freezing. Maintaining high membrane fluidity during freezing is necessary for proteins in membranes to change shape or position. Photosynthesis and respiration are both intimately associated with cell membranes. With a phase change, these processes are inhibited. Therefore, freezing tolerance involves membrane alterations that increase their fluidity at low temperatures. Increasing the double bonds in the fatty acids (unsaturation) lowers the phase transition temperature. The degree of unsaturation of membrane fatty acids is positively associated with membrane fluidity and stability and thus contributes to the ability of these plants to withstand prolonged exposure to low temperatures.

Freeze-tolerant seashore paspalum plants had a higher proportion of unsaturated fatty acids in their membranes than did freezing-sensitive plants (Cyril et al. 2002).

Plant hormone levels may also change during cold acclimation. However, little is known about the relationship between plant hormones and freezing tolerance in turfgrasses. In other species, abscisic acid (ABA) increases and gibberellin decreases during cold acclimation. The growth-promoting effect of gibberellin is negatively associated with freezing tolerance, whereas the quiescence or dormancy promoted by ABA is positively associated with tolerance. Abscisic acid increased the freezing tolerance of smooth bromegrass (*Bromus inermis* Leyss) cell suspension cultures and elicited many metabolic changes similar to those observed during cold acclimation (Lee and Chen 1993). Abscisic-acid-induced freezing tolerance has been associated with the expression of novel polypeptides (Robertson et al. 1988; Lee and Chen 1993). Abscisic acid may also promote freezing tolerance by increasing dehydration tolerance, as described in Chapter 3.

Genetic Variability in Freezing Resistance

Warm-Season Turfgrasses

Because they are best adapted to warm climates, warm-season grasses are less tolerant of freezing temperatures than cool-season grasses. The relative freezing resistance of warm-season grasses is indicated in Table 4-1. These killing temperatures represent the lowest reported temperatures at the tissue level that resulted in death.

Studies conducted to evaluate freezing resistance usually subject whole plants or crowns to freezing temperatures. Grasses are exposed to a range of temperatures, and some samples are removed at various points within the range to identify the killing temperature. Survival can be determined by evaluating recovery growth or measuring leakage of the cell contents when warmed. These controlled freezing tests usually measure plant responses to extra-cellular freezing. The lethal temperature is commonly reported as the temperature at which 50 percent of the crowns are killed (LT_{50}). Among warm-season turfgrasses, freezing tolerance varies from 23°F (–5°C) for Floratam St. Augustinegrass (Fry, Lang, and Clifton 1991) to 1°F (–17°C) for Brookings bermudagrass (Ibitayo, Butler, and Burke 1981).

Table 4-1
Relative freezing resistance of warm-season grasses according to the lowest estimated temperature resulting in death of the growing point (after Fry 1991)

Relative Freezing Resistance	Grass	Relative Killing Temperature	
		°F	°C
Excellent	Buffalograss	−10	−23
	Blue grama		
Very good	Zoysiagrass (Meyer)	6	−14
Good	Bermudagrass	18	−8
Poor	Centipedegrass	18	−8
	Seashore paspalum	19	−7
Very poor	St. Augustinegrass	23	−5
	Bahiagrass		

Rhizome-forming grasses, such as bermudagrass and zoysiagrass, maintain growing points that are insulated by the soil. Stoloniferous grasses, such as St. Augustinegrass and centipedegrass, have growing points that are less protected during cold winter days. As such, bermudagrass is considered to have better freezing resistance than centipedegrass, although centipedegrass crowns can survive tissue temperatures comparable to bermudagrass. An exception to this rule is buffalograss, which is stoloniferous yet more freezing resistant than other warm-season grasses.

There is little variability among cultivars of turfgrasses with poor or very poor freezing resistance. However, there are significant differences in the ability of cultivars of bermudagrass, zoysiagrass, and to a lesser extent buffalograss to endure freezing temperatures.

Bermudagrass

Bermudagrass freezing tolerance is quite variable depending upon the cultivar in question. Lowest killing temperatures reported for bermudagrass range from 1.2 to 24.8°F (−17.1 to −4°C) (Fry 1990;

Anderson, Taliaferro, and Martin, 1993; Ibitayo, Butler, and Burke 1981; Anderson and Taliaferro, 1995).

Among the vegetative bermudagrass cultivars presently used for golf course fairways and athletic fields, the most freezing resistant are Midlawn, Midfield, Patriot, Tifsport, and Quickstand. None of the bermudagrasses used on putting greens have good freezing resistance; Tifgreen and Tifdwarf are as hardy as any of the newer bermudagrasses that have been introduced for this purpose.

Seeded bermudagrasses generally lack good freezing resistance. Exceptions are Guymon and Wrangler, relatively coarse-textured, pasture-type bermudagrasses, and the turf-type cultivars, Yukon and Riviera, recently released by Oklahoma State University. The development of these cold-hardy bermudagrasses gives an additional option to transition zone turf managers who prefer the aggressive habit this species provides.

If bermudagrass is to be used in the transition zone, into USDA hardiness zone 5, selection of one of the freezing-resistant cultivars is critical. Although non-hardy cultivars may perform well during some years, a harsh winter could be devastating.

Zoysiagrass

Meyer has long been the standard zoysiagrass cultivar for use in the transition zone, and it appears to be as hardy as any of the other

Figure 4-3
Freezing injury on a bermudagrass athletic field in Kansas.

Table 4-2

Freezing tolerance of vegetative bermudagrasses adapted to maintenance at fairway or putting green height, and of seeded bermudagrass cultivars (after Anderson, Taliaferro, and Martin 2002)

Fairway		Putting Green		Seeded	
Cultivar	Killing Temperature, °F (°C)	Cultivar	Killing Temperature, °F (°C)	Cultivar	Killing Temperature, °F (°C)
GN-1	21.3 (–5.9) a[1]	Champion	23.4 (–4.8) a	AZ Common	21.9 (–5.6) a
Baby	19.9 (–6.7) ab	Floradwarf	23.2 (–4.9) a	Mirage	21.0 (–6.1) ab
Tifway	19.9 (–6.7) ab	MS-Supreme	22.6 (–5.2) ab	Jackpot	20.7 (–6.3) abc
Tifsport	19.0 (–7.2) bc	MiniVerde	21.6 (–5.8) bc	Guymon	18.7 (–7.4) bc
Quickstand	17.6 (–8.0) cd	Tifeagle	21.2 (–6.0) cd	Yukon	18.3 (–7.6) c
Midlawn	16.9 (–8.4) d	Tifdwarf	20.3 (–6.5) d		
		Tifgreen	20.3 (–6.5) d		

[1] Temperatures followed by the same letter within a column are not significantly different ($P < 0.05$).

Note: These are tissue temperatures that were estimated in the laboratory to result in death of the crown, not air temperatures. Ambient air temperatures would have to be significantly colder than this to cause tissue temperatures this low in the field, due to the insulating effects of the soil and thatch.

cultivars presently available (Table 4-3). Belair, a cultivar with a slightly darker color than Meyer, is another hardy vegetative cultivar, but it is not used extensively. Seeded zoysiagrass cultivars, including Korean Common and Zenith, have excellent freezing resistance.

Recent zoysiagrass releases from Texas A and M University, including Cavalier, Crowne, and Palisades, are not as hardy as Meyer and are better suited for use in the southern United States. Likewise, Emerald, a dense, dark green cultivar with fine texture, and El Toro, a fast-spreading cultivar with an appearance similar to Meyer, also lack cold hardiness.

■ *Buffalograss*

Concern regarding buffalograss freezing resistance was not an issue until improved cultivars were developed. Native buffalograss is well adapted to the climate in which it grows. However, when

Table 4-3

Approximate killing temperatures and spring recovery of zoysiagrass cultivars

Killing temperatures were determined by sampling rhizomes from the field, exposing them to low temperatures in a freezer, and regrowing.

Spring recovery was based upon a 0 to 9 rating taken in June in Columbia, Missouri (after Dunn et al. 1999).

Cultivar[1]	Killing Temperature, °F (°C)	Spring Recovery Rating
Cavalier		2.0
Crowne		3.0
El Toro	≥14 (−10)	2.3
Emerald		3.0
Palisades		2.7
Belair		8.0
Korean Common	0.4 (−18)	8.7
Meyer		6.7
Sunburst		6.7
LSD	6.8 (−14)	1.2

[1]Meyer, Belair, Sunburst, El Toro, Korean Common, Crowne, and Palisades are *Z. japonica*, Emerald is a *Z. japonica* × *Z. tenuifolia*, and Cavalier is a *Z. matrella*.

Note: These are tissue temperatures that were estimated in the laboratory to result in death of the crown, not air temperatures. Ambient air temperatures would have to be significantly colder than this to cause tissue temperatures this low in the field, due to the insulating effects of the soil and thatch.

Figure 4-4
Freezing injury of Emerald zoysiagrass is obvious during springtime in Silver Spring, Maryland.

improved cultivars were selected by plant breeders, some selections native to the southern United States that had high quality (e.g., 609, which originated from a female clone collected in Texas) sold and established in northern climates to which they were not well adapted.

Freezing tolerance studies with field-grown buffalograss in Colorado indicated that few differences among cultivars occurred in September, when no acclimation had occurred (Qian et al. 2001). Texoka and Tatanka experienced reduced growth and entered dormancy most quickly in autumn and were also most cold hardy. Stolons from both cultivars tolerated midwinter temperatures below –5.8°F (–21°C) in a controlled-environment test. Conversely, 609, UCR-95 and Stampede maintained color and growth longer into the autumn and were more freezing sensitive, tolerating temperatures no lower than 3.2°F (–16°C) in controlled-environment tests.

Tropical Warm-Season Grasses
All St. Augustinegrass cultivars have relatively poor freezing resistance. Raleigh was shown to acclimate to freezing temperatures, whereas Floratam and FX-332 did not (Maier, Lang, and Fry 1994). In the same test, the lethal midwinter temperature at the tissue level for Raleigh was approximately 21°F (–6°C), whereas that for Floratam was approximately 25°F (–4°C). Raleigh also survived in

Figure 4-5
Spring green-up of buffalograss cultivars in a National Turfgrass Evaluation Program trial. Note how some of the cultivars that originated in the south suffered greater freezing injury than others.

the field following a winter in which air temperatures were lower than 5°F (–15°C); Floratam did not (Wilson, Reinert, and Dudeck 1997).

Centipedegrass has slightly better freezing resistance than St. Augustinegrass, tolerating temperatures between 16 and 19°F (–7 and –9°C) (Fry et al. 1993). There has been no reported difference among genotypes of centipedegrass in freezing resistance (Johnston and Dickens 1977).

Cool-Season Turfgrasses One would surmise that freezing injury in cool-season grasses is not as great a concern as in warm-season grasses, and this is generally the case. However, in northern climates it is not unusual for some cool-season turfgrass species and cultivars to suffer freezing injury. The reported range of lethal freezing temperatures for hardened cool-season grasses in midwinter is 23°F (–5°C) for common perennial ryegrass to –31°F (–35°C) for creeping bentgrass (Gusta et al. 1980) (Table 4-4).

Grasses for which winter low temperature injury is most likely are annual bluegrass, perennial ryegrass, and tall fescue. Annual bluegrass ecotypes sampled from golf course putting greens have been shown to tolerate temperatures as low as –24°F (–31 °C) under controlled conditions (Dionne et al. 2001b). However, the freezing

Figure 4-6
Freezing injury on a St. Augustinegrass lawn in Baton Rouge, Louisiana.

Table 4-4

Cold hardiness of turfgrasses sampled from the field in February in Fort Collins, Colorado (after Gusta et al. 1980)

Turfgrass	Number of Cultivars Evaluated	Range of Lethal Temperatures, °F (°C)[1]
Perennial ryegrass	11	5 to 23 (−15 to −5)
Hard fescue	1	−5.8 (−21)
Creeping red fescue	2	−11.2 (−24)
Weeping alkaligrass	1	−16.6 (−27)
Kentucky bluegrass	7	−22 to −5.8 (−30 to −21)
Creeping bentgrass	3	−31 (−35)

[1] Lethal temperature is reported as the temperature at the crown at which at least 50 percent of the plant population died (LT_{50}).

injury commonly observed in annual bluegrass is likely the result of freezing following crown hydration. Crown hydration injury usually occurs in early spring, when snow and ice melt and crowns absorb water. Between late March and late April in Canada, a 4 percent increase in annual bluegrass crown hydration occurred (Tompkins, Ross, and Moroz 2000). Lack of insulation provided by snow cover during this period could predispose plants to freezing injury if freezing temperatures return.

Perennial ryegrass is the most freezing sensitive of the cultivated cool-season turfgrasses. Selection of hardy cultivars is important in northern climates. Evaluation of the best and poorest ryegrass cultivars from the National Turfgrass Evaluation Program test in Orono, Maine, indicated that performance was directly related to cold hardiness (Ebdon, Gagne, and Manley 2002). The best-performing cultivars had an average killing temperature (LT_{50}) of 13.5°F (−10.3°C), whereas the poorest-performing cultivars had a killing temperature of 19.6°F (−6.9°C).

Tall fescue is generally thought to have good cold temperature tolerance. However, in extreme northern climates, such as in the Dakotas, it may not survive as a perennial.

HEAT STRESS

Both air and soil temperatures often reach supraoptimal levels during summer months, which limits shoot and root growth and even plant survival, particularly for cool-season grasses. Heat stress occurs typically at temperatures greater than 86°F (30°C) for cool-season grasses and 113°F (45°C) for warm-season grasses. Heat stress has been considered to be the primary environmental factor, causing decline of cool-season grasses in the summer, although many other factors can be involved.

Types of Heat Stress

Temperature may rise slowly above the optimal temperature range and persist for prolonged periods of time during summer. This may not be immediately fatal to plants, but it eventually causes injury or death. This is referred to as indirect heat stress. Indirect heat stress negatively affects turfgrass physiological and metabolic functions, including photosynthesis, respiration, transpiration, and water and nutrient uptake.

Turfgrasses occasionally are subjected to sufficiently high temperatures to cause immediate cell death. This type of high tempera-

Figure 4-7
Scientists measure the soil surface temperature on creeping bentgrass green experiencing summer decline in Kansas.

ture stress is referred to as direct heat stress and is not as common as indirect heat stress. Direct heat stress occurs due to a rapid increase in temperature that lasts for a short period of time. This stress may cause immediate physical injury, such as denaturation of proteins and cellular enzymes, and rupture of cell membranes, leading to rapid cell death.

Heat Injury Symptoms   Typical symptoms of heat stress injury in turfgrasses include leaf chlorosis and a reduction in shoot density. Roots of cool-season grasses typically appear to be shorter and less extensive during summer compared to those in spring. Rooting decline at high temperatures is mainly due to dieback and reduction in new root formation. Root growth is more sensitive to high temperatures than shoot growth, consistent with its lower optimal temperature

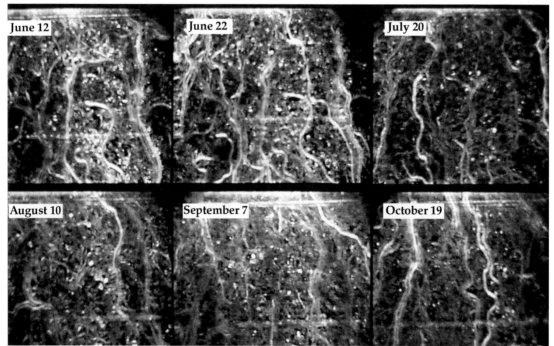

Figure 4-8
Root images recorded with a minirhizotron camera at a 3-cm soil depth from June to October 1998 on a Crenshaw creeping bentgrass green in Kansas mowed at ⅛ inch (3 mm). Note the decline in new root growth and increasing root mortality from July to September. New root production is noticeable in October.

requirement. For cool-season grasses such as creeping bentgrass, decline in root number, length, mass, and viability often precedes visual turf quality decline during high temperature exposure (Pote and Huang 2004).

Heat stress symptoms are often confused with pathological problems in cool-season turfgrasses. For example, creeping bentgrass on closely mowed putting greens often exhibits yellowing and thinning of the turf canopy and root dieback during summer months, a phenomenon known as summer bentgrass decline. Over the years, there has been much confusion about whether summer bentgrass decline is a pathological or physiological problem. The symptoms are not alleviated or reversed when fungicides are applied. In most situations, summer decline in turf quality and root growth is associated with deterioration or dysfunction of physiological processes rather than the presence of pathogens.

Physiological Responses and Mechanisms of Heat Resistance

Plants exposed to heat stress exhibit various physiological, metabolic, and cellular responses. Plants capture light energy and carbon (in the form of CO_2) from the air to produce carbohydrates that are used to maintain and produce new leaves, roots, stems, and stolons. Respiration consumes carbohydrates to generate energy to support the growth and development of plant organs. When temperatures are within the optimal range, cool-season grasses are able to maintain a positive balance between photosynthesis and respiration and thus provide for adequate carbohydrate storage. Photosynthesis is among the physiological processes most sensitive to high temperatures. Under high temperature exposure, net photosynthetic rate (P_n) decreases as temperature increases above 86°F (30°C) in cool-season turfgrasses, while respiration rates of both shoots and roots increase with temperature (Fig. 4-9). The imbalances between photosynthesis and respiration under high-temperature conditions can result in higher daily total carbon consumption than carbon production. Energy consumption often exceeds energy assimilation during hot summer months, especially at low mowing heights, which remove leaves that are otherwise available for energy production. Ultimately, this leads to the exhaustion of carbohydrate reserves via respiration and growth inhibition.

Carbohydrates make up the skeleton or structure of plants and are a source of metabolic energy, which is particularly important for

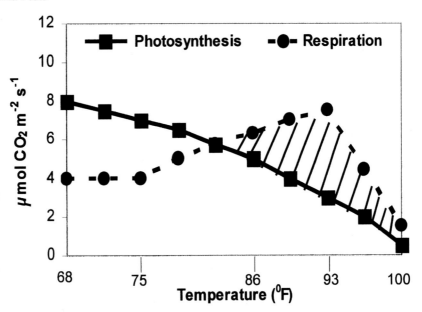

Figure 4-9
Changes in canopy
photosynthetic and
respiration rates with
increasing temperatures
(20°C = 68°F ; 38°C =
100°F) for Penncross
creeping bentgrass grown
in a growth chamber.
The shadowed area
indicates the period of
time when respiration
exceeded photosynthesis,
which could result in
carbohydrate depletion.

the regrowth of shoots and roots following defoliation or mowing. Nonstructural carbohydrates (TNC) (including starch, fructans, sucrose, and glucose) are the primary energy reserves for plants exposed to stressful conditions and are widely used as a measure of stress tolerance (Hull 1992). Total nonstructural carbohydrate availability decreases with increasing temperatures. The decrease in carbohydrate content is often more pronounced in roots than in shoots. The decline in carbohydrate availability has been associated with decreases in root growth (Carrow 1996; Xu and Huang 2000a, 2000b; Sweeney et al. 2001), tiller production, and leaf growth (Xu and Huang 2000a, 2000b, 2001b). Carbon allocation to roots in creeping bentgrass is also inhibited by heat stress, which could cause root dieback (Xu and Huang 2000b). Aldous and Kaufmann (1979) suggested that decline in carbohydrate content in roots appeared to be related to cessation of shoot growth at supraoptimal temperatures in Kentucky bluegrass.

Metabolic changes during heat stress include the induction of free radicals such as the superoxide radical ($\cdot O_2^-$), hydrogen peroxide (H_2O_2), hydroxyl free radical ($\cdot OH$), and singlet oxygen ($^1O_2$) inside cells. These free radicals are strong oxidizing agents and are highly toxic to cells. They can react with macromolecules such as unsaturated fatty acids and proteins to cause oxidative damage to cell membranes (lipid peroxidation). Oxidative stress can lead to inhibition of photosynthesis and respiration and thus plant growth. Plants develop defensive mechanisms against the attack of the free radicals by scavenging or eliminating these molecules using antioxidants and antioxidant enzymes. Oxidative protection is an important component in determining the survival of a plant during heat stress.

Activities of antioxidant enzymes, which help to protect plant tissues from the toxic free radicals, typically decrease during heat stress. Shoot injury and leaf senescence in cool-season grasses subjected to heat stress have been associated with oxidative damage induced by the suppression of antioxidant enzyme activity and the oxidation of lipids in cell membranes (lipid peroxidation) (Liu and Huang 2000b). Turf quality decline of creeping bentgrass was correlated with an increase in membrane leakage and lipid peroxidation during the summer months (Xu and Huang 2004). Heat-tolerant creeping bentgrass cultivars maintained higher antioxidant enzyme activity and lower lipid peroxidation than heat-sensitive ones (Liu and Huang 2000b).

Heat stress also alters patterns of gene expression. Heat injury is often associated with a decrease in the synthesis of normal proteins and an increase in protein degradation. Soluble protein content decreases during heat stress. This has been observed at temperatures above 86°F (30°C) in creeping bentgrass. However, the synthesis of another set of proteins is induced with increasing temperatures. These heat-inducible proteins are called heat shock proteins (HSPs) and are rapidly produced in response to a temperature increase of about 18°F (10°C) above normal (optimal) growth temperature. Some HSPs can be synthesized within minutes of heat shock. Heat shock proteins play an important role in protecting cells from heat damage by ensuring proper folding of other polypeptides. Plants can acquire thermotolerance if exposed to a short-term, non-lethal high temperature before encountering lethal high temperatures (heat acclimation). Synthesis of HSPs is involved in the process of heat acclimation. Plants acclimated to heat stress produce more HSPs and show improved tolerance to heat; they can even survive temperatures that previously would have been lethal.

Little is known about protein changes during heat stress and their contribution to heat tolerance in turfgrasses. Park and colleagues (1996) reported that more HSP25 was detected in heat-tolerant varieties of creeping bentgrass compared to heat-intolerant ones. Heat tolerance and the presence of the additional HSP25 polypeptides are linked traits in creeping bentgrass (Park et al. 1997). DiMascio and colleagues (1994) found detectable differences in the levels of heat-induced HSP26 between heat-tolerant and heat-sensitive cultivars of perennial ryegrass and suggested that analysis of HSP could provide the basis of a rapid and reliable characterization of heat tolerance.

Root Regulation of Plant Responses to High Soil Temperature

In warm climates, soil temperatures can rise to a point where cool-season turfgrass injury occurs and root and shoot survival are in jeopardy. Soil temperature has been found to be more critical than air temperature in controlling the growth of creeping bentgrass (Xu and Huang 2000a, 2000b, 2001a, 2001b). Exposing creeping bentgrass roots to a high soil temperature (95°F [35°C]) while maintaining shoots at an optimal air temperature (68°F [20°C]) reduced shoot and root growth. Lowering soil temperature from 95°F (35°C) to 68°F (20°C) while a high air temperature (95°F [35°C]) was maintained increased shoot and root growth, enhanced photosynthesis, and improved turf quality (Xu and Huang 2001a, 2001b).

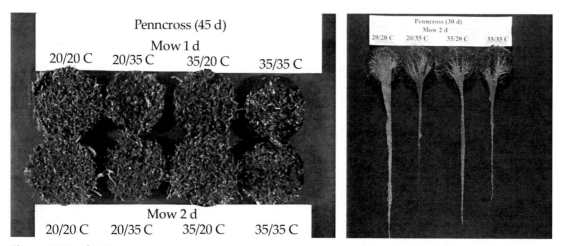

Figures 4-10 and 4-11
Effects of air and soil temperatures [70° and 70°F (20° and 20°C); 70° and 95°F (20° and 35°C); 95° and 70°F (35° and 20°C); and 95° and 95°F (35° and 35°C)] on shoots (Fig. 4-10, left) and roots (Fig. 4-11, right) of Penncross creeping bentgrass. Shoots were exposed to air temperatures in a growth chamber, while root temperatures were controlled using a water bath inside a growth chamber.

Although soil temperatures clearly influence shoot growth and performance of cool-season grasses, it is not clear what mechanisms allow roots to sense high soil temperatures and regulate shoot growth. Liu, Huang, and Banowetz (2002) reported that shoot injury and leaf senescence induced by high soil temperatures were associated with the inhibition of cytokinin production. Cytokinins, a class of hormones, are produced mainly in roots and may regulate shoot responses to high soil temperatures. Cytokinin content in both leaves and roots decreased when roots of creeping bentgrass were exposed to heat stress (95°F [35°C]); injection of zeatin riboside to the root zone alleviated leaf senescence (Liu, Huang, and Banowetz 2002; Liu and Huang 2002).

The adverse effects of high soil temperatures on shoot growth could also be attributed to decreased nutrient uptake by roots. Among the three major macronutrients (nitrogen, phosphorus, potassium) in creeping bentgrass, potassium was most sensitive to changes in soil temperature (Huang and Xu 2000). High potassium levels in leaves and roots may enhance turfgrass tolerance to high shoot or root temperatures by facilitating stomatal opening of leaves and water uptake of roots, thus increasing transpirational cooling. Studies with creeping bentgrass (Liu and Huang 2004) showed that the decline in cytokinin synthesis in roots preceded the decreases in water and nutrient uptake and leaf senescence when roots were exposed to high soil temperatures, suggesting that production of cytokinin may be the early root signal that induces changes in shoots, but this deserves further investigation.

Transpirational cooling is an important heat avoidance mechanism that is essential for turfgrass survival during exposure to high temperatures. Evaporative cooling associated with transpiration keeps leaves 5 to 18°F (3 to 10°C) cooler than air, but stomata must be open for cooling to occur. This requires a continuous water supply from roots to leaves. Bonos and Murphy (1999) reported that Kentucky bluegrass cultivars that were heat tolerant exploited soil moisture deep in the profile, exhibited significantly fewer summer stress symptoms, and maintained a canopy temperature 9°F (5°C) cooler than intolerant entries. This suggested that the maintenance of transpirational cooling is associated with better summer stress performance of Kentucky bluegrass during high temperature and drought stress. Extensive rooting and active water uptake are essential to meet the increased transpirational demand of turf during heat stress. Lehman and Engelke (1993) examined variability in rooting depth among cultivars of Kentucky bluegrass and found that Midnight exhibited both high heat resistance and long root extension, suggesting that screening for root extension could be used to hasten progress in selection for heat-tolerant genotypes.

Genetic Variability in Heat Resistance

Cool-Season Turfgrasses

Among the cool-season grasses, tall fescue has superior heat tolerance. Much of the heat tolerance exhibited by tall fescue is due to its deep root system. The deep-rooted nature of this species allows it to supply adequate water to the shoots. Hence, the ability of tall fescue's tissues to function at higher temperatures may be comparable to that of some other cool-season grasses, but it is able to maintain transpiration and avoid drought and heat stress after other grasses begin to suffer. Tall fescue's superior heat and drought resistance have contributed to its popularity in the transition zone and upper South.

Tests to compare heat resistance of Kentucky bluegrass and perennial ryegrass have shown that bluegrass is hardier than ryegrass (Minner et al. 1983; Wehner and Watschke 1981) (Table 4-6). Razmjoo, Kaneko, and Imada (1993) evaluated heat tolerance of perennial ryegrass, tall fescue, and Kentucky bluegrass in a controlled environment programmed to expose plants to several tem-

Table 4-5

Relative resistance of cool-season grasses to indirect heat stress

Turfgrass	Relative Heat Resistance
Tall fescue	Very good
Kentucky bluegrass	Good
Perennial ryegrass	Fair
Fine fescues	
Creeping bentgrass	
Annual bluegrass	Poor
Rough bluegrass	

Table 4-6

Comparative heat resistance of field-sampled Kentucky bluegrass and perennial ryegrass cultivars as measured by recovery after heat exposure in Maryland (after Minner et al. 1983)

Species	Cultivar	Recovery (%)[1]
Kentucky bluegrass	Sydsport	72.5 a
	Pennstar	66.9 b
	Vantage	65.6 b
Perennial ryegrass	Pennfine	59.9 c
	Citation	58.0 c
	Caravelle	56.3 c

[1] Mean recovery of whole plants sampled on three dates (June, July, August) over two years and subjected to temperatures of 108, 111, and 115°F (42, 44, and 46°C) and then allowed to recover in the greenhouse. Percentage was calculated as recovery weight of stressed plants compared to non-stressed plants. Means followed by the same letter are not significantly different ($P < 0.05$).

perature regimes ranging from 97 to 122°F (36 to 50°C) for about three weeks. They found that the perennial ryegrass cultivars Pinnacle and All Star survived 108°F (42°C), whereas Nugget and Bristol Kentucky bluegrass and Rebel Jr. and Mesa tall fescue survived 118°F (48°C). Midnight and Adelphi Kentucky bluegrass were found to be more heat tolerant than Fylking and Nugget (Lehman and Engleke 1993).

Fine fescues perform well in the transition zone until daytime temperatures exceed 95°F (35°C) for prolonged periods, and then quality quickly declines. As such, their resistance to high temperature stress might be considered inferior to that of perennial ryegrass.

For many years, Penncross creeping bentgrass was the cultivar of choice for putting greens. In the past twenty years, several new creeping bentgrass cultivars have been released that generally exhibit better heat tolerance than Penncross. In the South, Penn A-1, Penn A-4, Penn G-2, Penn G-6, Crenshaw, L-93, and Southshore all maintained higher turf quality than Penncross during summer (Bruneau et al. 2001). The inferior heat resistance of Penncross relative to newer cultivars has also been documented in several studies where turf was subjected to supraoptimal temperatures in a controlled environment (Huang, Liu, and Xu 2001; Xu and Huang 2001b). These new cultivars have higher tiller density and narrower leaves than Penncross. High tiller density is associated with high canopy photosynthetic rate by providing more leaves available for light interception.

The true annual type of annual bluegrass avoids heat stress by completing its life cycle in late spring. Perennial strains of annual bluegrass often decline in midsummer in localized areas on golf putting greens. If annual bluegrass occupies a significant portion of the green surface area, superintendents can reseed only when autumn returns. No doubt there is a range of heat tolerances among perennial types of annual bluegrass. Sampling of 115 annual blue-grass clones in Canada resulted in the identification of 26 that had fair to good heat stress tolerance (Cordukes 1977). It is possible that even on a single golf course there may be some annual bluegrass clones with better heat tolerance than others. The genetic variability in heat tolerance among strains of annual bluegrass is just another factor that superintendents use in building their case for eliminating it from their golf course.

Rough bluegrass often goes unnoticed until it declines during midsummer heat. At that time, segregated patches of this species are often evident in stands of other cool-season turfgrasses. Rough bluegrass usually recovers, however, once cool autumn temperatures return.

Warm-Season Turfgrasses   High temperatures should not be a concern with warm-season grasses. Buffalograss and bermudagrass leaf tissues tolerated temperatures of approximately 140°F (60°C) for over 600 minutes in a controlled-environment test (Wallner, Becwar, and Butler 1982).

REFERENCES

Aldous, D. E., and J. E. Kaufmann. 1979. Role of root temperature on shoot growth of two Kentucky bluegrass cultivars. *Agron. J.* 71:545–47.

Anderson, J. and C. Taliaferro. 1995. Laboratory freeze tolerance of field-grown bermudagrass cultivars. Agron. J. 87:1017–1019.

Anderson, J., C. Taliaferro, and D. Martin. 1993. Evaluation of freeze tolerance of bermudagrass in a controlled environment. *HortScience* 28:955.

_____. 2002. Freeze tolerance of bermudagrasses: vegetatively propagated cultivars intended for fairway and putting green use, and seed-propagated cultivars. *Crop Sci.* 42:975–77.

_____. 2003. Longer exposure durations increase freeze damage to turf bermudagrasses. *Crop Sci.* 43:973–77.

Beard, J. B. 1973. *Turfgrass: Science and culture.* Englewood Cliffs, NJ: Prentice-Hall.

Bonos, S., and J. A. Murphy. 1999. Growth responses and performance of Kentucky bluegrass under summer stress. *Crop Sci.* 39:770–74.

Bredemeijer, G. M. M., and G. Esselink. 1995. Sugar metabolism in cold-hardened *Lolium perenne* varieties. *Plant Varieties and Seeds* 8:187–95.

Bruneau, A. H., C. A. Bigelow, R. J. Cooper, and D. C. Bowman. 2001. Performance of creeping bentgrass cultivars maintained at two mowing heights and under two fungicide regimes in North Carolina. *Int. Turf. Soc. Res. J.* 9:835–42.

Bush, E., P. Wilson, D. Shepard, and J. McCrimmon. 2000. Freezing tolerance and nonstructural carbohydrate composition of carpetgrass (*Axonopus affinis* Chase). *HortScience* 35:187–89.

Cardona, C. A., R. R. Duncan, and O. Lindstrom. 1997. Low temperature tolerance assessment in paspalum. *Crop Sci.* 37:1283–91.

Carrow, R. N. 1996. Summer decline of bentgrass greens. *Golf Course Management* 64:51–56.

Cordukes, W. E. 1977. Growth habit and heat tolerance of a collection of *Poa annua* plants in Canada. *Can. J. Plant Sci.* 57:1201–3.

Cyril, J., G. L. Powell, R. R. Duncan, and W. V. Baird. 2002. Changes in membrane polar lipid fatty acids of seashore paspalum in response to low temperature exposure. *Crop Sci.* 42: 2031–7.

Dunn, J. H., S. S. Bughrara, M. R. Warmund, and B. F. Fresenburg. 1999. Low temperature tolerance of zoysiagrasses. *HortScience* 34:96–99.

DiMascio, J. A, P. M. Sweeney, T. K. Danneberger, and J. C. Kamalay. 1994. Analysis of heat shock in perennial ryegrass using maize heat shock protein clones. *Crop Sci.* 34:798–804.

Dionne, J., Y. Castonguay, P. Nadeau, and Y. Desjardins. 2001a. Amino acid and protein changes during cold acclimation of green-type annual bluegrass (*Poa annua* L.) ecotypes. *Crop Sci.* 41:1862–70.

_____. 2001b. Freezing tolerance and carbohydrate changes during cold acclimation of green-type annual bluegrass (*Poa annua* L.) ecotypes. *Crop Sci.* 41:443–51.

Ebdon, J. S., R. A. Gagne, and R. C. Manley. 2002. Comparative cold tolerance in diverse turf quality genotypes of perennial ryegrass. *HortScience* 37:826–30.

Fry, J. 1990. Cold temperature tolerance of bermudagrass. *Golf Course Management* 58 (10):26, 28, 32.

———. 1991. Freezing resistance of southern turfgrasses. *Lawn and Landscape Maint.* 12 (1):48, 50–51.

Fry, J. D., N. S. Lang, and R. G. P. Clifton. 1991. Freezing resistance and carbohydrate composition of Floratam St. Augustinegrass. *HortScience* 26:1537–39.

Fry, J. D., N. S. Lang, R. G. P. Clifton, and F. P. Maier. 1993. Freezing tolerance and carbohydrate content of low-temperature-acclimated and nonacclimated centipedegrass. *Crop Sci.* 33:1051–5.

Gatschet, M. J., C. M. Taliaferro, D. R. Porter, M. O. Anderson, J. A. Anderson, and K. W. Jackson. 1996. A cold-regulated protein from bermudagrass crowns is a chitinase. *Crop Sci.* 36:712–18.

Gusta, L. V., J. D. Butler, C. Rajashekar, and M. J. Burke. 1980. Freezing resistance of perennial turfgrasses. *HortScience* 15:494–96.

Huang, B., X. Liu, and Q. Xu. 2001. Supraoptimal temperatures induced oxidative stress in leaves of creeping bentgrass cultivars differing in heat tolerance. *Crop Sci.* 41:430–435.

Huang, B., and Q. Xu. 2000. Root growth and nutrient element status of creeping bentgrass cultivars differing in heat tolerance as influenced by supraoptimal shoot and root temperatures. *J. Plant Nutrition* 23:979–90.

Hull, R. 1992. Energy relations and carbohydrate partitioning in turfgrass. Pp. 175–205 in D. V. Waddington, R. N. Carrow, and R. C. Sherman, eds., *Turfgrass*. Madison, WI: American Society of Agronomy.

Ibitayo, O. O., J. D. Butler, and M. J. Burke. 1981. Cold hardiness of bermudagrass and *Paspalum vaginatum* Sw. *HortScience* 16:683–84.

Johnston, W. J., and R. Dickens. 1977. Cold tolerance evaluation of several centipedegrass selections. *Agron. J.* 69:100–3.

Lee, S. P., and T. H. Chen. 1993. Molecular cloning of abscisic acid–responsive mRNAs expressed during the induction of freezing tolerance in bromegrass (*Bromus inermis* Leyss) suspension culture. *Plant Physiol.* 101:1089–96.

Lehman, V. G, and M. C. Engelke. 1993. Heat resistance and rooting potential of Kentucky bluegrass cultivars. *Int. Turf. Soc. Res. J.* 7:775–79.

Levitt, J. 1980. *Responses of plants to environmental stresses*. New York: Academic Press.

Liu, X., and B. Huang. 2000a. Carbohydrate accumulation in relation to heat stress tolerance in two creeping bentgrass cultivars. *J. Am. Soc. Hort. Sci.* 125:442–47.

———. 2000b. Heat stress injury of creeping bentgrass in relation to membrane lipid peroxidation. *Crop Sci.* 40:503–10.

———. 2002. Cytokinin effects on creeping bentgrass responses to heat stress II. Antioxidant enzyme activities and lipid peroxidation. *Crop Sci.* 42:466–72.

Liu, X., and B. Huang. 2004b. Root physiological factors involved in creeping bentgrass response to high temperature. *Environmental and Experimental Botany* 51:in press.

Liu, X., B. Huang, and G. Banowetz. 2002. Cytokinin effects on creeping bentgrass responses to heat stress I. Shoot and root growth. *Crop Sci.* 42:457–65.

Maier, F. P., N. S. Lang, and J. D. Fry. 1994. Freezing tolerance of three St. Augustinegrass cultivars as affected by stolon carbohydrate and water content. *J. Am. Soc. Hort. Sci.* 119:473–76.

Minner, D. D., P. H. Dernoeden, D. J. Wehner, and M. S. McIntosh. 1983. Heat tolerance screening of field-grown cultivars of Kentucky bluegrass and perennial ryegrass. *Agron. J.* 75:772–75.

Nilsen, E. T., and D. M. Orcutt. 1996. *The physiology of plants under stress*. New York: John Wiley and Sons.

Park, S. Y., K. C. Chang, R. Shivaji, and D. S. Luthe. 1997. Recovery from heat shock in heat-tolerant and nontolerant variants of creeping bentgrass. *Plant Physiol.* 115:229–40.

Park, S. Y., R. Shivaji, J. V. Krans, and D. S. Luthe. 1996. Heat-shock response in heat-tolerant and nontolerant variants of *Agrostis palustris* Huds. *Plant Physiol.* 111:515–24.

Pollock, C. J., C. F. Eagle, and I. M. Sims. 1988. Effect of photoperiod and irradiance changes upon development of freezing tolerance and accumulation of soluble carbohydrate in seedlings of *Lolium perenne* grown at 2 C. *Ann. Bot.* 62:95–100.

Pomeroy, K. M., C. J. Andrews, K. P. Stanley, and J. Y. Gao. 1985. Physiological and metabolic responses of winter wheat to prolonged freezing stress. *Plant Physiol.* 78:207–10.

Pote, J., and B. Huang. 2004. Timing and temperature of physiological decline for creeping bentgrass. *J. Am. Soc. Hort. Sci.* 129:in press.

Qian, Y., S. Ball, Z. Tan, A. J. Koski, and S. J. Wilhelm. 2001. Freezing tolerance of six cultivars of buffalograss. *Crop Sci.* 41:1174–78.

Razmjoo, K., S. Kaneko, and T. Imada. 1993. Varietal differences of some cool-season turfgrass species in relation to heat and flood stress. *Int. Turf. Soc. Res. J.* 7:636–42.

Robertson, A. J., Gusta, L. V., M. J. T. Reaney, and M. Ishikawa. 1988. Identification of proteins correlated with increased freezing tolerance in Bromegrass (*Bromus inermis* Leyss. cv. Manchar) cell cultures. *Plant Physiol.* 86:344–47.

Stier, J. C., D. L. Filiault, M. Wisniewski, and J. P. Palta. 2003. Visualization of freezing progression in turfgrasses using infrared video thermography. *Crop Sci.* 43:415–20.

Sweeney, P., K. Danneberger, D. Wang, and M. McBride. 2001. Root weight, nonstructural carbohydrate content, and shoot density of high-density creeping bentgrass cultivars. *HortScience* 36:368–70.

Tompkins, D. K., J. B. Ross, and D. L. Moroz. 2000. Dehardening of annual bluegrass and creeping bentgrass during late winter and early spring. *Agron. J.* 92:5–9.

Wallner, S. J., M. R. Becwar, and J. D. Butler. 1982. Measurement of turfgrass heat tolerance in vitro. *J. Am. Soc. Hort. Sci.* 107:608–13.

Wehner, D. J., and T. L. Watschke. 1981. Heat tolerance of Kentucky bluegrasses, perennial ryegrasses, and annual bluegrass. *Agron. J.* 73:79–84.

Wilson, C. A., J. A. Reinert., and A. E. Dudeck. 1977. Winter survival of St. Augustinegrass in north Mississippi. *Quarterly News Bul. of Southern Turfgrass Assn.* V:12.

Xu, Q., and B. Huang. 2000a. Growth and physiological responses of creeping bentgrass to changes in air and soil temperatures. *Crop Sci.* 40:1363–68.

———. 2000b. Effects of differential air and soil temperature on carbohydrate metabolism in creeping bentgrass. *Crop Sci.* 40:1368–74.

———. 2001a. Lowering soil temperature under supraoptimal air temperature improved shoot and root growth in creeping bentgrass. *Crop Sci.* 41:1878–83.

———. 2001b. Morphological and physiological characteristics associated with heat tolerance in creeping bentgrass. *Crop Sci.* 41:127–33.

———. 2004. Seasonal changes in antioxidant enzyme activities for three creeping bentgrass cultivars. *Crop Sci.*, in press.

5

Shade

It is estimated that 20 to 25 percent of all turfgrasses are maintained under some degree of shade, whether from buildings or trees. Shade affects plant growth by influencing light intensity, quality, and duration. In addition, shade alters the turf microclimate, including temperature, relative humidity, and air movement. Trees above and surrounding turfgrass not only cast shade but may also affect grass growth through competition for light, water, and nutrients. Some trees may also have allelopathic effects on turfgrasses, that is, chemicals may be released from roots or leaves that inhibit turfgrass growth.

Turfgrass Shade Stress Is Affected By:	See Information Beginning on Page:
Irrigation	153
Mowing	193
Fertilization	217
Cultivation	249
Plant growth regulators	277

SHADE AND TURFGRASS GROWTH

Light Quality Sunlight that reaches the earth's surface is composed of a wide spectrum of energy, with wavelengths ranging from 200 to 1,800 nm. Plants use light energy particles called photons, with wave-

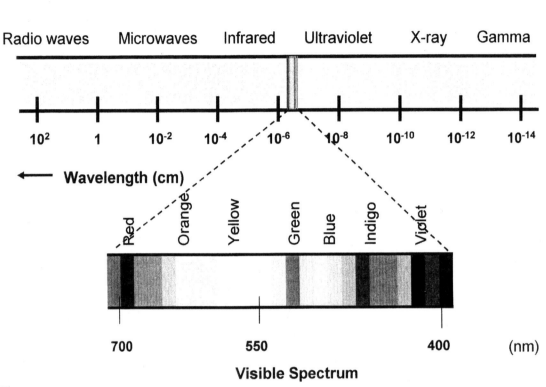

Figure 5-1
The electromagnetic spectrum, with visible, photosynthetically active radiation magnified.

lengths between 400 and 700 nm, for photosynthesis and growth. Consequently, this wavelength band is called photosynthetically active radiation (PAR).

Plant pigments, including chlorophylls and carotenoids, have maximum PAR absorption at specific wavelengths. Chlorophyll a has a peak spectral absorption at wavelengths of 410, 430, and 660 nm. Chlorophyll b absorbs most effectively at 430, 455, and 640 nm. Peak absorption of carotenoids is near 450 nm. For photosynthesis, the most important light spectra are at 400 to 500 nm, referred to as blue light, and 600 to 700 nm, referred to as red light. The PAR from 500 to 600 nm, green light, has essentially no effect on plant growth and development. Far-red irradiance occurs in a spectral band from 700 to 800 nm and is not active in photosynthesis but may influence germination, flowering, and stem growth.

Turfgrass growth and survival under trees is largely dependent on the intensity and quality of light passing through a tree's canopy. Turfgrass under trees receives the transmitted light, which is less intense and contains less-effective wavelengths. Spruce (*Picea* spp.), oak (*Quercus* spp.), and maple (*Acer* spp.) absorb a large amount of blue light, leaving a red shade. As the tree canopy becomes denser, all wavelengths are filtered to a greater degree. Warm-season turfgrasses respond well to reduced light as long as it is composed largely of the short wavelengths (blue region of the spectrum). For example, bermudagrass can grow at 40 to 50 percent of full sunlight if blue light is transmitted.

Light filtered by deciduous trees and conifers had significantly more high activity (red plus blue) quanta than shade produced by a building. Relative to total irradiance, the percentage of blue wavelengths increases and that of red wavelengths decreases with increasing shade. Levels of blue, red, and far-red light were affected by both shade source and shade intensity (Bell, Danneberger, and McMahon 2000).

Light Intensity   Only 37 percent of the energy in sunlight is within the wavelengths useful for photosynthesis; 62 percent is infrared (>700 nm), and the remaining 0.6 percent is ultraviolet (200 to 400 nm). Of the sunlight that reaches the plant leaf, approximately 1 to 5 percent is used for photosynthesis, 10 percent is reflected, and 10 percent is transmitted through the leaf. Most of the sunlight is reradiated or used for powering transpiration. Sunlight reaching the ground at sea level has a PAR intensity of about 1,800 to 2,300 µmol per m^2 per second on a cloudless day. Saturation point for photosynthesis ranges from 534 to 1,072 µmol per m^2 per second for cool-season grasses and from 1,794 to 2,139 µmol per m^2 per second for warm-season grasses. The levels of light that cause adverse effects on plant growth vary with shade duration, species, cultivar (see discussion below on genetic variability in shade tolerance), and environmental conditions.

Light Duration   Turfgrasses require a minimum daily duration of light for growth. Duration is affected by the time of year (the sun's angle), latitude, and size and location of the tree or structure creating shade. Most turfgrasses require four to five hours of full sun per day or an entire day of filtered light. Prolonging light duration promotes leaf growth, tiller production, and dry matter accumulation and may increase environmental stress resistance (Hay and Heide 1983; Hay and Pedersen 1986; Aamlid 1992). Xu and Huang (2004) reported that extending the light duration from 14 to 22 hours significantly increased turf quality, tiller density, root length, and root number for creeping bentgrass exposed to heat stress. Improved turf performance associated with extended light duration was related to increases in carbohydrate content.

Supplemental lighting has been used to increase light duration on creeping bentgrass putting greens at some U.S. golf courses, including Augusta National's hole 12 and Riviera Country Club's hole 6, which are situated in shaded areas (Kind 2001). Some golf courses employ grow lights to promote recovery from other stresses. Leaving lights on for 24 hours each day in late winter 1999 assisted in the recovery of Penn A-4 creeping bentgrass from a root Pythium outbreak in Mississippi (Kind 2001).

The minimum light duration for maintenance of turf quality varies with species and cultivar. Density of tall fescue and colonial bentgrass was significantly reduced when turf was covered continuously with 30 percent shade or for shorter periods with higher (70 percent) shade levels (Cereti and Rossini 1997). Perpetual shade (35 percent of full sunlight) caused creeping bentgrass color and density to decline, but shade applied at 31 percent of full sunlight for up to six hours per day did not affect turf performance (Bell and Danneberger 1999).

In some shaded areas, light may be available only during morning or afternoon hours. However, whether shade in the morning or afternoon influences turfgrass quality and growth is not clear. Bell and Danneberger (1999) compared effects of 69 percent morning or afternoon shade and observed no difference in creeping bentgrass growth. Seashore paspalum exposed to 90 percent of full sunlight in the morning or afternoon for five hours exhibited no detrimental growth effects in the absence of traffic stress; however, afternoon shade was more detrimental than morning shade when plants were subjected to wear stress or wear plus soil compaction (Jiang, Duncan, and Carrow 2004).

Effects of Shade on the Turf Microclimate

Shade limits turfgrass growth not only by altering irradiance but also by modifying other micro-environmental conditions. Water transpired from trees and grasses in enclosed, shaded areas leads to high relative humidity. The shade canopy moderates temperature fluctuations by lowering temperatures during daytime and increasing temperatures during nighttime by retaining heat. Shade from trees or other structures usually has little influence on grass canopy temperature, but soil temperature is typically much lower under shade than areas exposed to full sun during summer months. Reduced soil temperatures are beneficial to cool-season turfgrasses growing in hot, dry environments. However, lower soil temperatures under heavy shade may restrict growth earlier in fall and delay recovery in spring. Shaded areas may maintain longer dew coverage than exposed, sunny areas, which promotes diseases. The concentration of carbon dioxide often increases in shaded areas with restricted air movement, which may increase photosynthesis.

Plant Competition and Allelopathy

The competition for light, nutrients, and water between turf and surrounding shade plants weakens turfgrass plants and reduces their growth potential. Trees with large leaves and thick branches, such as some oaks and maples, intercept most of the sunlight before it reaches the ground, thus creating a poor environment for turfgrass growth. Some evergreens, such as firs and spruces, have very dense canopies but usually affect only small areas of turf because of their narrow canopy. Pines (*Pinus* spp.), poplars (*Populus* spp.), ashes (*Fraxinus* spp.), and birches (*Betula* spp.) produce a more open shade than maples and oaks.

Shrubs and trees that develop a dense, shallow, fibrous root system, such as some maples, willows (*Salix* spp.), and beeches (*Fagus* spp.), are extremely competitive with turfgrass for moisture and nutrients. The primary root structure in nearly all plants, including large trees, is located in the upper eight inches of the soil and competes very effectively with turf for nutrients and water.

Silver maple (*Acer saccharinum*) and honeylocust (*Gleditsia triacanthos*) are allelopathic to Kentucky bluegrass. Allelochemicals produced by plants may be in the form of terpenes, phenolic compounds, organic acids, tannins, steroids, or other compounds. Evidence also exists that grasses can inhibit the germination and development of young trees. For example, dogwood (*Cornus florida*) and forsythia (*Forsythia intermedia*) exhibited poor establishment when planted in mature sods of Kentucky bluegrass and red fescue (Fales and Wakefield 1981).

TURFGRASS PHYSIOLOGICAL, MORPHOLOGICAL, AND ANATOMICAL RESPONSES TO SHADE

Anatomical, morphological, and physiological changes of plants exposed to shade are summarized in Table 5-1. Typical shoot and root characteristics of shaded turfgrass plants include shortened roots, reduced shoot density, erect and elongated growth of stems and leaves, thin leaves, and decreased plant vigor. The reduced sunlight leads to decreased carbohydrate production under shade. Therefore, leaves of shaded turfgrasses have delicate, succulent structures (thin cell walls) and less developed vascular tissues. Shade-adapted plants also have lower light requirements, respiration rates, and water and nutrient requirements.

Dudeck and Peacock (1992) and Beard (1997) presented extensive reviews of previous research on growth and physiological responses of turfgrass to shading. Van Huylenbroeck and Van Bockstaele (2001) reported that average leaf elongation was 35 percent higher under reduced irradiance (65 percent) compared to full light in several grass species, and perennial ryegrass had the highest plant height and lowest relative grass cover under shade. The enhanced shoot growth under shade was most likely due to

Table 5-1

Anatomical, morphological, and physiological effects of shade on turfgrasses

Anatomical	Morphological	Physiological
Thinner cuticle layer	Thinner, narrower leaves	Higher chlorophyll content
Lower stomatal density	Longer leaves and internodes	Lower respiration rate
Fewer chloroplasts	Lower shoot density	Lower photosynthetic rate
	Fewer tillers	Lower transpiration rate
	Thinner stems	Greater succulence
	More upright growth	Lower carbohydrate reserves

increased endogenous gibberellin (GA1) levels found in Kentucky bluegrass (Tan and Qian 2003). Jiang, Duncan, and Carrow (2004) reported that canopy height of bermudagrass under low light conditions increased over 100 percent relative to plants exposed to full light; the reduced shoot density was paralleled with diminished canopy coverage (density). Turf density decline in shade is likely due to decreased tiller or leaf area. Moreover, the reduced shoot density has adverse effects on canopy physiological processes, photosynthesis in particular.

Maintaining high photosynthetic capacity under low light is important for turfgrass performance because leaves are removed due to regular mowing. For grasses adapted to full sunlight, the photosynthetic rate decreases with increasing shade, especially in C_4 grasses. Cool-season grasses approach light saturation at only moderate intensity. Jiang, Duncan, and Carrow (2004) reported that net photosynthetic rate decreased with 70 percent and 90 percent of full light for seashore paspalum and bermudagrass, respectively. Seashore paspalums generally had a higher photosynthetic rate than bermudagrasses, particularly under 90 percent light. This suggested that a higher photosynthetic rate contributed to tolerance of low light in seashore paspalums. Van Huylenbroeck and Van Bockstaele (2001) also demonstrated significant differences in photosynthetic rate among perennial ryegrass, red fescue, and crested hairgrass (*Koeleria macrantha* L.), and a relationship between tolerance of low light and photosynthetic features of the species. However, leaf anatomical and physiological responses to shade were both shown to influence photosynthesis in tall fescue leaves (Allard, Nelson, and Pallardy 1991).

A reduced respiration rate is often considered a major physiological adaptation, allowing plants to conserve carbohydrates in shade. Reduced leaf respiration at low light levels has been well documented (Givnish 1988). The photosynthetic-respiratory balance is a critical factor in shade tolerance, and a positive CO_2 balance contributed to shade adaptation in red fescue (Wilkinson, Beard, and Krans 1975). A low ratio of photosynthesis to respiration in response to stress conditions may result in a reduced total nonstructural carbohydrate content and inferior turf recovery from stress. Qian and Engelke (1999) found that total nonstructural carbohydrate content decreased in Diamond zoysiagrass under 87 percent shade, resulting in poor turf density and stand persistence.

SHADE EFFECTS ON STRESSES AND PESTS

Shaded turfgrasses under relatively constant temperature, high humidity, and subdued light are susceptible to environmental stresses such as heat, cold, and drought. Warm-season grasses, in particular, often suffer more winter injury in shaded areas.

Diseases including Pythium blight, brown patch, and dollar spot (see Chapter 6) are enhanced by higher relative humidity, extended periods of dew cover, and reduced photosynthetic irradiance under shade. Overall, shaded turf is less able to compete with weeds, although there is only a select group of weeds that is competitive in shaded conditions.

GENETIC VARIABILITY IN SHADE TOLERANCE

Cool-Season Turfgrasses The fine fescues are considered the most shade tolerant of the cool-season grasses. After fourteen years of evaluating thirty-five species and cultivars under moderate to heavy tree shade in Ames, Iowa, the top thirteen grasses in 2001 were fine fescues (Christians and Li 2002). The Chewings fescues, in particular, exhibited excel-

Figure 5-2
Fine fescue species and tall fescue have exhibited good shade tolerance in shade studies done in Iowa and Ohio.

Table 5-2

Shade tolerance of commonly used cool-season turfgrasses

Turfgrass	Ranking
Chewings fescue	Excellent
Red fescue Hard fescue Sheep fescue Tall fescue	Very good
Kentucky bluegrass Rough bluegrass	Fair to Good
Perennial ryegrass	Poor

lent shade tolerance over the duration of this study and also performed well when evaluated in a long-term test under moderate tree shade in Ohio (Gardner and Taylor 2002) (Table 5-3). Creeping red fescue, Chewing's fescue, sheep fescue, and hard fescue all have shown promise in heavily shaded areas.

Tall fescue cultivars were superior to all grasses evaluated in the Ohio shade evaluation (Gardner and Taylor 2002) (Table 5-3). Environmental conditions and maintenance of the shade-grown turf play a critical role in how species perform. In the Ohio test, no supplemental irrigation was applied after turf was established; the drought-avoidance characteristics of tall fescue favored its performance under these conditions. Evaluation of tall fescue in the Iowa test indicated that some cultivars, including Rebel II and Apache, performed relatively well. Under tree shade in California, the tall fescue cultivars Falcon, Rebel, and Houndog outperformed Alta (Wu, Huff, and Davis 1985). All cultivars produced a reasonable stand of turf under 70 percent shade.

Kentucky bluegrass and rough bluegrass have fair to good shade tolerance. Some cultivars of Kentucky bluegrass and turf-type tall fescue have performed well in moderate shade. Rough bluegrass has good shade tolerance but prefers moist soil conditions. Tree-shaded sites with significant root competition become drier than it prefers. Results from tests in Iowa and Ohio (Table 5-3) indicated that rough bluegrass had relatively poor quality when grown in

Table 5-3

Cover and quality of turfgrass species after six years of evaluation in Ohio (after Gardner and Taylor 2002)

Species	Number of Cultivars Tested	Mean Cover in 2000 (%)	Change in Cover, 1994–2000 (%)	Mean Quality[1]	Change in Quality, 1994–2000
Tall fescue	9	72.2	9.5	6.1	0.4
Chewings fescue	5	62.7	−4.6	4.6	−2.3
Red fescue	3	50	−14	4.1	−2.7
Kentucky bluegrass	6	32.5	8.7	3.7	−0.1
Hard fescue	3	27.2	−34.3	4.2	−2.4
Rough bluegrass	1	10	−45	3.6	−2.3
Perennial ryegrass	3	8.9	−65.7	2.9	−4.1

[1] Turf quality was rated on a 1 to 9 scale, where 1 = poorest quality, 6 = acceptable quality, and 9 = best quality based on overall color, cover, and density.

shade for a prolonged period of time and was comparable in performance to some of the Kentucky bluegrass cultivars evaluated.

Warm-Season Turfgrasses

Shade-tolerant warm-season grasses include centipedegrass, St. Augustinegrass, and zoysiagrass. Centipedegrass and St. Augustinegrass are commonly used in moderate shade in the southern United States. There are important cultivar differences in shade tolerance, however, particularly in St. Augustinegrass. Oklawn centipedegrass exhibited an 8 percent reduction in quality under 63 percent shade in Louisiana compared to a 35 percent reduction in quality for Floratam St. Augustinegrass (Barrios et al. 1986). Comparison of four St. Augustinegrass cultivars for shade tolerance indicated that Seville was least affected by low light levels, Floratine was intermediate, and Floratam exhibited the greatest growth reductions when shading reduces light levels to less than 45 percent of full sunlight (Peacock and Dudeck, 1993). Floratam was also inferior to Floratine when evaluated under shade cloth in Louisiana (Barrios et al. 1986).

There is also much variability among zoysiagrass cultivars in shade resistance. Meyer is relatively shade intolerant. Emerald and

Table 5-4

Shade tolerance of commonly used warm-season turfgrasses

Turfgrass	Ranking
St. Augustinegrass (with the exception of the cultivar Floratam) Centipedegrass	Very good
Emerald zoysia Diamond zoysia Seashore paspalum	Good
Other zoysia cultivars	Fair
Bermudagrass Buffalograss	Poor

Diamond, however, have good shade tolerance and are commonly used in low light conditions in the southern United States. In a Louisiana evaluation, Emerald had shade tolerance that was inferior to that of Oklawn centipede but better than Floratam St. Augustine's (Barrios et al. 1986). Diamond zoysia is used under relatively low light conditions in Bank One Ballpark in Phoenix, Arizona, where the Arizona Diamondbacks play.

Although bermudagrass has poor shade tolerance, there may be potential for improvement through breeding. A comparison of thirty-two bermudagrass clones in a greenhouse study indicated that vegetative growth characteristics of at least five were less affected than others when compared in low light and high light environments (Gaussoin, Baltensperger, and Coffey 1988). Boise, No Mow, R9-P1, NM1-3, and NM3 bermudagrass clones were moderately insensitive to reduced light intensity. In the same test, Tifsport generally exhibited better performance than Tifeagle under both full light and low light conditions. McBee (1969) found that Tifdwarf was slightly more shade tolerant than Tifway.

REFERENCES

Aamlid, T. S. 1992. Effects of temperature and light duration on growth and development of tillers and rhizomes in *Poa pratensis* L. ecotypes. *Ann. Bot. 69*:289–96.

Allard, G., C. J. Nelson, and S. G. Pallardy. 1991. Shade effects on growth of tall fescue: II. Leaf gas exchange characteristics. *Crop Sci.* 31:167–72.

Barrios, E. P., F. J. Sundstrom, D. Babcock, and L. Leger. 1986. Quality and yield response of four warm-season lawngrasses to shade conditions. *Agron. J.* 78:270–73.

Beard, J. B. 1997. Shade stresses and adaptation mechanisms of turfgrasses. *Int. Turfgrass Soc. Res. J.* 8:1186–95.

Bell, G. E., and T. K. Danneberger. 1999. Temporal shade on creeping bentgrass turf. *Crop Sci.* 39:1142–6.

Bell, G. E, T. K. Danneberger, and M. J. McMahon. 2000. Spectral irradiance available for turfgrass growth in sun and shade. *Crop Sci.* 40:189–95.

Cereti, C. P., and F. Rossini. 1997. Effect of intensity and duration of shade on turfgrasses in a Mediterranean environment. *Int. Turfgrass Soc. Res. J.* 8:1260–6.

Christians, N., and D. Li. 2002. Shade adaptation study. *Iowa Turfgrass Research Report*, 21–22.

Dudeck, A. E., and C. H. Peacock. 1992. Shade and turfgrass culture. Pp. 269–84 in D. V. Waddington, R. N. Carrow, and R. C. Shearman, eds., *Turfgrass*. Madison, WI: American Society of Agronomy.

Fales, S. L., and R. C. Wakefield. 1981. Effects of turfgrass on the establishment of woody plants. *Agron. J.* 73:605–10.

Gardner, D. S., and J. A. Taylor. 2002. Change over time in quality and cover of various turfgrass species and cultivars maintained in shade. *HortTechnology* 12:465–69.

Gaussoin, R. E., A. A. Baltensperger, and B. N. Coffey. 1988. Response of 32 bermudagrass clones to reduced light intensity. *HortScience* 23:178–79.

Givnish, T. J. 1988. Adaptation to sun and shade: a whole-plant perspective. *Aust. J. Plant Physiol.* 15: 63–92.

Hay, R. K. M., and O. M. Heide. 1983. Specific photoperiodic stimulation of dry matter production in a high-latitude cultivar of *Poa pratensis*. *Physiol. Plant.* 57:135–42.

Hay, R. K. M., and K. Pedersen. 1986. Influence of long photoperiod on the growth of timothy (*Phleum pratense* L.) varieties from different latitudes in northern Europe. *Grass and Forage Sci.* 41:311–17.

Jiang, Y. W., R. R. Duncan, and R. N. Carrow. 2004. Assessment of low light tolerance of seashore paspalum and bermudagrass. *Crop Sci.* 44, in press.

Kind, M. 2001. Turf talk—greens lights get green light. *Golf Course Management*, January.

McBee, G. G. 1969. Association of certain variations in light quality with the performance of selected turfgrasses. *Crop Sci.* 9:14–17.

Peacock, C. H., and A. E. Dudeck. 1993. Response of St. Augustinegrass cultivars to shade. *Intl. Turfgrass Res. J.* 7:657–63.

Qian, Y. L., and M. C. Engelke. 1999. 'Diamond' zoysiagrass as affected by light intensity. *J. Turfgrass Management* 3:1–13.

Tan, Z. G., and Y. L. Qian. 2003. Light intensity affects gibberellic acid content in Kentucky bluegrass. *HortScience* 38:113–16.

Van Huylenbroeck, J. M., and E. Van Bockstaele. 2001. Effects of shading on photosynthetic capacity and growth of turfgrass species. *Int. Turf. Soc. Res. J.* 9:353–59.

Wilkinson, J. F., J. B. Beard, and J. V. Krans. 1975. Photosynthetic-respiratory responses of 'Merion' Kentucky bluegrass and Pennlawn red fescue at reduced light intensities. *Crop Sci.* 15: 165–68.

Wu, L., D. Huff, and W. B. Davis. 1985. Tall fescue turf performance under a tree shade. *HortScience* 20:281–82.

Xu, Q., and B. Huang. 2004. Physiological responses to extended photoperiod under heat stress for creeping bentgrass. *J. Am. Soc. Hort. Sci.*, in press.

6

Pests

Turfgrass cultural practices can significantly impact susceptibility to weed encroachment and insect and disease infestations. In Part III of this text, some of the specific responses of turfgrass pests to cultural practices are discussed. Our objective here is to provide a brief synopsis of the characteristics of each of the pests that has been to be influenced by one or more cultural practices. What follows is not intended to be a comprehensive review of the weeds, insects, and diseases commonly found in turf. Furthermore, other cultural practices than those highlighted here may impact a particular pest, but research-based results may be limiting, which precluded presentation here.

While some research projects have addressed specific weed problems, there are myriad weed species that are affected by turfgrass cultural practices. Furthermore, it is common for numerous weed species to infest a turf once turf density begins to decline. In some cases researchers report the percentage of weed infestation without listing specific weeds. As such, some of the common weed species are discussed in broad terms, such as summer annual grasses and broadleaf weeds. Other weeds, such as annual and rough bluegrass, are addressed specifically.

Although only a few projects have addressed cultural practices and their influence on insect infestations in turf, numerous studies have been done on diseases. Specific insects and diseases addressed by researchers are highlighted below.

WEEDS

Annual bluegrass (*Poa annua*)

Affected By:	See Page:
Irrigation	184
Mowing	208
Fertilization	234
Cultivation	261
Plant growth regulators	277

See description on pages 24–25 (Fig. 2-4).

Roughstalk bluegrass (*Poa trivialis*)

Affected By:	See Page:
Irrigation	184

See description on pages 27–29 (Fig. 2-7).

Bermudagrass (*Cynodon dactylon*)

Affected By:	See Page:
Mowing	208
Fertilization	234

See description on pages 41–44.

Figure 6-1
Bermudagrass encroaching in a perennial ryegrass golf course fairway.

Summer annual grasses, including crabgrass (*Digitaria* spp.), goosegrass (*Eleusine indica*), and foxtails (*Setaria* spp.)

Affected By:	See Page:
Irrigation	184
Mowing	208
Fertilization	234
Cultivation	261

- *Life Cycle:* All of these grasses are summer annuals, meaning that seed germinates in late spring, plants grow vegetatively during the summer, and flowering occurs in early autumn. Germination time depends upon latitude. For example, over a three-year period, the earliest date for crabgrass emergence in thin turf was May 5 in Manhattan, Kansas, and June 1 in Lincoln, Nebraska (Fry et al. 2001). Goosegrass generally germinates a few weeks after crabgrass.

- *Preferred growing conditions:* Crabgrass, foxtails, and goosegrass are warm-season C_4 plants and grow best in midsummer.

- *Characteristics:* Smooth (*D. ischaemum*) and large (*D. sanguinalis*) crabgrass differ in that the former has no hair on leaf sheaths or blades. Large crabgrass has prominent hairs on the leaf sheath and on both sides of the leaf blade. Both species produce seedheads from midsummer into autumn that have two or more spiked branches.

  Foxtails, including yellow (*S. glauca*) and green (*S. viridis*), produce characteristic seedheads, resembling a fox's tail, that are bristly panicles, 1 to 3 inches (2.5 to 7.5 cm) long.

  Goosegrass is sometimes referred to as "silver crabgrass," as its center is silver when leaf sheaths are growing horizontally. Goosegrass is commonly found in compacted soils and is more difficult to control with preemergence herbicides than crabgrass.

Figures 6-2, 6-3, and 6-4
Summer annual
grasses: large crabgrass
(Fig. 6-2, above, left),
goosegrass (Fig. 6-3,
opposite), and yellow
foxtail (Fig. 6-3, above,
right). (Goosegrass and
yellow foxtail
photographs courtesy
of Ward Upham.)

Broadleaf weeds, including dandelion (*Taraxacum officinale*), white clover (*Trifolium repens*), broadleaf plantain (*Plantago major*), and prostrate knotweed (*Polygonum aviculare*)

Affected By:	See Page:
Irrigation	184

■ *Characteristics:* Dandelion is a cool-season perennial recognized by its bright yellow flower that emerges from the center of a rosette of leaves that are deeply cut. Mature flowers form a puff-ball that consists of "parachutes" that transport wind-borne seed. Leaves and flower stalks contain a milky sap that is exuded when tissue is torn.

White clover is a stoloniferous, cool-season perennial legume that produces round, white flowers in spring and fall. Clover possesses the characteristic three leaflets on each stem, with leaves sometimes exhibiting a white, angled band encircling the base of each leaflet.

Broadleaf plantain is a cool-season perennial herb that has a distinctive rosette of waxy leaves. The seedhead is a spike produced on a leafless stem, which appears from mid-spring into summer.

Prostrate knotweed is a warm-season summer annual that germinates as early as mid-February in the Midwest. It develops a long taproot and exhibits good tolerance to soil compaction, wear, and drought. Knotweed forms inconspicuous flowers in leaf axils from late spring until frost.

Figures 6-5, 6-6, 6-7, and 6-8
Broadleaf weeds: dandelion (Fig. 6-5, top, left), white clover (Fig. 6-6, top, right), broadleaf plantain (Fig. 6-7, bottom, left), and seedling prostrate knotweed (Fig. 6-8, bottom, right). (Dandelion, broadleaf plantain, and prostrate knotweed photographs courtesy of Ward Upham.)

INSECTS

Black cutworm (*Agrotis ipsilon*)

Black cutworms often cause damage around core aerification holes.

Affected By:	See Page:
Mowing	210

- *Grasses most commonly affected:* Creeping bentgrass
- *Symptoms:* Black cutworm larvae burrow in aerification holes or other spaces on bentgrass putting surfaces and emerge at night to chew plants at the base and cause small, circular areas of scalped turf. Turf may eventually die. Close inspection of damaged areas or flushing with soapy water may reveal the presence of the cutworm just below the surface.
- *Characteristics:* The black cutworm is the larva of a night-flying moth found throughout the United States. Moths are robust and hairy with a wingspan of 1 to 1.75 inches (35 to 45 mm) (Potter 1998). Several generations occur each year, depending upon latitude. Larvae go through six or seven instars and range from 1.25 to 1.75 inches (30 to 45 mm) long and 0.25 inches (7 mm) wide (Potter 1998).

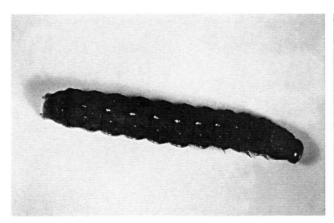 

Figures 6-9 and 6-10
Black cutworm larva (Fig. 6-9, left) and damage on a creeping bentgrass putting green (Fig. 6-10, right). (Photographs courtesy of the Crop Science Society of America, Turfgrass Insects slide set, 1990.)

Chinch bugs (*Blissus* spp.)

Affected By:	See Page:
Irrigation	185

- *Grasses most commonly affected:* Zoysia, St. Augustinegrass, and buffalograss
- *Symptoms:* Water and sap are sucked from turfgrass stems, leading to wilt and eventually a necrotic, scorched appearance. Symptoms often appear first in areas that are the first to heat up, including south-facing slopes or areas near sidewalks or driveways. When damaging levels of chinch bugs are present, the symptoms will expand over a turf area relatively quickly.
- *Characteristics:* In the Northeast, the hairy chinch bug causes damage to cool-season grasses. The southern chinch bug is a destructive pest of St. Augustinegrass lawns. In the Midwest, the common chinch bug causes significant damage to zoysia, and the buffalograss chinch bug causes damage specific to buffalograss. Chinch bug adults are approximately 1/16 inch (3.5 mm) long and have piercing-sucking mouthparts that remove water and juice from the turfgrass stems (Potter 1998). Adults and instars cause injury and are commonly found together in on the interface between damaged and unaffected turf areas.

Figures 6-11 and 6-12
Chinch bug instars from egg to adult (Fig. 6-11, left) and chinch bug damage on a zoysiagrass lawn (Fig. 6-12, right). (Chinch bug photograph courtesy of the Crop Science Society of America, Turfgrass Insects slide set, 1990; damage photograph courtesy of Steve Keeley.)

Southern masked chaffer (*Cyclocephala lurida*) and Japanese beetle (*Popilla japonica*)

Affected By:	See Page:
Irrigation	185
Mowing	210
Fertilization	235
Cultivation	262

■ *Grasses affected:* All grasses

■ *Symptoms:* Roots are severed by larvae residing in the soil, which may initially cause turf to suffer from drought stress even though soil may be moist. Eventually large areas will become necrotic, and pulling on the turf allows it to roll up like a carpet.

■ *Characteristics:* Larvae of both species are white, C-shaped grubs that arise from eggs laid by adult beetles. Masked chaffer larvae cause damage to turf, but adults do not injure plants. The masked chaffer has a one-year life cycle. Adults lay eggs in late June or early July in the transition zone (Potter 1998). Eggs hatch in about two weeks, and young larvae begin feeding on turfgrass roots. Feeding continues through several molts in autumn, when larvae go deeper in the soil below the frost line (Potter 1998). Grubs return to the surface early the following spring to resume feeding. Then, the larvae go deeper into the soil in late spring to pupate. Adults begin emerging in early June.

The Japanese beetle adult feeds on the foliage of ornamentals, and the larvae cause damage to turf. It is primarily a problem in the eastern United States, and significant efforts have been made to avoid introducing the Japanese beetle in other areas of the country. The Japanese beetle also has a one-year life cycle that resembles that of the southern masked chaffer (Potter 1998).

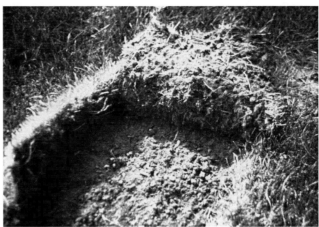

Figures 6-13 and 6-14
Southern masked chaffer larva (Fig. 6-13, left) and damage caused to a home lawn (Fig. 6-14, right). (Southern masked chaffer larva photograph courtesy of Ward Upham.)

DISEASES

Foliar-Infecting Fungi

Brown patch (*Rhizoctonia solani*)
(description after Tisserat 2003i)

Affected By:	See Page:
Irrigation	185
Mowing	211
Fertilization	236
Plant growth regulators	291
Biostimulants	293

■ *Grasses affected:* Primarily bentgrasses, perennial ryegrass, and tall fescue

■ *Symptoms:* Brown patch symptoms develop rapidly (in twenty-four to forty-eight hours) during warm, humid weather and can result in blighting of large areas of the turf. Symptoms vary depending on the grass, weather, and management practices. In some cases, the disease appears as distinct circular patches of blighted turf that range in size from a few inches (several cm) to several feet (up to 1 m or more) in diameter. Patches initially are dark purple-green but then quickly fade to light tan or brown as the diseased leaves dry out. In most cases, however, blighting tends to occur in a more irregular or diffuse pattern, without formation of circular patches. Diseased turf may appear droughty even though sufficient soil moisture is present. In most cases, the fungus attacks only the leaves, but during severe disease pressure, the crowns may also be killed.

Conditions favoring disease development: Nighttime temperatures above 70°F (21°C) and leaf wetness periods exceeding ten hours contribute to disease development. This may occur anytime from early May through mid-September.

Figure 6-15
Rhizoctonia solani mycelium infecting leaves of perennial ryegrass. (Photograph courtesy of Derek Settle.)

Figure 6-16
Brown patch symptoms on perennial ryegrass.

Dollar spot (*Sclerotinia homoeocarpa*)
(description after Tisserat 2003a, 2003b)

Affected By:	See Page:
Irrigation	185
Mowing	211
Fertilization	236
Topdressing	274
Plant growth regulators	291
Biostimulants	293

▦ *Grasses most commonly affected:* Nearly all grasses, but a significant problem on creeping bentgrass, annual bluegrass, and Kentucky bluegrass

▦ *Symptoms:* On turfgrass mowed at 0.5 inches (1.3 cm) or less, the disease results in the formation of small bleached spots that rarely exceed 2 inches (5.1 cm) in diameter. During favorable weather hundreds of spots may coalesce to blight large, irregular areas of the turf. Severe dollar spot outbreaks result in a pock-marked or craterlike surface to putting greens. Individual infected leaves exhibit light tan lesions surrounded by a dark reddish brown border. These lesions may be difficult to see on closely mowed bentgrass without the aid of a hand lens.

On longer turf, patches are more numerous in areas where there is poor air circulation or drainage. Most spots are only a few inches (cm) in diameter. However, under favorable environmental conditions and mowing heights greater than 2 inches (5.1 cm), individual spots may exceed 6 inches (15.2 cm) in diameter. Affected plants within the diseased spots wilt and eventually turn tan or brown. During outbreaks of the disease, numerous spots on the turfgrass coalesce into large irregular dead areas. It rarely infects the roots, although fungal toxins produced may affect root formation.

▦ *Conditions that favor disease development:* Dollar spot can occur at a range of 59 to 86°F (15 to 30°C). It is most common during periods of humid weather when days are warm and significant dew deposition occurs in the evening.

Figure 6-17
Characteristic "hour glass" pattern of dollar spot injury on Kentucky bluegrass.

Figure 6-18
Dollar spot symptoms on perennial ryegrass.

Gray leaf spot (*Pyricularia grisea*)
(description after Tisserat 2003h)

Affected By:	See Page:
Mowing	211
Fertilization	236
Plant growth regulators	291

- *Grasses most commonly affected:* Perennial ryegrass, tall fescue, and St. Augustinegrass
- *Symptoms:* Gray leaf spot, also called blast, was first observed on perennial ryegrass throughout the eastern half of the United States in 1992. The epidemic resulted in extensive damage to golf fairways and athletic fields. The disease now is established in most areas of the country where perennial ryegrass is grown. Gray leaf spot symptoms initially develop in late summer. Small, chocolate brown spots approximately $\frac{1}{16}$ inch (1.6 mm) in diameter develop on leaves. During early disease development these leaf spots may not be numerous and can be easily overlooked. The spots expand slightly with age and develop a gray center

surrounded by a yellow halo. Depending on weather, multiple coalescing leaf spots will girdle and kill both leaf and crown tissue. Dying leaves tend to develop a characteristic twist at the leaf tip that helps differentiate this disease from brown patch or Pythium blight. Gray leaf spot often develops first in heat- or drought-prone areas such as the tops of small mounds or on steep slopes. The diseased turf first appears to be under drought stress even though soil moisture is sufficient, but it soon collapses and turns a dull brown. The fungus sporulates profusely from leaf lesions, and vast quantities of spores can be spread by wind, splashing water, and equipment to infect new leaves. New leaf symptoms appear within a few days of infection. The combination of quick symptom development and massive spore production are reasons why gray leaf spot epidemics progress rapidly and are so destructive.

■ *Conditions that favor disease development:* Factors that eventually trigger epidemics are not completely understood, but temperatures of 77 to 86°F (25 to 30°C) in combination with extended periods of leaf wetness interspersed with intermittent dry periods favor disease development.

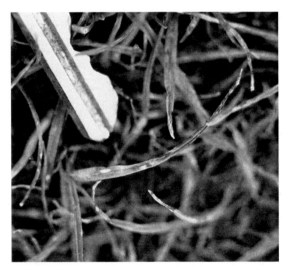

Figure 6-19
Grey leaf spot lesions on perennial ryegrass.

Figure 6-20
Damage to a perennial ryegrass fairway caused by grey leaf spot. The darker, unaffected areas are bermudagrass. (Photograph courtesy of Dr. Steve Keeley.)

Large patch (*Rhizoctonia solani*)
(description after Tisserat 2003c)

Affected By:	See Page:
Mowing	211

■ *Grasses most commonly affected:* Zoysia

■ *Symptoms:* Symptoms may occur anytime during the growing season, but are most common in spring and fall as zoysia enters or breaks winter dormancy. Circular, slightly matted areas of straw-yellow zoysia initially develop in early to during cool, rainy weather. Leaf blades, particularly those near the patch margin, may develop a yellow-orange color. Individual shoots within the patch exhibit reddish brown to black lesions at the base of leaf sheaths. As its name implies, the disease results in the formation of large patches of blighted turf that may exceed 20 feet (6.1 m) in diameter. Crown infection may continue into November as long as soil temperatures remain above 50°F (10°C) and soil moisture is high. Patch enlargement after fall dormancy (October) may not be noticed until zoysia resumes spring growth. In the spring, patches of zoysia damaged by large patch

Figure 6-21
Necrosis of zoysiagrass leaf sheaths caused by *Rhizoctonia solani*, the fungus that incites large patch disease. (Photograph courtesy of Dr. Ned Tisserat.)

Figure 6-22
Symptoms of large patch disease on a zoysiagrass golf course fairway. (Photograph courtesy of Dr. Ned Tisserat.)

reappear in spring as light brown, sunken areas that are slower to recover from dormancy than surrounding, healthy turfgrass. Patch expansion may continue into the spring and early summer if environmental conditions are favorable.

▨ *Conditions favoring disease development:* Temperatures of 68 to 77°F (20 to 25°C) are optimal for infection, in conjunction with prolonged wet periods (Green et al. 1993).

Pink snow mold (*Microdochium nivale*)

Affected By:	See Page:
Fertilization	236

▨ *Grasses most commonly affected:* Nearly all grasses grown in temperate climates

▨ *Symptoms:* Damage appears as patches of varying sizes from 2 to 8 inches (5 to 20 cm) in diameter that may have a pink outer margin.

▨ *Conditions favoring disease development:* Prolonged periods of cool (32 to 46°F [0 to 8°C]), wet weather (Smiley, Dernoeden, and Clarke 1992). Although it is often associated with the presence of snow, symptoms may also be evident without it.

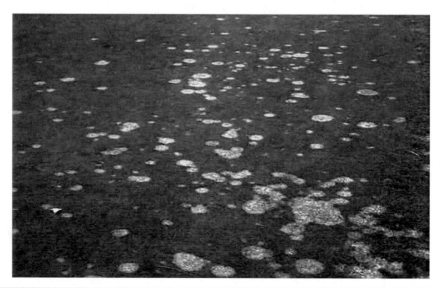

Figure 6-23
Symptoms of pink snow mold damage on creeping bentgrass. (Photograph courtesy of Dr. Ned Tisserat.)

Pythium blight (*Pythium*)
(description after Tisserat 2003e)

Affected By:	See Page:
Irrigation	185
Mowing	211
Fertilization	236

■ *Grasses most commonly affected:* Perennial ryegrass, creeping bentgrass, and tall fescue

■ *Symptoms:* Symptoms of Pythium blight are variable depending on the turfgrass species affected and the height at which the grass is cut. On bentgrass and perennial ryegrass mowed at fairway height, the first symptoms are small, irregularly shaped, water-soaked, greasy patches up to 4 inches (10.2 cm) in diameter. A cottony growth may be present in patches early in the morning. The patches may merge and form streaks, since the fungus-like organism may be spread by mowing equipment or water. Diseased plants eventually turn the color of straw and wither, resulting in craterlike depressions in the turf. Symptoms progress rapidly during favorable weather, and large areas may be extensively damage within a matter of days. In tall fescue, softball-sized patches of water-soaked turfgrass form during hot, wet conditions. Diseased grass blades within the patch tend to stick to one another and have a mushy texture. Spots may coalesce and streaks may also form. Pythium blight will commonly develop along water drainage patterns in the turf. Affected plants eventually wilt and die to the crown. However, crowns and roots may not be killed and plants may recover after several weeks.

■ *Conditions favoring disease development:* Pythium blight is most active when air temperatures are 86 to 95°F (30 to 35°C) with minimum night temperatures of 68°F (20°C). The disease usually occurs when soil is saturated with water following extended periods of rain. Long dew periods, high relative humidity, and lush, dense turfgrass growth also favors disease development.

Figure 6-24
Pythium mycelium in tall fescue. (Photograph courtesy of Dr. Ned Tisserat.)

Figure 6-25
Pythium blight injury to a creeping bentgrass putting green collar and perennial ryegrass on the perimeter of the green.

Figure 6-26
Pythium blight injury to roughstalk bluegrass overseeded on a bermudagrass putting green in Louisiana. Note the streaking pattern, as this fungus is mobile and damage often follows water drainage patterns.

Red thread (*Laetisaria fuciformis*)

Affected By:	See Page:
Fertilization	236

- *Grasses most commonly affected:* Bentgrasses, fescues, ryegrasses, and bluegrasses (Smiley, Dernoeden, and Clarke 1992)
- *Symptoms:* Circular or irregular patches that may range from 2 to 10 inches (5 to 25 cm) in diameter. Mycelium produced by the fungus is visible to the naked eye as red or orange strands of thread in the patch areas. Infected leaves become water-soaked and quickly die. Only the foliage is affected.
- *Conditions favoring disease development:* Red thread may appear anytime during the growing season but is most prevalent when turf is growing slowly and there is heavy dew formation.

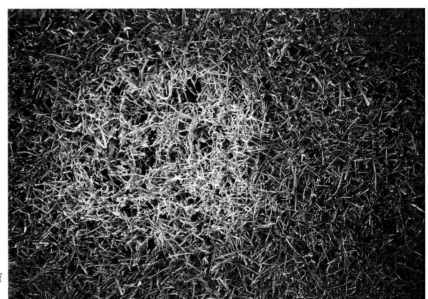

Figure 6-27
Red thread mycelium infecting a stand of perennial ryegrass. (Photograph courtesy of Dr. Peter Dernoeden.)

Rust (*Puccinia*, *Uromyces*, *Physopella*, and *Uredo* spp.)

Affected By:	See Page:
Fertilization	236

■ *Grasses most commonly affected:* All grasses

■ *Symptoms:* Light yellow flecks on leaves may become enlarged in rust or orange-colored pustules that break through the leaf's epidermis (Smiley, Dernoeden, and Clarke 1992). Walking through rust-infested turf results in the orange spores being deposited over shoes and socks. Severe rust outbreaks result in yellowing and thinning of the turf.

■ *Conditions favoring disease development:* Growth of the fungus is generally favored at temperatures between 68 and 86°F (20 and 30°C) (Smiley, Dernoeden, and Clarke 1992). Turf that is subjected to stresses such as drought and nutrient deficiencies is most susceptible to infection.

Figures 6-28 and 6-29
Rust pustules on leaves of perennial ryegrass (Fig. 6-28, left) create a lighter appearance to the turf (Fig. 6-29, right).

Root-Infecting Fungi

Necrotic ring spot (*Ophiosphaerella korrae*)
(description after Tisserat 2003d)

Affected By:	See Page:
Irrigation	185

- *Grasses most commonly affected:* Kentucky bluegrass, red fescue, and annual bluegrass
- *Symptoms:* Necrotic ring spot results in numerous circular to arc-shaped patches of dead or dying turfgrass roughly 1 foot (30.5 cm) or more in diameter. The affected turf in the ring is slightly matted, whereas the turfgrass in the middle of the "frog eye" remains healthy and green. Affected plants exhibit extensive root discoloration and rot.
- *Conditions favoring disease development:* Necrotic ring spot symptoms usually appear in late spring or early fall, but they may continue into the summer months. The disease often shows up two years after sodding and may reappear in the same location year after year.

Figure 6-30
Symptoms of necrotic ring spot on a Kentucky bluegrass lawn. (Photograph courtesy of Dr. Noel Jackson.)

Spring dead spot (*Ophiosphaerella herpotricha*, *O. korrae*, and *O. narmari*) (description after Tisserat 2003f)

Affected By:	See Page:
Mowing	211
Fertilization	236
Cultivation	263

- *Grasses most commonly affected:* Bermudagrass
- *Symptoms:* Spring dead spot may occur on bermudagrass lawns of all ages, although it typically appears three to four years after the turf has been established. The disease results in the formation of circular or arc-shaped patches of dead turf in early spring as bermudagrass breaks winter dormancy. The dead patches, which are slightly depressed and straw-colored, may range in size from several inches to several feet in diameter. The patches normally are randomly distributed throughout the lawn. Roots and stolons of affected plants are dark brown to black and are severely rotted. It may be necessary to dig up a piece of sod near the margin of the dead area and wash it in water to observe this symptom. During the summer, broadleaf weeds and other weedy grasses invade and colonize the bare soil, resulting in a clumpy or patchy appearance to the lawn. Bermudagrass slowly colonizes the bare areas, and by late summer there may be little or no evidence of the disease. Dead patches reappear the following spring in the same locations. Over a number of years, the patches can become quite large, coalesce, and develop arc-like patterns in the lawn. After seven to ten years, disease severity may begin to decrease to the point where the disease no longer appears in the lawn.
- *Conditions favoring disease development:* Spring dead spot fungi colonize roots, stolons, and crowns of bermudagrass plants in late summer or fall. During winter dormancy, infected bermudagrass roots or crowns are either killed directly by the fungus or are predisposed to desiccation or cold temperature injury. Root colonization by the pathogen decreases the cold hardiness of the bermudagrass.

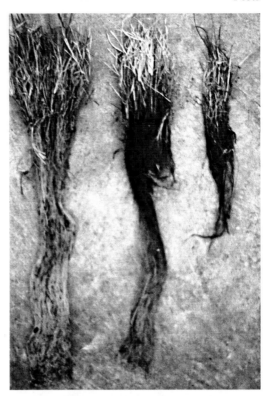

Figure 6-31
Necrotic roots resulting from inoculation of bermudagrass roots with the fungus that causes spring dead spot. (Photograph courtesy of Dr. Ned Tisserat.)

Figure 6-32
Symptoms of spring dead spot on bermudagrass. (Photograph courtesy of Dr. Ned Tisserat.)

Summer patch (*Magnaporthe poae*)
(description after Tisserat 2003g)

Affected By:	See Page:
Irrigation	185
Mowing	211
Cultivation	263

- *Grasses most commonly affected:* Kentucky bluegrass and annual bluegrass

- *Symptoms:* Summer patch symptoms in Kentucky bluegrass initially develop in June through August as small patches of turf, 2 to 6 inches (5.1 to 15.2 cm) in diameter. Grass blades in the patch change to a dull reddish brown, then tan, and finally a light straw color. In the final stages of the disease, doughnut-shaped patches of dead grass form throughout the lawn. Healthy grass may occur within patch centers, resulting in a characteristic "frog eye" pattern. When weather conditions are ideal for disease development, affected areas may overlap and blight large areas of the lawn. Roots of affected plants are discolored, although this symptom may be difficult to see without the aid of a hand lens. On annual bluegrass growing on putting greens symptoms are

Figure 6-33
Symptoms of summer patch on Kentucky bluegrass.

not presented as uniform, frog eye patches; rather, damage is more diffuse.

▩ *Conditions favoring disease development:* Root infection is favored by moist conditions in the spring. Despite root infection at this time, symptoms don't appear until summer months.

Take-all patch (*Gaeumannomyces graminis*)

Affected By:	See Page:
Fertilization	236

▩ *Grasses most commonly affected:* Creeping bentgrass

▩ *Symptoms:* Small, light brown patches appear in spring and continue to spread throughout the growing season. Patches may enlarge up to 6 inches (15 cm) per year, reaching up to 3 feet (1 m) in diameter (Smiley, Dernoeden, and Clarke 1992). Stolons, roots, and the bases of leaf sheath appear brown to black before turf dies.

▩ *Conditions favoring disease development:* The disease spreads and infects new tissues during cool, wet weather. Symptoms usually appear when the weather warms and the turf is subjected to stress. The disease is favored by soils that have a relatively high pH.

Figure 6-34
Symptoms of take-all patch on creeping bentgrass. (Photograph courtesy of Dr. Peter Dernoeden.)

REFERENCES

Fry, J., S. Rodie, R. Gaussoin, S. Wiest, W. Upham, and A. Zuk. 2001. Using flowering ornamentals to guide applications of preemergence herbicides in the Midwestern U.S. *Int. Turfgrass Soc. Res. J.* 9:1009–18.

Green, D. E. II, J. D. Fry, J. C. Pair, and N. A. Tisserat. 1993. Pathogenicity of *Rhizoctonia solani* AG-2-2 and *Ophiosphaerella herpotricha* on zoysiagrass. *Plant Disease* 77:1040–44.

Potter, D. A. 1998. *Destructive turfgrass insects: Biology, diagnosis, and control.* Chelsea, MI: Ann Arbor Press.

Smiley, R. W., P. H. Dernoeden, and B. B. Clarke. 1992. *Compendium of turfgrass diseases,* 2nd ed. St. Paul, MN: American Phytopathological Society.

Tisserat, N. 2003a. Dollar spot of creeping bentgrass putting greens. Fact sheet, Kansas State University Research and Extension. Available at http://www.oznet.ksu.edu/path-ext

————. 2003b. Dollar spot in home lawns. Fact sheet, Kansas State University Research and Extension. Available at http://www.oznet.ksu.edu/path-ext

————. 2003c. Large patch. Fact sheet, Kansas State University Research and Extension. Available at http://www.oznet.ksu.edu/path-ext

————. 2003d. Necrotic ring spot of Kentucky bluegrass. Fact sheet, Kansas State University Research and Extension. Available at http://www.oznet.ksu.edu/path-ext

————. 2003e. Pythium blight of turfgrasses. Fact sheet, Kansas State University Research and Extension. Available at http://www.oznet.ksu.edu/path-ext

————. 2003f. Spring dead spot of bermudagrass. Fact sheet, Kansas State University Research and Extension. Available at http://www.oznet.ksu.edu/path-ext

————. 2003g. Summer patch. Fact sheet, Kansas State University Research and Extension. Available at http://www.oznet.ksu.edu/path-ext

————. 2003h. Gray leaf spot of perennial ryegrass. Fact sheet, Kansas State University Research and Extension. Available at http://www.oznet.ksu.edu/path-ext

————. 2003i. Rhizoctonia brown patch of tall fescue. Fact sheet, Kansas State University Research and Extension. Available at http://www.oznet.ksu.edu/path-ext

Cultural Practices and Their Effects upon Growth, Environmental Stresses, and Pests

Grasses were initially identified for use as turfs because they tolerated grazing. From the early days of grazing, humans have made tremendous strides in the cultural practices they impose on grasses in order to provide a quality turf. The following chapters integrate the information covered in earlier chapters with irrigation (Chapter 7), mowing (Chapter 8), fertilization (Chapter 9), cultivation (Chapter 10), and plant growth regulators and biostimulants (Chapter 11). In each, we cover available information on how each cultural practice influences turfgrass growth (shoots and roots), resistance to environmental stresses, and responses to turfgrass pests.

7

Irrigation

EVAPOTRANSPIRATION

Transpiration is the primary means whereby water leaves a dense sward of turf. However, in all turf areas, evaporation of water from the soil surface also contributes to the total water loss of the stand. The sum of water lost from evaporation and transpiration is referred to as evapotranspiration (ET). The turf manager's ultimate goal should be to select grasses and cultural strategies that result in the lowest possible ET rate that still allows turf quality to be maintained at a desired level. There are a number of environmental and

Figure 7-1
Irrigation has tremendous effects on turfgrass growth and responses to environmental stresses and pests.

cultural factors that influence ET. Of course, the turf manager has limited ability to control the environmental factors, but greater control over cultural factors.

Environmental Factors Influencing ET

Environmental factors that have the greatest effect on ET include temperature, day length, relative humidity, wind, and soil water content. Evapotranspiration increases with increasing temperature. The longest sustained periods of relatively high temperature occur around the summer solstice, and ET rates are generally highest at this time. As water evaporates, heat is released and the plant is cooled. Hence, there is a greater demand for cooling as temperatures rise.

Relative humidity has a large effect on ET. Evapotranspiration increases with decreasing relative humidity. A large vapor pressure gradient between the leaf and air encourages transpiration and minimizes leaf temperature. Creeping bentgrass is routinely used on putting greens in the southwestern United States, where temperatures may exceed 100°F (38°C) during the summer. However, at the same time, relative humidity may be less than 10 percent. This results in a large vapor pressure gradient between water in the stomata and that in the atmosphere, and ET occurs at a rapid rate. Hence, the plant can cool itself efficiently even when temperatures are very high. Conversely, high relative humidity, common in the southeastern United States, lessens the vapor pressure gradient between the stomata and atmosphere, and the plant is less efficient at cooling itself. As a result, creeping bentgrass is (almost) never grown as a perennial in Florida.

Wind disturbs the thin layer of water vapor that hovers above the turfgrass leaf blade, referred to as the boundary layer. This disturbance results in an increased gradient between water vapor in the stomata and that in the atmosphere, increasing water loss. In the transition zone and southern United States, bentgrass putting greens that are situated in low areas or surrounded by vegetation are most susceptible to heat stress due to lack of wind movement. Addition of fans to move air will increase ET and result in a cooler turf canopy.

Evapotranspiration is highest when the soil is at field capacity. As time from irrigation increases and soil dries, ET decreases. Free soil water is easily lost by evaporation or absorbed by roots to enter

Figure 7-2
Fans may be used to
encourage air movement,
promote ET, and reduce
heat stress on creeping
bentgrass putting greens.

the transpiration stream. As water use progresses, however, the remaining water molecules are more tightly bound to soil, thereby reducing ET. Hence, turf managers watering on a relatively deep, infrequent schedule should anticipate lower ET rates than those watering on a frequent schedule that results in a consistently high soil water content.

Table 7-1
Environmental factors and their effect on turfgrass ET

As This Environmental Factor Increases:	ET:
Air and soil temperature	Increases
Solar radiation	Increases
Day length	Increases
Wind	Increases
Relative humidity	Decreases

Plant and Cultural Factors Influencing ET

Turfgrasses vary widely in ET rates, both among and within species. Grasses that grow fastest and that have upright growth habits tend to use more water than those that grow slowly and have more prostrate habits. Grasses that reach taller heights more quickly are more greatly influenced by the advective forces of wind. Shearman (1986) observed a positive correlation between vertical extension rate and ET of twenty Kentucky bluegrass cultivars. Evaluation of zoysiagrass and bermudagrass ET rates in Texas indicated that they were significantly lower than those measured in St. Augustinegrass and tall fescue (Kim and Beard 1988). This was attributed, in part, to their more prostrate growth habits and dense canopies. In addition, warm-season grasses generally exhibit ET rates at least 10 to 15 percent lower than those observed in cool-season grasses. This is likely due to greater photosynthetic efficiency in warm-season grasses and their capacity to continue carbon fixation even when stomata are closed.

Average water use rates for cool-season grasses during active growth and under well-watered conditions range from 0.10 to 0.3 inches (2.5 to 8 mm) per day (Huang and Fry 1999). Tall fescue, a relatively fast-growing species with an upright growth habit, has been reported to have an ET rate up to 20 percent greater than other cool-season grasses (Qian et al. 1996; Minner 1984; Biran et al. 1981).

Average ET rates for warm-season grasses range from 0.08 to 0.20 inches (2 to 5 mm) per day (Huang and Fry 1999). Warm-season grasses with relatively low ET rates are bermudagrass, zoysiagrass,

Table 7-2

Evapotranspiration of tall fescue and three warm-season turfgrasses under well-watered conditions at Manhattan, Kansas (after Qian et al. 1996)

Turfgrass	Mowing Height (in inches [cm])	Mean ET (in inches per day [mm per day])[1]	ET Range (in inches per day [mm per day])
Mustang tall fescue	2.6 (6.5)	0.27 (6.9)	0.05–0.47 (1.3–11.9)
Meyer zoysiagrass	1.8 (4.5)	0.22 (5.5)	0.04–0.31 (1.0–8.0)
Prairie buffalograss	1.8 (4.5)	0.20 (5.1)	0.04–0.29 (0.9–7.3)
Midlawn bermudagrass	1.8 (4.5)	0.20 (5.0)	0.04–0.31 (1.0–7.8)

[1] Mean of 39 dates between 1 June and 20 August, 1994.

and buffalograss. Centipedegrass, St. Augustinegrass, seashore paspalum, and bahiagrass have higher ET rates.

Differences among turfgrass cultivars in ET has also been reported. For example, Shearman (1986) evaluated twenty Kentucky bluegrass cultivars in a growth chamber and found that ET rates ranged from 0.15 to 0.24 inches (3.9 to 6.3 mm) per day. Field studies in Nebraska indicated differences in ET among cultivars of tall fescue (Kopec and Shearman 1987) and perennial ryegrass (Shearman 1989).

Warm-season grass cultivars appear to have less variability in ET rates. No differences in ET were reported during field evaluations of eleven zoysiagrass (Green et al. 1991) or ten St. Augustinegrass cultivars in Texas (Atkins et al. 1991). The greatest differences among cultivars and species are likely to occur near the end of a mowing respite. Differences between fast- and slow-growing tall fescue cultivars were not obvious for the three or four days after mowing at the same height; however, ET differences were observed five to seven days after the initial mowing (Fry and Upham 1993). As time had progressed since mowing, differences in canopy heights between fast- and slow-growing cultivars were more significant and were reflected in ET measurements.

FACTORS TO CONSIDER IN DETERMINING IRRIGATION NEED

There are many factors that should be considered in determining water needs of turf. The turf manager has many tools available to help guide irrigation amounts and frequencies. In most cases, an integrated approach is used to couple common sense with one or more science-based tools.

Visible Turf Response Turfgrass leaf blades roll or fold when a water deficit occurs. Rolling and folding may also allow the plant to reduce additional water loss by lessening the amount of leaf surface area exposed. Turf often takes on a darker, bluish appearance when this happens. Walking across a turf area under drought stress results in footprinting—tracks are left when drought stressed plants are compressed but lack the turgidity needed to spring back up.

Figure 7-3
A Kentucky bluegrass
at the onset of wilt.
(Photo courtesy of Dr.
Steve Keeley.)

**Turfgrass
Rooting Depth**

Rooting depth can serve as a gauge of how deeply and frequently one should irrigate. There is usually no benefit wetting soil well below the maximum rooting depth. A soil probe can be used to periodically measure rooting depth, and determine the depth of the wetting front after irrigation. Rooting depth may change through the growing season. For example, in spring or fall, a creeping bentgrass green may have roots extending to depths of 8 inches (20 cm) or more. In midsummer, however, rooting depth may be reduced to 2 inches (5 cm) or less. Hence, irrigation could be done on a deeper, more infrequent schedule in spring or fall but would have to be done more frequently during summer months.

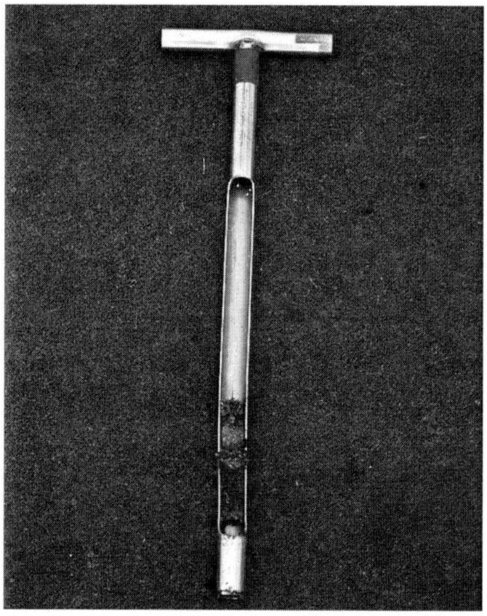

Figure 7-4
Periodically sampling to determine
rooting depth can help guide irrigation
strategies.

Soil Water Content   Soil matric potential, an indication of how tightly water is bound to soil particles, can be measured using tools including tensiometers or gypsum blocks. Dual heat probes and sensors that use time domain reflectometry can be used to measure volumetric soil water content. Tensiometers have a porous ceramic cup at one end that is fed by a column of water. The ceramic end is buried in the soil at the preferred depth and allowed to reach equilibrium with the soil water content. Multiple tensiometers may be installed at a single location to get soil water content measurements over a range of depths. A drier soil results in more water exiting the ceramic cup, creating a vacuum that is recorded by a gauge on the opposite end. Tensiometers are capable of measuring soil matric potential down to –1.0 bar (–100 kPa). A reading of –0.1 to –0.3 bars (–10 to –30 kPa) indicates soil is at field capacity, whereas a reading of –0.7 bar (–70 kPa) indicate reduced availability of soil water (Turgeon 1999). Tensiometers are not effective when the soil dries extensively, and are better for use on relatively high-maintenance turf.

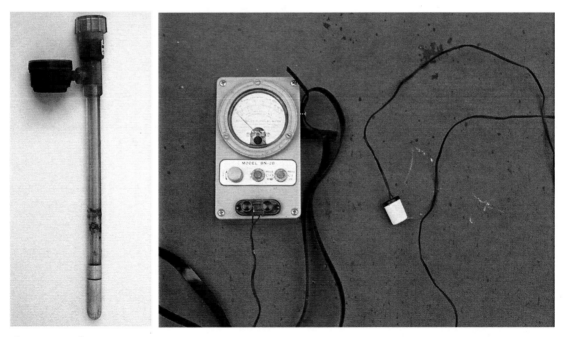

Figures 7-5 and 7-6
Tensiometers (Fig. 7-5, left) and gypsum blocks (Fig. 7-6, right) are commonly used to measure soil water potential.

Gypsum blocks use electrical conductivity to provide an estimate of soil water content. Two electric probes are buried in a block of gypsum, which is set at the preferred soil depth. The gypsum block then comes into equilibrium with the soil water. Higher soil water contents are reflected by higher electrical conductivity readings. Gypsum blocks are better than tensiometers for measuring soil water contents during significant dry-downs.

Dual heat probes and time domain reflectometers (TDR) have been used primarily for research up until now, but these technologies are now being marketed to turfgrass managers. Both methods provide a very accurate estimate of soil water content. The dual heat probe measures the time required for a pulse of heat to traverse two steel probes. A higher soil water content results in greater capacity of the soil to conduct heat. Comparison of soil water content measured using the dual heat probe to gravimetric measurements indi-

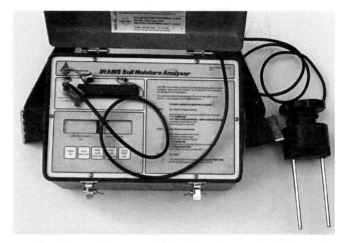

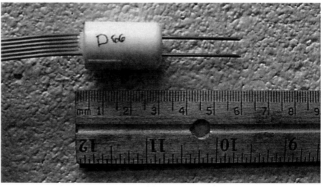

Figures 7-7 and 7-8
The time domain reflectometer (Fig. 7-7, top) and dual heat probe sensor (Fig. 7-8, bottom) employ more advanced technology to provide an accurate measurement of soil water content.

cated a very high correlation between the two (Dale Bremer, personal communication). The TDR measures the dielectric constant of soil, which is directly affected by its water content. Both the dual probe and TDR technologies provide accurate estimates of the volumetric soil water content across a range of soil moisture levels.

Evapo-transpiration Since the Last Irrigation

Turfgrass water use rates in research studies are frequently measured using lysimeters, which provide the most accurate measurement of water requirements under well-watered conditions. Lysimeters are pots that contain a soil medium (preferably fritted clay) on which grasses are established. Lysimeters are set in sleeves in the ground so that the canopy of turf growing in the lysimeter is experiencing nearly the same environment as turf in a natural setting. To measure ET, soil in lysimeters is soaked and allowed to drain to field capacity, and lysimeters are then weighed to determine reference weights. After the lysimeters have been in the field for a given period of time (usually twenty-four hours), they are removed and weighed again. By taking the difference between the lysimeter's reference weight and its mass at the subsequent weighing, ET can be calculated.

Figures 7-9 and 7-10
Lysimeters are used by researchers to determine turfgrass ET rates. A lysimeter containing tall fescue has been removed from its sleeve in the field prior to weighing (Fig. 7-9, left). Creeping bentgrass growing in a lysimeter set in position on a putting green (Fig. 7-10, right).

Although lysimeters are accurate in providing ET information, they are too laborious for the turf manager to maintain. Therefore, scientists have developed other tools to estimate turfgrass reference ET. Atmometers can be used to measure evaporation of water and then correlate this to turf ET. The most well known example of an atmometer is the evaporation pan. Daily measurements of evaporation from the pan are converted to turf ET with a crop coefficient, or multiplier. Coefficients vary greatly depending upon turf species and environmental conditions. Qian and colleagues (1996) found that the evaporation pan provided turfgrass ET estimates that were inferior to the Bellani plate, but better than the Penman-Monteith empirical model.

A second type of atmometer commonly used to estimate turf ET is the Bellani plate. This is a flat, circular plate of porous porcelain that encloses the large end of a funnel-like base. A reservoir below the plate supplies water to the apparatus. Water evaporates through micropores on the surface of the plate at a rate determined by prevailing weather conditions. Researchers in Kansas indicated that ET estimates provided by the black Bellani plate were better correlated to lysimeter-measured turfgrass ET than to ET estimated via pan evaporation or the Penman-Monteith model (Qian et al. 1996). Another positive aspect of the Bellani plate is that it can be set out at numerous locations across a large piece of property (such as a

Figure 7-11
Water evaporation from a Class A pan can easily be converted to turfgrass ET estimates.

Figure 7-12
The Bellani plate atmometer provides a relatively accurate estimate of turfgrass ET under well-watered conditions, and can be used to measure variability in turfgrass ET across a large property, such as a golf course.

golf course) if one is interested in knowing how water demand varies across the area. Microclimates across one Kansas golf course caused evaporative demand to vary by as much as 20 percent from one location to another (Jiang, Fry, and Wiest 1998). Of course, there are some disadvantages to the Bellani plate that limits its use, including periodic cleaning that is required, and damage that may result if the temperature drops below freezing. Bellani plates are sold commercially under the trade name ET Gauge.

New irrigation systems on golf courses, in particular, are often accompanied by weather stations. Besides providing valuable information on current weather conditions, weather stations also collect data that can be incorporated into empirical models that serve to predict ET. Many such models exist, all with their own particular nuances. Most use temperature, solar radiation, relative humidity, wind speed, and sometimes other weather data to generate a predicted ET value. For example, the Penman-Monteith model provides an estimate of reference ET from a hypothetical 5-inch-tall

Figure 7-13
Weather stations often accompany
installation of large-scale irrigation
systems and provide weather data that
can be used in empirical models to
generate estimates of turfgrass ET.

(12 cm) grass surface with a given surface resistance and albedo
(Allen 2000).

Qian and colleagues (1996) evaluated the accuracy of all the
above ET estimators for grasses commonly planted in Manhattan,
Kansas, in the transition zone. The equations outlined in Table 7-3
can be used to generate turfgrass ET estimates for turf in comparable climates, assuming the turf is growing under well-watered conditions. For example, using the equation from Table 7-3, if 8 mm of
evaporation occurred from a Class A evaporation pan, the ET rate
of Mustang tall fescue mowed at 2.5 inches would be calculated as:

$$ET = 1.08 + (0.83 \times 8 \text{ mm})$$

$$ET = 7.72 \text{ mm}$$

$$ET = 7.72 \text{ mm} \div 25.4 \text{ mm/inch}$$

$$ET = 0.30 \text{ inches}$$

Assuming well-watered conditions, the ET for the Mustang tall
fescue was 0.30 inches (7.72 mm) over the previous twenty-four
hours.

Table 7-3

The simple equations below can be used to convert atmometer evaporation and empirical model ET estimates to ET values for the four turfgrasses grown in the Midwest transition zone (after Qian et al. 1996)[1]

Turfgrass	Mowing Height (inches [cm])	Evaporation Pan	Bellani Plate	Penman-Monteith Model
Mustang tall fescue	2.50 (6.5)	ET = 1.08 + 0.83 × pan evaporation in mm	ET = 0.51 + 0.57 × plate evaporation in mm	ET = 0.21 + 1.02 × model estimated ET in mm
Meyer zoysiagrass	1.75 (4.5)	ET = 1.53 + 0.57 × pan evaporation in mm	ET = 1.07 + 0.39 × plate evaporation in mm	ET = 0.64 + 0.89 × model estimated ET in mm
Prairie buffalograss	1.75 (4.5)	ET = 1.22 + 0.54 × pan evaporation in mm	ET = 0.81 + 0.37 × plate evaporation in mm	ET = 0.58 + 0.82 × model estimated ET in mm
Midlawn bermudagrass	1.75 (4.5)	ET = 1.05 + 0.58 × pan evaporation in mm	ET = 0.64 + 0.39 × plate evaporation in mm	ET = 0.43 + 0.86 × model estimated ET in mm

[1] Models provide ET estimates in mm. To convert to inches of ET, divide by 25.4.

Irrigation systems can then be set to deliver all or a fraction of the total ET that occurred since the last irrigation.

The models generally provide the turf manager with good guidelines on how much water should be applied. As discussed above, they may provide a less accurate measurement of ET than evaporation pans or atmometers, because the models estimate evaporation rather than providing an actual measurement. Accuracy of the model used varies depending upon the species of turf used and the height at which it is maintained. For example, in Kansas the Doorenbos-Pruitt-Makkink, FAO-Penman, and Penman models provide the best ET estimates for buffalo, bermudagrass, and zoysiagrass, but other models were more effective for tall fescue (Fry et al. 1997).

Special care should be taken to locate the weather station, which provides the data for the model, in an area representative of the majority of the turf to be irrigated. For example, a weather station that will be used to collect data to empirically estimate ET for an open, windy golf course should not be situated near a windbreak.

Furthermore, if the area around the weather station is not irrigated and becomes droughty, ET estimates may be as much as 22 percent higher than actual ET in irrigated areas (Jiang, Fry, and Wiest 1998), due principally to higher air temperatures around the weather station. As with all ET estimators, it is important to note that numbers provided assume that the turf is managed under well-watered conditions, that is, the soil is at or near field capacity at all times. Because ET declines as soil dries, turf managers irrigating on a deep, infrequent schedule may find that these models overestimate water requirements.

Soil Type and Rate of Water Depletion

The volumetric soil water content at field capacity and permanent wilting point varies among soils of different textures. As such, the available water differs among soil types as well.

By knowing the average daily ET rate and plant-available water, an estimate of the required irrigation frequency can be made. This requires a series of simple calculations (divide inches by 2.54 to convert to cm in all steps below):

1. Determine the amount of water held by each soil type by multiplying plant available water by the depth of the root zone (we'll assume it's 12 inches for this example).

   For sand: 0.06×12 inches = 0.72 inches
   For clay: 0.16×12 inches = 1.92 inches

2. Most turf managers irrigate when 25 to 50 percent of the plant available water has been depleted. Let's assume 50 percent

Table 7-4

Hypothetical representation of water-holding capacities of sand and clay at field capacity and permanent wilting point, and plant-available water in each

	Water Retained (% by volume)	
Soil Water Level	**Sand**	**Clay**
Field capacity (FC)	10	40
Permanent wilting point (PWP)	4	24
Plant available water (= water content at FC − water content at PWP)	6	16

depletion for this example. Amount of water depleted before irrigation would be calculated as follows:

| For sand: | 0.72 inches × 0.50 = 0.36 inches |
| For clay: | 2.92 inches × 0.50 = 0.96 inches |

3. Estimate the average daily ET rate and divide plant available water by the daily ET rate to determine irrigation frequency in days. For this example, we'll assume that the average ET rate is 0.20 inches.

| For sand: | 0.36 inches ÷ 0.20 inches/day = 3.6 days |
| For clay: | 0.96 inches ÷ 0.20 inches/day = 4.8 days |

Hence, more frequent irrigation is required to replenish the depleted water reservoir in the sandy soil. Fine-textured soils, such as the clay in this example, have a greater water holding capacity; thus irrigation may be applied less frequently. However, infiltration rates on fine-textured soils high in clay content can be less than 0.10 inches (0.25 cm) per hour. As such, irrigation may have to be applied cyclically to fine-textured soils to prevent runoff. On coarse-textured soils with high sand content, infiltration rates are commonly greater than 1 inch (2.5 cm) per hour.

DETERMINING IRRIGATION REQUIREMENTS: A CASE STUDY

Colbert Hills is an eighteen-hole championship course located in Manhattan, Kansas, and the home of Kansas State University. Irrigated turf on the course consists of 5 acres of L-93 creeping bentgrass greens mowed at 0.130 inches (3 mm), 45 acres of Meyer zoysiagrass fairways and tees mowed at 0.5 inches (1.3 cm), and 100 acres of turf-type tall fescue mowed at 2.5 inches (6.1 cm). Water requirements for large expanses of turf and other crops are expressed as acre-feet (1 acre-foot = 325,851.43 gallons [equivalent to 1,233,445.4 liters of water to a depth of 30.5 cm over 0.4047 hectares]).

By knowing the area of turfgrass to be irrigated, estimates of turfgrass ET through the season, and the amount of water in one acre-foot, it is possible to estimate the annual water requirements for any large expanse of turf.

In Table 7-5, turf ET values for June to September were based upon turfgrass research data conducted at Kansas State University.

Table 7-5

Estimating water requirements in acre-feet for Colbert Hills Golf Course in Manhattan, Kansas (after Fry 2002)

Months	(1) Average Daily ET (inches)	(2) No. Days	(3) Total ET (inches) (col. 1 × col. 2)	(4) Acre-feet/acre (col. 3 ÷ 12)	(5) Acres	(6) Total Acre-feet (col. 4 × col. 5)	(7) Usable Precip. (acre-feet over the area given)	(8) Net Acre-feet (col. 6 − col. 7)
Creeping Bentgrass Greens								
Mar.–May	0.1	92	9.2	0.77	5	3.85	2.06	1.79
Jun.–Sep.	0.2	122	24.4	2.03	5	10.15	3.39	6.76
Oct.–Nov.	0.1	61	6.1	0.51	5	2.55	1.01	1.54
Total								10.09
Zoysiagrass Fairways and Tees								
Mar.–May	0.08	92	7.36	0.61	45	27	18.5	8.5
Jun.–Sep.	0.17	122	20.74	1.73	45	77.78	30.5	47.28
Oct.–Nov.	0.08	61	4.88	0.41	45	18.45	9.09	9.36
Total								65.14
Tall Fescue Roughs								
Mar.–May	0.12	92	11.04	0.92	100	92	41.13	50.87
Jun.–Sep.	0.27	122	32.94	2.75	100	275	67.8	207.2
Oct.–Nov.	0.12	61	7.32	0.61	100	61	20.2	40.8
Total								298.87

Note: Convert ET in inches to mm by multiplying by 25.4. The term *acre-foot* does not convert well to international units. One acre-foot is equivalent to 1,233,445.4 liters of water to a depth of 30.5 cm over 0.4047 hectares.

Using the zoysiagrass fairway data for the 122-day period from June through September, the steps for determining water requirements are as follows:

1. Total ET for time period in inches

= average daily ET in inches × number of days in period
= 0.17 inches × 122 days
= 20.74 inches

2. Total ET for time period in feet

$$= \text{inches} \div 12$$
$$= 20.74 \text{ inches} \div 12$$
$$= 1.73 \text{ feet ET}$$

3. Acre-feet of ET over the time period

$$= \text{feet of ET} \times \text{number of acres of turf}$$
$$= 1.73 \text{ feet ET} \times 45 \text{ acres}$$
$$= 77.78 \text{ acre-feet ET}$$

4. Subtract usable precipitation to determine net acre feet

$$77.78 \text{ acre-feet} - 30.5 \text{ acre-feet} = 47.28 \text{ net acre feet}$$

It was assumed that the turfgrass plant would use 50 percent of the precipitation that fell. This is a conservative estimate, for as much as 75 percent may be available for use. Weather-based estimates were used to determine values for March-May and October-November. Based upon the calculations outlined in the tables, the annual irrigation requirement for Colbert Hills is 374.10 acre-feet, or 121,901,019 gallons.

Water estimates such as provided by this case study may be fairly accurate during a dry year but overestimate water needs during a wet year. Nevertheless, it is better to err on the high side than to submit a request that will not allow for sufficient water. Actual water use could be less because ET values used in the tables assumed that turf was growing under well-watered conditions. As discussed earlier, ET declines as the soil dries between irrigation or precipitation events, which would mean less water would be required than estimated.

Table 7-6
Estimated total annual water requirements of Colbert Hills Golf Course, Manhattan, Kansas, in acre-feet (after Fry 2002)

Area	Acre-feet
L-93 creeping bentgrass	10.09
Meyer zoysiagrass fairways and tees	65.14
Turf-type tall fescue rough	298.87
Total	374.10

It is also important to note that the steps outlined above to determine annual irrigation requirements do not account for inefficiencies in the way water is delivered to the turf. Poor water distribution will increase the amount of water required to maintain turf quality (Wilson and Zoldoske 1997). Once again, a higher rather than lower estimate of irrigation need may help to account for minor problems with distribution uniformity.

IRRIGATION MANAGEMENT

The debate regarding whether the turfgrass plant is best served by relatively deep, infrequent irrigation or light, frequent irrigation has gone on for decades and likely will continue. First, let's differentiate between the two irrigation strategies. Deep, infrequent irrigation is probably better defined as irrigation to replenish the root zone at or just before the time when the first signs of leaf wilt are evident. To simplify, we will refer to this as wilt-based irrigation. For tall fescue growing on a deep, fertile soil, this may mean watering every two weeks during midsummer. However, on a heat-stressed creeping bentgrass putting green with shallow roots, wilt-based irrigation may require irrigating more than once a day.

In our context, light, frequent irrigation refers to applying water well before wilt is evident in an effort to maintain soil water content at or near field capacity at all times. We will refer to this as field-capacity irrigation. Often this means irrigating every day. Research has demonstrated that the plant is probably best served by using wilt-based irrigation. There are, however, benefits to field-capacity irrigation that should be recognized.

Positive Aspects of Wilt-Based Irrigation

Positive plant growth responses that have been observed when turf is watered on a wilt-based schedule versus a field-capacity schedule include reduced clipping production and shoot growth, enhanced rooting, lower leaf water and osmotic potentials, better turf quality during dry-down, and leaching of growth-inhibiting salts.

Irrigation promotes root water uptake, leading to increased cell division and elongation in shoots, thereby promoting shoot growth and clipping production. In zoysiagrass, shoot growth rate was up to 40 percent higher in turf watered daily compared to that watered at the onset of wilt (Qian and Fry 1996). As such, one should expect mowing requirements to increase as irrigation frequency increases.

Irrigation management has a direct influence upon rooting, and several researchers have reported enhanced rooting when a wilt-based strategy was employed. Bennett and Doss (1960) and Doss, Ashley, and Bennett (1960) observed that rooting of cool- and warm-season forage grasses was enhanced by allowing the surface 23.6 inches (60 cm) of soil to dry to 15 percent versus 70 percent of available water content. Likewise, Madison and Hagan (1962) reported that Kentucky bluegrass rooting was enhanced by watering every twenty days compared to three days per week in California. Soil under zoysiagrass watered at the onset of wilt had up to 19 percent lower volumetric water content at soil depths of 21.6 and 29.5 inches (55 and 75 cm) than that watered daily when turf was allowed to dry down for more than forty days in the greenhouse (Qian and Fry 1996). This suggested that more zoysiagrass roots were present deep in the profile in turf irrigated using a wilt-based irrigation regime compared to turf watered using a field capacity scheme. When kikuyugrass (*Pennisetum clandestinum*) was watered on schedules ranging from seven to thirty days, turf watered less frequently extracted proportionately more water from deep in the root zone (Mantell 1966). Jaguar III tall fescue exhibited superior quality when watered twice weekly, compared to three or four times per week, in southern California (Richie et al. 2002).

Figure 7-14
Kentucky bluegrass irrigated using a wilt-based approach (center) had turf quality levels similar to turf irrigated using a field-capacity approach (far right). That on the far left was exposed to severe drought.

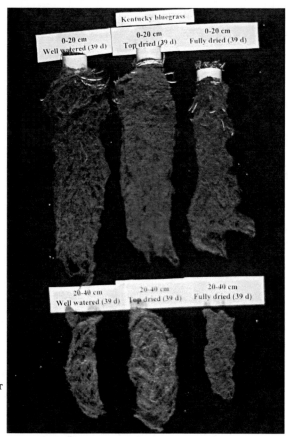

Figure 7-15
Kentucky bluegrass irrigated using a field capacity-approach (left) had fewer and shallower roots than turf irrigated using a wilt-based strategy (center). Kentucky bluegrass subjected to severe wilt (right) also had inferior rooting compared to turf watered on a wilt-based schedule.

In Kansas, Fu (2003) evaluated rooting of tall fescue irrigated twice weekly at 20, 60, and 100 percent ET. Turf irrigated at 20 percent ET had significantly higher root number, length, and surface area at a 5- to 7-inch (13–18 cm) depth in consecutive years compared to turf irrigated at other levels, despite turf quality ratings that fell below a minimum acceptable level (Fu 2003).

Even in creeping bentgrass managed under putting green conditions, irrigation every four days resulted in higher turf quality, shoot density, and root length density than irrigation applied every one or two days (Jordan et al. 2003).

Rooting is directly proportional to shoot growth, and, as discussed earlier, shoots respond readily to field-capacity-based irrigation. Therefore, by reducing shoot growth with wilt-based irrigation, the plant has the capability to redirect photosynthates to roots.

Soil drying has also been shown to encourage the development of root hairs in tall fescue (Huang and Fry 1998), presumably an effort by the plant to maximize water uptake. The mechanism for this response is not understood, but it may be related to hormone production.

Severe drought conditions will obviously result in root injury, and this varies among species and cultivars. In tall fescue, root cells collapsed and an increase in root electrolyte leakage was observed beginning at fourteen days without irrigation in the greenhouse (Huang and Fry 1998). The dwarf cultivar M1C18 exhibited greater root death than did Kentucky-31, a forage-type cultivar.

Leaf, and possibly root, tissues of plants subjected to a wilt-based regime will generally be more physiologically prepared for drought than will be those of plants subjected to field-capacity irrigation. Zoysiagrass irrigated daily over a three-month period exhibited higher leaf water potentials and less osmotic adjustment than turf watered at the onset of wilt (Qian and Fry, 1996). Lower water and osmotic potentials arise when there is an accumulation of solutes in the cell, including potassium, chloride, and sugars. Plants that osmotically adjust are better prepared for a drought if it occurs. For this reason, and the other positive plant responses to wilt-based irrigation discussed above, the turf manager can also expect better turf

Figure 7-16
"Meyer" zoysia on the left was irrigated daily for three months before watering ceased. Turf on the right was irrigated using a wilt-based schedule over the same period before irrigation ceased.

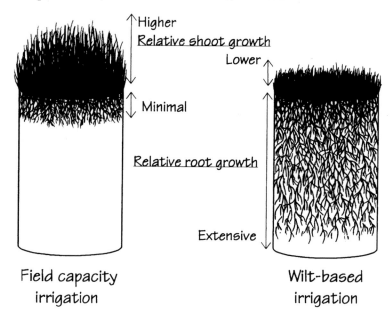

↑ Higher
<u>Relative shoot growth</u>
Lower ↑
↕ Minimal
<u>Relative root growth</u>
Extensive ↕

Field capacity irrigation

Wilt-based irrigation

Figure 7-17
Field-capacity based irrigation promotes shoot growth and detracts from root growth (drawing by Angie Settle).

quality into dry-down, if water restrictions occur, than would be observed with a field-capacity irrigation strategy.

Wilt-based irrigation also allows for greater potential to move growth-inhibiting salts deeper into the root zone. Salts reduce the osmotic potential of water and may actually draw water out of plant roots, causing drought symptoms. Superintendents irrigating turf growing on saline soils must periodically leach salts through the root zone. Even routine fertilization can result in salt accumulation over time if leaching is not done periodically. Hence, an indirect benefit of a wilt-based irrigation strategy is to satisfy this leaching requirement.

Positive Aspects of Field-Capacity-Based Irrigation

Although field-capacity-based irrigation is generally not necessary from the perspective of plant health, research has demonstrated that there are some benefits, including less potential for nutrient and pesticide leaching, fewer problems with localized dry spot on sand-based soils, maintenance of turf quality when water availability is restricted, and potential reduction in some turf diseases.

The benefits of wilt-based irrigation as they relate to leaching of salts may also increase the likelihood of groundwater contamination if water-soluble fertilizers or pesticides move vertically through the soil profile. Hence, there may be benefits to using a field capacity irrigation strategy to minimize the leaching of fertilizers and pesticides. Starrett, Christians, and Austin (1996) found that leaching of pesticides through a fine, loamy soil averaged from 0.2 to 7.7 percent of that applied when a heavy irrigation (four 1-inch [2.54 cm] applications of water) regime was employed. Leaching ranged from 0 to 0.4 percent on average when a light (sixteen 0.25-inch [0.64 cm] applications of water) irrigation strategy was used. The risk of leaching in following a wilt-based irrigation strategy may be most important on sand-based root zones, where the potential to hold nutrients and organic pesticides is greatly reduced.

Localized dry spot is a common problem with sand-based root zones and is affected by irrigation management. The decomposition of organic matter can result in sand particles becoming coated with hydrophobic organic chemicals. Hydrophobicity may affect only the top inch (2.5 cm) of the root zone or may extend several inches deep. Researchers in Georgia (Karnok and Tucker 1999) found that symptoms of localized dry spot on creeping bentgrass putting greens were reduced if turf was watered using a field-capacity-based strategy. Golf course superintendents who allow soil to dry down between irrigations are often required to use a wetting agent to minimize the nuisance of localized dry spot on sandy soils.

Field-capacity-based irrigation may also provide benefits as they relate to getting turf through periods of water restrictions and in battling some turfgrass diseases. These situations are discussed more below.

Preparing for Drought and Water Restrictions

When water suppliers are unable to keep up with water demand, or when extended drought has resulted in reduced water availability, water restrictions may be imposed. Turf can be managed to maximize drought resistance, as discussed above. In addition, steps can be taken to maintain turf quality during periods when water availability is reduced.

Use Deficit Irrigation

Deficit irrigation is defined as irrigating turf with some fraction of water that is less than the estimated reference ET. Most turfgrass managers are irrigating at levels less than estimates of reference ET, for these estimates assume turf is always growing in well-watered

Figure 7-18
An aerial view of a linear gradient irrigation system in Dallas, Texas, that allows evaluation of grasses subjected to deficit irrigation. Turf growing closest to the center irrigation line receives the most water, and water supply decreases with distance from that line. Note how the grasses farther away from the center line differ in quality. (Photo courtesy of Dr. Yaling Qian.)

soil. Soil dry-down results in lower turf water requirements relative to reference ET. Generally, warm-season grasses are more amenable to deficit irrigation than cool-season grasses. Bermudagrass has been shown to maintain quality at levels as low as 40 percent of actual ET (Fu, Fry, and Huang 2002) and 35 percent of pan evaporation (Qian and Engelke 1999). Buffalograss quality was maintained at 26 percent of pan evaporation in Dallas, Texas (Qian and Engelke 1999).

Figure 7-19
"Rebel" tall fescue subjected to a deficit irrigation level of 50% of actual ET and watered every 14 days (left) or every 4 days (right) in Colorado.

Of the cool-season grasses, tall fescue has shown the most promise for tolerating deficit irrigation, particularly if there is subsurface moisture present when the deficit regime begins. When a two-day irrigation frequency was employed, Rebel tall fescue quality remained acceptable when irrigated at 50 percent of actual ET (Fry and Butler 1989).

Table 7-7

Turfgrass responses to deficit irrigation at various locations in the United States

Grass	Location	Soil Type	Irrigation Frequency	Deficit Irrigation Level Required to Maintain Quality[1]	Reference
Rebel tall fescue	Fort Collins, Colorado	Sandy clay loam	2 days	50 percent of ET_a	Fry and Butler 1989
Rebel tall fescue	Fort Collins, Colorado	Sandy clay loam	4, 7, or 14 days	75 percent of ET_a	Fry and Butler 1989
Rebel II tall fescue	Dallas, Texas	Clay	3 days	67 percent of E_{pan}	Qian and Engelke 1999
Falcon II tall fescue	Manhattan, Kansas	Silt loam	Twice weekly	60 percent of ET_a	Fu et al. 2002
Waldina hard fescue	Fort Collins, Colorado	Sandy clay loam	2, 4, or 7 days	75 percent of ET_a	Fry and Butler 1989
Meyer zoysiagrass	Manhattan, Kansas	Silt loam	Twice weekly	80 percent of ET_a	Fu et al. 2002
Meyer zoysiagrass	Dallas, Texas	Clay	3 days	68 percent of E_{pan}	Qian and Engelke 1999
Nortam St. Augustinegrass	Dallas, Texas	Clay	3 days	44 percent of E_{pan}	Qian and Engelke 1999
Tifway bermudagrass	Dallas, Texas	Clay	3 days	35 percent of E_{pan}	Qian and Engelke 1999
Midlawn bermudagrass	Manhattan, Kansas	Silt loam	Twice weekly	40 percent of ET_a	Fu et al. 2002
Prairie buffalo	Dallas, Texas	Clay	3 days	26 percent of E_{pan}	Qian and Engelke 1999

continued on next page

Grass	Location	Soil Type	Irrigation Frequency	Deficit Irrigation Level Required to Maintain Quality[1]	Reference
Santa Ana bermudagrass, Adalyd seashore paspalum, Jade zoysiagrass	Santa Ana, California	Sandy loam	not reported	60 percent of ET_o	Gibeault et al. 1985
Merion Kentucky bluegrass	Fort Collins, Colorado	Clay loam	2, 4, or 7 days	75 percent ET_a	Minner 1984
Brilliant Kentucky bluegrass	Manhattan, Kansas	Silt loam	Twice weekly	100 percent ET_a	Fu et al. 2002
Kentucky bluegrass blend; perennial ryegrass blend, Kentucky-31 tall fescue	Santa Ana, California	Sandy loam	not reported	80 percent of ET_o	Gibeault et al. 1985

[1] Deficit irrigation: E_{pan} based upon evaporation from a Class A evaporation pan; ET_o based upon reference ET calculated using an empirical model; ET_a based upon actual ET measured using turf growing in lysimeters under well-watered conditions.

Manipulate Irrigation Frequency to Maintain Quality

As discussed earlier, there are positives to watering on a wilt-based schedule. However, it may be desirable to increase irrigation frequency when water is limiting. Water can be applied in lesser amounts but more frequently to maintain visual quality of some grasses when amount of total water applied is restricted. Research has shown that quality of tall fescue and zoysiagrass can be maintained with less water if it is applied at more frequent intervals. For example, tall fescue maintained high quality turf by watering at 50 percent of estimated ET every two days during summer months in Colorado (Fry and Butler 1989). Watering once weekly at this same level resulted in unacceptable quality. There are obvious public perception difficulties that would have to be considered when watering frequently during a period in which water restrictions are in force. Nevertheless, public education regarding this issue might be worthwhile in order to nurse a turf area through a drought period.

Water-Saving Alternatives

Many turfgrass managers have adapted the idea of expanding native areas or partitioning off portions of the course as "no mow" areas. On some golf courses, the majority of the irrigated area is composed of rough. Planting drought-resistant native turfgrasses in these areas can result in tremendous water savings. For example, the water use illustration above for Colbert Hills Golf Course indicated that it had 100 acres of tall fescue rough. This turf alone receives approximately 300 of the 374 total annual acre-feet required to irrigate the golf course. Using a drought-resistant native turfgrass species, such as buffalograss, in place of tall fescue would allow the golf course superintendent to be selective in levels of irrigation applied to the turf without compromising the plant's ability to recover. The result would have been tremendous water savings.

Alternatively, non-native species can be allowed to go unmowed in selected areas, which will result in significant water savings and reduce labor costs associated with irrigating and mowing. Plant materials other than grasses may also be considered for water savings, but be careful. Select plant materials that have proven drought resistance, for some ornamentals may require more water than turfgrasses.

Figure 7-20
Incorporating unmowed native grass areas can help to save water, such as was done at Prairie Dunes Country Club in Hutchinson, Kansas.

INTERACTIONS WITH ENVIRONMENTAL STRESSES

Because shoot and root growth is so substantially influenced by irrigation management, one would suspect that it also affects resistance to environmental stresses other than drought. In fact, irrigation plays a significant role in the turfgrass plant's ability to tolerate temperature extremes and shade.

Temperature Stresses

Freezing

Freezing injury increases as cell water content increases; therefore, excessive rainfall or irrigation in the fall may reduce the ability of the turfgrass plant to acclimate to cold temperatures. Freezing resistance of Raleigh St. Augustinegrass has been shown to be directly related to stolon water content (Meier, Lang, and Fry 1994). As water level increases, survivability decreases. As such, turf growing in areas where water puddles and drainage is poor will be more susceptible to direct freezing stress, for crowns become hydrated. Dehardened perennial ryegrass that was irrigated in early spring exhibited greater freezing injury of crowns compared to turf that had been subjected to drought stress prior to freezing (Welterlen and Watschke 1985).

Figure 7-21
In areas where dry winter conditions with no snow cover are common, desiccation injury is common, as evident on this creeping bentgrass green in Kansas.

Although overwatering during the winter acclimation period should be avoided, the turfgrass plant should enter winter months with an adequate amount of water. Winter desiccation is commonly misdiagnosed as low temperature injury. For example, creeping bentgrass is very cold hardy but often suffers from winter desiccation in Midwestern and Western states. In some cases, irrigation may be required in midwinter to avoid desiccation.

Heat   Drought contributes to "summer decline" of cool-season turfgrass stands. Adequate soil water is required if the plant is to transpire and keep itself cool. It is likely that a cool-season grass that experiences some degree of drought stress during a hot summer day could also suffer from direct or indirect effects of high temperatures. In fact, the combination of heat and drought stresses is more deleterious than either stress alone. Kentucky bluegrass exposed to heat and drought stresses in a growth chamber experienced a greater reduction in photosynthesis and photochemical efficiency than when either stress was applied alone (Jiang and Huang 2000).

In general, cool-season grasses have better heat tolerance when soil is allowed to dry down between irrigations compared to those that receive frequent watering. Kentucky bluegrass plants that were preconditioned to drought by watering on a wilt-based schedule in the growth chamber were better able to tolerate subsequent heat stress compared to plants that had been irrigated using a field-capacity strategy (Jiang and Huang, 2000 and 2001). Drought-preconditioned plants exhibited higher quality and better photosynthesis, stomatal conductance, transpiration, leaf relative water content, and osmotic adjustment after two and three weeks of heat stress than those that were not preconditioned. Soluble carbohydrates were up to 44 percent higher in drought-preconditioned plants. Preconditioned plants also had higher root weights after the heat stress period.

Syringing, a light application of water to wet the leaf surface, is commonly used to reduce the potential detrimental effects of heat on cool-season grasses (particularly creeping bentgrass and annual bluegrass). In theory, water evaporates from the leaf surface and compliments transpiration to aid in cooling the plant. Greatest benefits from syringing will occur in semiarid and arid regions, where relative humidity is generally low and the leaf-to-air vapor pressure gradient is greatest. Research indicates that the benefits afforded by

Figure 7-22
Syringing is used to
wet the surface of the
turfgrass leaf and cool
the plant via
evaporation.

syringing are fleeting. Analysis of the effects of application of various amounts of water throughout the day on bentgrass canopy temperature in North Carolina indicated there was little effect one hour after treatment (DiPaola 1984). The author suggested that, without plant wilt, there may be little benefit to syringing greens under the conditions of their test. Researchers in Michigan also reported little effects of syringing on temperatures in the mat and at a 2-inch (5 cm) depth. However, they suggested that syringing prevented the soil and mat temperatures from reaching levels that might be observed had no syringing been applied (Duff and Beard 1966).

Syringing   Hand-watering

Figure 7-23
A hose-end nozzle that produces a fine mist with small water droplets, such as on the left, should be selected for syringing (drawing by Angie Settle).

In Alabama, syringing was most effective at reducing soil surface temperatures under a bentgrass green when it was done in combination with fans. When soil surface temperatures were highest, using a fan plus syringing resulted in a decrease in soil temperature at a 0.5-inch (1.3 cm) depth of about 7°F (4°C) (Dr. Elizabeth Guertal, personal communication).

Special care should be taken to select the correct hose-end nozzle when syringing is done by hand. Use of a nozzle that delivers large water droplets is better at delivering water to the soil than to the leaf surface. In fact, this often results in overirrigation of bentgrass greens and can lead to turf decline. Instead, a nozzle that produces a fine mist should be used to syringe.

Shade Turf in shade doesn't experience high daytime temperatures like that growing in full sun, is less dense, and lacks vigor. Hence, ET rates of shaded turf will be lower than those of that growing in full sun. Kentucky bluegrass ET increased linearly with the amount of solar radiation received (Feldhake, Danielson, and Butler 1983). Nevertheless, tree roots compete with turf for water, and periodic irrigation is required. Shaded turf also experiences reduced air movement and higher humidity, increasing the likelihood of diseases. As such, a wilt-based irrigation schedule is recommended in shaded areas.

Figure 7-24
Kentucky bluegrass was grown under shade structures in Colorado to determine effects on ET.

INTERACTIONS WITH PESTS

Irrigation influences pest incidence in turf directly and indirectly. The biology and life cycle of nearly all pests are affected by water. Turfgrass vigor indirectly affects pest problems, and plants subjected to drought stress, or overwatering, may be predisposed to pest problems.

Weeds   Weed infestations are greatly affected by irrigation management. Annual weeds, like newly seeded turfgrass stands, require water for germination and emergence. Furthermore, there is a relatively narrow window during which winter or summer annuals emerge. Hence, irrigation management during these windows may help to encourage or discourage these problems.

A field-capacity-based irrigation regime would have the potential to promote weed seed germination. Nevertheless, Jiang, Fry, and Tisserat (1998) found that ryegrass irrigated on a field-capacity basis had similar levels of smooth crabgrass (Fig. 6-2) and dandelion (Fig. 6-5) as turf irrigated on a regime resembling a wilt-based schedule.

A scenario likely to favor establishment of summer annual weeds is one where turf is first subjected to drought stress, and as a result, density declines. Then, in an attempt to rescue drought-ridden turf, irrigation is applied on a field-capacity schedule. Germination of crabgrass, goosegrass (Fig. 6-3), and other summer annuals is then ensured, as turf competition is reduced, more light reaches the soil surface, and soil surface temperatures are higher.

Ecological evolution of some weed species determines their competitiveness under specific irrigation management regimes. For example, annual bluegrass (Fig. 2-4) is favored when soils are consistently moist (Sprague and Burton 1937). Rough bluegrass (Fig. 2-7) plot coverage was over 20 percent greater in perennial ryegrass watered daily compared to that watered three days weekly (Settle, Fry, and Tisserat 1998). Although research information is not available, weeds such as sedges and rushes also prefer wet soil conditions, and field-capacity-based irrigation will likely favor their competitiveness. Other weed species, such as prostrate spurge, exhibit exceptional drought resistance. Once established, this species is more competitive in turf that is exposed to drought.

Insects   Little information is available on how insects respond to irrigation. Studies on the behavior of root-feeding insects, including white grubs (Fig. 6-13 and 6-14) and mole crickets, indicate that they respond positively to moisture (Potter 1998). For example, when the soil surface is relatively moist, they move nearer the surface. When the surface dries down, grubs and mole crickets move downward. As such, it is important to consider irrigation as an important tool in improving insecticide efficacy. Irrigation before insecticide application will help to bring the target nearer to the surface. Watering after insecticide application is important to move the chemical down to where the target is.

Soil moisture levels also seem to influence behavior of egg-laying adult insects. Irrigation of Kentucky bluegrass or tall fescue prior to beetle flights resulted in higher densities of Japanese beetle and masked chaffer grubs than in nonirrigated plots (Potter et al. 1996). These researchers recommended lengthening the interval between irrigations during peak flights of adult beetles. Theoretically, however, wilt-based irrigation may also result in an earlier display of grub damage, such as wilting turf. Although turf irrigated on a field-capacity-based strategy may harbor more grubs, symptoms may be delayed or never expressed, for the plant may not suffer a water deficit. Indeed, greater grub population densities are necessary to cause symptom development on well watered versus water-deprived turf (Potter 1998).

There is less information concerning irrigation management effects on surface-feeding insects. Chinch bugs (Fig. 6-11) prefer hot and dry conditions, and survival of young nymphs can be reduced by overirrigation (Potter 1998).

Diseases   Nearly all turfgrass diseases are caused by fungi that infect shoots, roots, or both. Because fungi require water in order to proliferate, irrigation management can play a significant role in symptom development.

Until recently, any irrigation regime that encouraged wet conditions was thought to promote diseases. Wet conditions could arise from a field-capacity-based irrigation regime or nighttime irrigation. Research has shown that pathogens respond differently to irrigation practices, with many, as expected, suppressed under a wilt-based irrigation regime but others, surprisingly, suppressed by a field-capacity-based scheme.

Irrigation schedules that resemble wilt-based regimes have been shown to suppress some turf diseases. Summer patch (Fig. 6-33), a root-infecting fungus, caused more pronounced injury in Kentucky bluegrass when turf was irrigated using a field capacity versus wilt-based strategy in a Maryland study (Davis and Dernoeden 1991). Interestingly, a field-capacity-based schedule reduced symptoms of necrotic ring spot (Fig. 6-30), another root-infecting pathogen, in Michigan (Melvin and Vargas, 1994).

Perennial ryegrass exhibited 2 to 9 percent less brown patch (Fig. 6-16) when irrigated daily using a field capacity-based schedule compared to a wilt-based schedule (Jiang, Fry, and Tisserat 1998). This was curious, for brown patch is generally thought be encouraged by frequent irrigation. Early research (Oakley 1924) suggested that morning irrigation reduced brown patch on bentgrass putting greens. Rowell (1951) also reported that turf inoculated with the brown patch fungus failed to develop symptoms when receiving overhead irrigation. The initial Kansas work, and the aforementioned reports of earlier researchers, led investigators to conduct more studies to better understand how brown patch responds to irrigation (Settle, Fry, and Tisserat 2001a). They found that brown patch symptoms in growth-chamber-grown ryegrass could be allayed by using a wilt-based strategy or by watering every hour with 0.5 inches (1.3 cm) of water. The former strategy likely provided too little water for the fungus to thrive, whereas the latter caused a physical removal of the fungal mycelium. When projects were conducted in the field, however, brown patch symptoms were similar whether a wilt-based or field capacity strategy was used. Poling to remove dew and disturb the fungal mycelium reduced brown patch by about 10 percent.

Daily, field-capacity-based irrigation did not increase brown patch in tall fescue any more than irrigation applied three days weekly (Settle, Fry, and Tisserat 2001b). Pythium blight (Fig. 6-25 and 6-26), evaluated in the same test, was exacerbated by daily irrigation, particularly when treated turf was treated with the fungicide azoxystrobin.

Dollar spot (Fig. 6-18), which usually increases dramatically when dew presence increases, is favored by a field capacity-based irrigation strategy (Jiang, Fry, and Tisserat 1998).

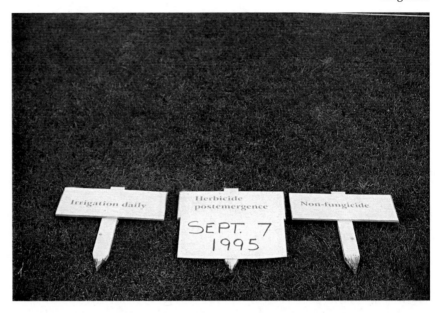

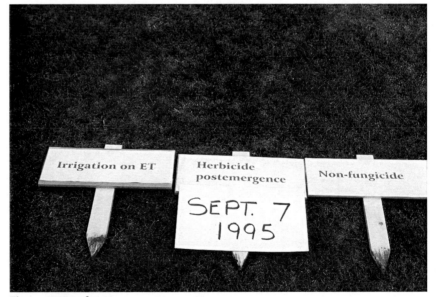

Figures 7-25 and 7-26
Daily-irrigated perennial ryegrass (Fig. 7-25, top) exhibited reduced brown patch injury compared to turf watered on a wilt-based schedule (Fig. 7-26, bottom) in Kansas.

Table 7-8
Summary of research results from projects that compared irrigation frequency effects on turfgrass diseases. The citation is listed in the respective irrigation treatment column where least disease occurred

Disease	Turfgrass	Strategy That Reduces Disease Symptoms	
		Wilt-Based	**Field Capacity**
Dollar spot	Perennial ryegrass	Jiang, Fry, and Tisserat (1998)	
	Creeping bentgrass	Irrigation amount 60 percent versus 100 percent ET_{pan} had no effect (Watkins et al. 2001)	
	Bermudagrass	Observed at 115 percent of ET_{pan} but not at lower levels (frequency not evaluated) (Qian and Engelke 1999)	
Brown patch	Perennial ryegrass		Jiang, Fry, and Tisserat 1998
		Brown patch was discouraged by wilt-based irrigation or heavy, hourly irrigation in the growth chamber, but no effect with frequency in the field (Settle et al. 2001a)	
	Tall fescue	No difference reported between irrigation daily or three times weekly (Settle et al. 2001b).	
	St. Augustinegrass	Observed only at > 80 percent of ET_{pan} (frequency not evaluated) (Qian and Engelke 1999)	
Gray leaf spot	St. Augustinegrass	Observed only at 10 percent of ET_{pan}, not at higher irrigation levels (frequency not evaluated) (Qian and Engelke 1999)	
Necrotic ring spot	Kentucky bluegrass		Melvin and Vargas 1994
Pythium blight	Tall fescue	Settle, Fry, and Tisserat 2001b	
Summer patch	Kentucky bluegrass	Davis and Dernoeden 1991	

The time of day during which irrigation is applied obviously has a significant effect on foliar diseases. Irrigating in the evening causes the turf canopy to remain wet until the next morning. Brown patch will not develop unless there has been more than 10 hours of leaf wetness; hence, evening irrigation contributes to the development of this disease (Fidanza and Dernoeden 1996).

REFERENCES

Allen, R. G. 2000. Using the FAO-56 dual crop coefficient method over an irrigated region as part of an evapotranspiration intercomparison study. *J. Hydrol.* 229:27–41.

Atkins, C., R. Green, S. Sifers, and J. Beard. 1991. Evapotranspiration rates of ten St. Augustinegrass genotypes. *HortScience* 26:1488–91.

Bennett, O., and B. Doss. 1960. Effect of soil moisture level on root distribution of cool-season species. *Agron. J.* 52:204–7.

Biran, I., B. Bravado, I. Bushkin-Harav, and E. Rawitz. 1981. Water consumption and growth rate of eleven turfgrasses as affected by mowing height, irrigation frequency, and soil moisture. *Agron. J.* 73:85–90.

Davis, D. B., and P. H. Dernoeden. 1991. Summer patch and Kentucky bluegrass quality as influenced by cultural practices. *Agron. J.* 83:670–77.

DiPaola, J. 1984. Syringing effects on canopy temperatures of bentgrass greens. *Agron. J.* 76:951–53.

Doss, B. D., D. A. Ashley, and O. L. Bennett. 1960. Effect of soil moisture regime on rooting distribution of warm-season forage species. *Agron. J.* 52:569–72.

Duff, T., and J. Beard. 1966. Effects of air movement and syringing on the microclimate of bentgrass turf. *Agron. J.* 58:495–97.

Feldhake, C. M., R. E. Danielson, and J. D. Butler. 1983. Turfgrass evapotranspiration. I. Factors influencing rate in urban environments. *Agron. J.* 75:824–30.

Fidanza, M., and P. Dernoeden. 1996. Brown patch severity in perennial ryegrass as influenced by irrigation, fungicide, and fertilizers. *Crop Sci.* 36:1631–38.

Fry, J. 2002. How much is a year's worth of water? *Golf Course Management* 70 (11): 85–88.

Fry, J., and J. Butler. 1989. Responses of tall and hard fescue to deficit irrigation. *Crop Sci.* 29:1536–41.

Fry, J., and W. Upham. 1993. Rooting, drought resistance, and water use of three tall fescue cultivars. Kansas State University Agricultural Experiment Station, Report of Progress no. 685, pp. 34–38.

Fry, J., S. Wiest, Y. Qian, and W. Upham. 1997. Evaluation of empirical models for estimating turfgrass water use. *Int. Turfgrass Soc. Res. J.* 8:1268–73.

Fu, J. 2003. Growth and physiological responses of turfgrasses to deficit irrigation. Ph.D. dissertation, Dept. of Horticulture, Forestry and Recreation Resources, Kansas State University.

Fu, J., J. Fry, and B. Huang. 2002. Water savings and performance of four turfgrasses under deficit irrigation. Kansas State University Research and Extension, Report of Progress no. 894, pp. 1–5.

Gibeault, V. A., J. L. Meyer, V. B. Youngner, and S. T. Cockerham. 1985. Irrigation of turfgrass below replacement of evapotranspiration as a means of water conservation: Performance of commonly used turfgrasses. Pp. 347–56 in F. Lemaire, ed., *Proceedings of the Fifth International Turfgrass Research Conference*. Versailles: INRA.

Green, R., S. Sifers, E. Atkins, and J. Beard. 1991. Evapotranspiration rates of eleven zoysiagrass genotypes. *HortScience* 26:264–66.

Huang, B., and J. Fry. 1998. Root anatomical, physiological, and morphological responses to drought stress for tall fescue cultivars. *Crop Sci.* 38:1017–22.

———. 1999. Turfgrass evapotranspiration. *J. Crop Prod.* 2:317–33.

Jiang, H., J. Fry, and N. Tisserat. 1998. Assessing irrigation management for its effects on disease and weed levels in perennial ryegrass. *Crop Sci.* 38:440–45.

Jiang, H., J. Fry, and S. Wiest. 1998. Variability in turfgrass water requirements on a golf course. *HortScience* 33:689–91.

Jiang, Y., and B. Huang. 2000. Effects of drought or heat stress alone and in combination on Kentucky bluegrass. *Crop Sci.* 40:1358–62.

———. 2001. Osmotic adjustment and root growth associated with drought preconditioning-enhanced heat tolerance in Kentucky bluegrass. *Crop Sci.* 41:1168–73.

Jordan, J., R. White, D. Vietor, T. Hale, J. Thomas, and M. Engelke. 2003. Effect of irrigation frequency on turf quality, shoot density, and root length density of five bentgrass cultivars. *Crop Sci.* 43:282–87.

Karnok, K., and K. Tucker. 1999. Dry spots return with summer: Localized dry spot and water-repellent soils require careful, constant management. *Golf Course Management* 67:49–52.

Kim, K., and J. Beard. 1988. Comparative turfgrass evapotranspiration rates and associated plant morphological characteristics. *Crop Sci.* 28:328–31.

Kopec, D., and R. Shearman. 1987. Evapotranspiration of tall fescue turf. *HortScience* 23:300–1.

Madison, J., and R. Hagan. 1962. Extraction of soil moisture by Merion bluegrass turf as affected by irrigation frequency, mowing height, and other cultural operations. *Agron. J.* 54:157–60.

Mantell, 1966. Effect of irrigation frequency and nitrogen fertilization on growth and water use of kikuyugrass turf. *Agron. J.* 58:559–61.

Meier, F., N. S. Lang, and J. Fry. 1994. Freezing tolerance of three St. Augustinegrass cultivars as affected by stolon carbohydrate and water content. *J. Amer. Soc. Hort. Sci.* 119:473–76.

Melvin, B. P., and J. M. Vargas. 1994. Irrigation frequency and fertilizer type influence necrotic ring spot of Kentucky bluegrass. *HortScience* 29:1028–30.

Minner, D. 1984. Cool season turfgrass quality as related to evapotranspiration and drought. Ph.D. dissertation, Colorado State University, Fort Collins, Colorado.

Oakley, R.A. 1924. Brown-patch investigation. *Bulletin of the Green Section of the U.S. Golf Association* 4:87–92.

Potter, D. 1998. *Destructive turfgrass insects: Biology, diagnosis, and control.* Chelsea, MI: Ann Arbor Press.

Potter, D. A., A. J. Powell, P. G. Spicer, and D. W. Williams. 1996. Cultural practices affect root-feeding white grubs (Coloeoptera: Scarabaeidae) in turfgrass. *Hort. Entom.* 89:156–64.

Qian, Y., and M. Engelke. 1999. Performance of five turfgrasses under linear gradient irrigation. *HortScience* 34:893–96.

Qian, Y., and J. Fry. 1996. Irrigation frequency affects zoysiagrass rooting and plant water status. *HortScience* 31:234–37.

Qian, Y., J. Fry, S. Wiest, and W. Upham. 1996. Estimating turfgrass evapotranspiration using atmometers and the Penman-Monteith model. *Crop Sci.* 36:699–704.

Richie, W., R. Green, G. Klein, and J. Hartin. 2002. Tall fescue performance influenced by irrigation scheduling, cultivar, and mowing height. *Crop Sci.* 42:2011–7.

Rowell, J. 1951. Observations on the pathogenicity of *Rhizoctonia solani* on bentgrasses. *Plant Dis. Rep.* 35:240–42.

Settle, D., J. Fry, and N. Tisserat. 1998. Influence of irrigation management on disease development in perennial ryegrass. Kansas State University Agricultural Experiment Station, Report of Progress no. 812, pp. 31–33.

_____. 2001a. Effects of irrigation frequency on brown patch in perennial ryegrass. *Int. Turfgrass Res. J.* 9:710–13.

_____. 2001b. Development of brown patch and Pythium blight in tall fescue as affected by irrigation frequency, clipping removal, and fungicide application. *Plant Dis.* 85:543–46.

Shearman, R. 1986. Kentucky bluegrass cultivar evapotranspiration rates. *HortScience* 21:455–57.

_____. 1989. Perennial ryegrass cultivar evapotranspiration rates. *HortScience* 24:767–69.

Sprague, H. B., and G. W. Burton. 1937. Annual bluegrass (*Poa annua* L.) and its requirements for growth. New Jersey Agricultural Experiment Station publication no. 630.

Starrett, S., N. Christians, and T. Austin. 1996. Soil processes and chemical transport, movement of pesticides under two irrigation regimes applied to turfgrass. *J. Env. Qual.* 25:566–71.

Turgeon, A. 1999. *Turfgrass management*, 5th ed. Upper Saddle River, NJ: Prentice-Hall.

Watkins, J. E., R. C. Shearman, R. E. Gaussoin, W. K. Cecil, M. Vaitkus, and L. A. Wit. 2001. An integrated approach to dollar spot management on a bentgrass fairway. *Int. Turfgrass Soc. Res. J.* 9:729–35.

Welterlen, M. S., and T. L. Watschke. 1985. Influence of drought stress and fall nitrogen fertilization on cold deacclimation and tissue components of perennial ryegrass turf. Pp. 831–40 in F. Lemaire, ed., *Proceedings of the Fifth International Turfgrass Research Conference.* Versailles: INRA.

Wilson, T., and D. Zoldoske. 1997. Evaluate sprinkler irrigation uniformity. *Grounds Maint,* June.

8

Mowing

Of all the cultural practices used to maintain turf stands, it is likely that none affects plant growth and physiology, and ability to tolerate biotic and abiotic stresses, to the degree that mowing does. Mowing is a human-imposed cultural practice that is stressful to the turfgrass plant. Over centuries of grazing, some grasses have evolved to tolerate frequent partial removal of leaves. Scientists have selected grasses for use as turfs based in large measure upon their ability to tolerate clipping. Many of these grasses perform exceptionally well under mowed conditions. In fact, turfgrass breeders have developed grasses that can tolerate mowing heights lower than 0.2 inches (5 mm).

Leaves, lateral stems, and roots of grasses arise from the crown, a stem that is hidden by thatch, soil, and surrounding leaf sheaths, and whose processes are not fully understood.

The crown is a dynamic structure that serves as the source for new roots, leaves, tillers, and rhizomes and stolons (in sod-forming grasses). It is also a primary storage organ for carbohydrate reserves that the plant may harbor for later use. The crown respires twelve months a year, regardless of the turf species or which latitude it is located. Once the crown dies, whether a result of biotic or abiotic stresses, the plant dies.

The crown itself is an elongating stem that has an apical meristem. As the crown elongates, it has the potential to produce new leaf primordia at nodes. Meristematic areas at each of these nodes give rise to leaves, with the initial cells produced resulting in

Figure 8-1
Mowing influences many physiological functions, but its importance is often not recognized by turfgrass managers.

formation of the leaf blade, and the later-formed cells eventually resulting in the leaf sheath. After the elongating shoot reaches a point where the blade differentiates from the leaf sheath, another meristem develops at the base of the blade, referred to as the intercalary meristem. Hence there are three meristems that serve important roles in the growth of the shoot.

During routine mowing, it is the leaf blades that are removed, assuming the standard one-third rule is observed. The intercalary meristem then provides new leaf tissue, primarily through cell elongation, causing the severed end of the leaf blade to grow taller until mowing is again required Seed stalks result when the apical meristem on the crown differentiates and begins to grow upward.

Mowing clearly has an effect on the longevity of shoots. Spak, DiPaola, and Anderson (1993) studied the initiation and death of shoots in a stand of Kentucky-31 tall fescue in North Carolina. About 36 percent of the shoots survived for two years when turf was mowed at 3.75 inches (9.5 cm). Conversely, only 4 percent of shoots in an unmowed area of turf lived for two years. Stand density declined by 31 percent from April to September for mown turf and by 63 percent for unmowed turf. The benefits of mowing in terms of retaining density in a stand of turf seem to have been clearly outlined in this test.

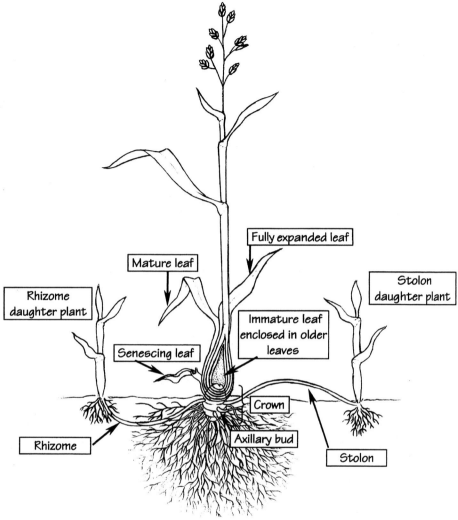

Figure 8-2
The turfgrass plant, including the crown, leaves, and lateral shoots (drawing by Angie Settle).

EFFECTS ON PLANT GROWTH AND CARBOHYDRATE METABOLISM

Shoot Responses Repeated removal of leaf tissue causes numerous growth responses in the plant. Some of these seem to be an attempt by the plant to maximize photosynthesis while enduring the mowing stress. For example, shoot density increases as mowing height declines. Early

Table 8-1

Standard mowing heights for commonly grown turfgrasses

Turfgrass	Mowing Height (inches [cm])
Bahiagrass	2–5 (5.1–7.6)
Bermudagrass	0.125–2 (0.318–5.1)
Buffalograss	1–2 (2.5–5.1)
Creeping bentgrass	0.125–1 (0.3–1.3)
Centipedegrass	1–2 (2.5–5.1)
Fine fescues	1–2.5 (2.5–6.4)
Kentucky bluegrass	0.5–2.5 (1.3–6.4)
Perennial ryegrass	0.5–2 (1.3–5.1)
St. Augustinegrass	2–4 (5.1–10)
Tall fescue	2–3 (5.1–7.6)
Zoysiagrass	0.5–3 (1.3–7.6)

research in mowing responses of turfgrass shoots indicated that Kentucky bluegrass had about 59 percent more tillers if mowed at a 1-inch (2.5 cm) height five days weekly compared to a 2-inch (5.1 cm) height once weekly (Juska and Hanson 1961). Hence, lowering the height promotes tillering in some fashion that is not yet clearly understood. One possible explanation is that there is a hormonal response that encourages tillering in an attempt by the plant to make up for the leaf area lost by the reduction in height. This increase in tillering, however, does not allow for the same level of carbon acquisition and rooting as would otherwise be observed at the higher mowing height. In dicots, removal of the apical meristem also removes an auxin-induced inhibition of lateral branching. However, in grasses routine mowing should not result in meristem removal.

Leaf blade width is also reduced as mowing height goes down. This response likely results because density increases and competition among plants is greater.

Leaf chlorophyll content in leaves increases (per unit area) with a decline in mowing height. Chlorophyll is the molecule that captures the energy of the sun. Again, the plant seems to account for the reduction in leaf area by maximizing its ability to capture sunlight.

Shoot succulence (water content) increases at lower mowing heights. Succulent tissues typically have cells with thinner walls. Greater shoot succulence is commonly associated with increased susceptibility to foliar diseases and environmental stresses. This may explain, in part, the reduced tolerance of low-mowed turf stands to biotic and abiotic stresses.

The turfgrass plant's ability to spread laterally via rhizomes or stolons decreases with mowing height. The recovery of turf that has been damaged, which depends upon rhizome or stolon growth in sod-forming grasses, is sped by maximizing leaf area. Therefore, to enhance the rate of coverage during establishment or recovery from injury, the mowing height should be at the higher end of the recommended range.

Decreasing mowing height also reduces the storage of carbohydrate reserves. Mowing removes plant cells that contain chloroplasts and chlorophyll, and stomata that allow the entrance of CO_2 into the plant for photosynthesis. At higher mowing heights the plant not only meets the day-to-day maintenance needs of tissues and growth but is also able to store some valuable carbohydrates that it could draw upon later in the season should the need arise.

Because maximizing leaf area enhances food storage reserves, adjustments in mowing height should be done only with good reason. For example, some publications suggest that mowing heights for cool-season grasses can be lower during cool times of the year, spring and autumn. Although it is true that cool-season grasses better tolerate lower mowing during these times of year, it is also important to recognize they are also better able to store carbohydrates if given the opportunity during these seasons. In other words, the carbohydrates cool-season turfgrasses can store during autumn and spring may be the key to survival during hot summer

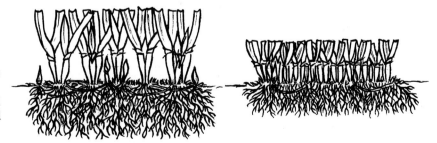

Figure 8-3
Lower mowing heights increase turf density, but reduce rooting and the potential for lateral spread via stolons and rhizomes (drawing by Angie Settle).

Higher mowing height   Lower mowing height

Figure 8-4
Higher mowing results in greater ability to store carbohydrates, represented as money in the bank (left). Maximizing the storage of these "funds" in the fall and spring reduces the likelihood they will be depleted during the summer (drawing by Angie Settle).

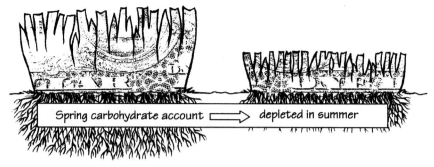

Spring carbohydrate account ⟹ depleted in summer

months. This is illustrated in the discussion of maintaining a balance between photosynthesis and respiration in Chapter 1.

Root Responses

Roots have no ability to make food on their own and rely upon leaf tissue to provide them with carbohydrates needed for maintenance and growth. Leaf tissue removal through mowing reduces availability of photosynthates for root growth and maintenance.

Rooting depth decreases and root growth rate and production are reduced as mowing height goes down. Root initiation and growth are dependent upon photosynthates produced by leaves. Removing leaf area by mowing reduces the plants potential to produce carbohydrates used to drive root growth. Early work indicated that Kentucky bluegrass root weights were reduced by 34 percent when the mowing height was reduced from 2 inches (5.1 cm) to 1 inch (2.5 cm) (Juska and Hanson 1961). However, on closely mown turf, even small reductions in mowing height can significantly affect rooting and plant performance. A 0.04 inch (1 mm) reduction in mowing height caused significant declines in Penncross and Crenshaw creeping bentgrass total root length, cumulative new root length, and rooting depth (Liu and Huang 2002). In the same test, concomitant increases in root mortality, new root length, and the ratio of dead-to-living roots were also observed as the mowing height was reduced from 0.16 to 0.12 inches (4 to 3 mm).

Low mowing heights also increase the likelihood of root death during high temperature stress. Most cool-season grasses experience some degree of root decline during summer months. This is likely due in part to reduced supplies of photosynthates, increased respiration rates, and the direct effect of high temperatures on root

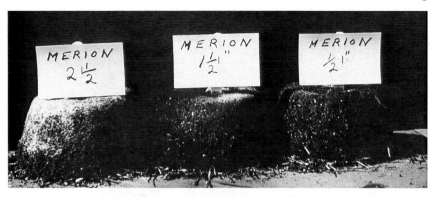

Figure 8-5
Kentucky bluegrass grown in pots and turned upside down. Note the greater mass of white roots where turf was mowed at 2.5 inches (6.4 cm) compared to 1.5 (3.8 cm) or 0.5 inches (1.3 cm) (middle and right, respectively).

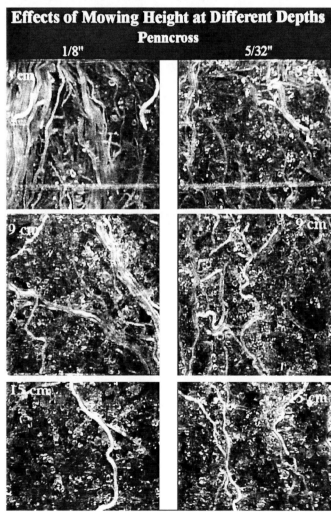

Figure 8-6
Images of creeping bentgrass roots taken with a minirhizotron imaging system at 1.2-, 3.5-, and 5.9-inch (3-, 9-, and 15-cm) soil depths when mowed daily at 0.125 inch (3.2 mm) (left) or 0.156 inch (4 mm) (right) in July 1998 in Manhattan, Kansas. Note that more roots are present, particularly at the deeper soil depths, at the higher mowing height.

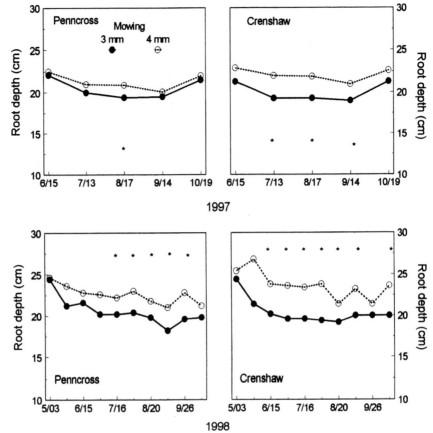

Figure 8-7
Effects of mowing height on root depth of Penncross and Crenshaw creeping bentgrass mowed at 0.125 and 0.156 inches (3 and 4 mm) at Manhattan, Kansas, in 1997 and 1998. (After Liu and Huang, 2002.)

metabolic processes. Reducing bentgrass mowing height from 0.156 to 0.125 inches (4 to 3 mm) resulted in a 5°F (3°C) increase in the soil temperature within the surface 5 cm of soil (Liu and Huang 2002).

Mowing Frequency Turfgrass managers are familiar with the one-third rule, which suggests that the plant is best able to tolerate mowing if no more than one-third of the canopy height is removed at any one time. The rule was developed by Franklin Crider in 1955 while evaluating Kentucky bluegrass growing in pots in the greenhouse, but his techniques for determining the maximum amount of foliage that should be removed during mowing were quite different from those we now employ (Minner 1993). Crider actually measured the volumetric displacement of water that resulted after inverting the bluegrass

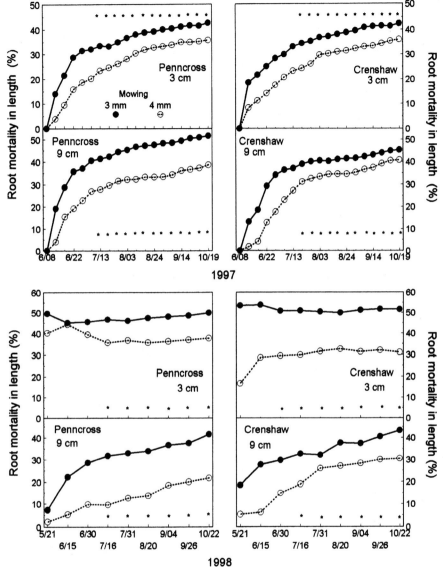

Figure 8-8
Effects of mowing height on root mortality in length of Penncross and Crenshaw creeping bentgrass mowed at 0.125 and 0.156 inches (3 and 4 mm) at Manhattan, Kansas, in 1997 and 1998. (After Liu and Huang, 2002.)

pots and dipping the foliage in the water. Once a given volume of water had been displaced, he trimmed the foliage at the water level. His results indicated that turf performed best when bluegrass was trimmed when no more than about 40 percent of the water had been displaced. Exactly how well 40 percent displacement of water compares to removing 40 percent of plant height has never been determined. Nevertheless, for nearly 50 years turfgrass managers have followed Crider's one-third rule and had good success.

Turf maintained at higher mowing heights requires less frequent mowing to meet the one-third rule. For example, Kentucky-31 tall fescue maintained at a 1.5-inch height in Missouri required mowing every six days compared to every ten days at a 4-inch height (Minner 1993). Hence, in addition to the physiological benefits that higher mowing allows, it also results in labor savings.

Removing greater than one-third of the plant height may result in scalping, which exposes leaf sheaths and results in a bleached appearance of the turf canopy. This often occurs when mowing has been delayed, perhaps due to inclement weather, and mowing then resumes at the original height. During the period since the previous mowing, the sheath has elongated and most of the foliage is above this point. Hence, mowing at the original height results in scalping.

Turf that has been scalped is immediately under stress, for it no longer possesses foliage needed for photosynthesis. As such, the plants must draw down their stored carbohydrates to produce a new canopy. Measurable responses to scalping include reductions in plant density, vertical growth rate, and stolon and rhizome growth. If a delay in mowing occurs or if a reduction of mowing height is desired, scalping can be avoided by reducing the mowing height gradually and staying within the one-third rule.

Table 8-2

Mowing frequency and weed encroachment of turfgrass species maintained at two mowing heights in Columbia, Missouri[1]

	1.5-inch (3.8 cm) Mowing Height		4-inch (10.2 cm) Mowing Height	
Grass	**Days between mowing**	**Weeds (%)**	**Days between mowing**	**Weeds (%)**
Aurora hard fescue	11	52	22	4
Kentucky-31 tall fescue	6	46	10	8
Rebel tall fescue	7	45	14	2
Merion Kentucky bluegrass	9	64	17	15
Pennfine perennial ryegrass	7	57	24	52

[1] After Minner 1993; republished here with permission of PRIMEDIA Business Magazines and Media Inc., copyright 1993, all rights reserved.

Figure 8-9
Scalping bermudagrass turf resulted in this bleached-white appearance as leaf sheaths, and not blades, were visible.

INTERACTIONS WITH ENVIRONMENTAL STRESSES

Water Use and Drought Resistance

Water conservation is increasingly becoming a critical issue throughout the world. The turfgrass manager should use cultural practices that can be employed to conserve water and maximize drought resistance. Mowing plays a large part in influencing water requirements of the turfgrass sward.

Evapotranspiration (ET) increases with mowing height because there is more leaf area exposed to the environment. Greater leaf area translates into more stomata through which water transpires. A taller canopy is also more influenced by wind, which disturbs the boundary layer, thereby increasing the vapor gradient between the stomatal cavity and atmosphere. Higher vapor pressure gradients result in higher water use rates. Merion Kentucky bluegrass used 15 percent more water when cut at 2 inches (5.1 cm) compared to 0.8 inches (2 cm) in Colorado (Feldhake, Danielson, and Butler 1983). A 6 percent increase in ET occurred for both annual bluegrass and Penncross creeping bentgrass maintained at 0.5 inches (1.3 cm) compared to that kept at a 0.24 inch (6 mm) mowing height in Colorado (Fry and Butler 1989).

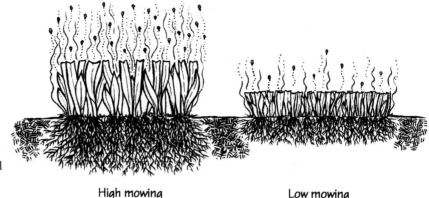

Figure 8-10
As mowing height increases, evapotranspiration increases in response to greater leaf area and environmental exposure (drawing by Angie Settle).

High mowing   Low mowing

Despite the fact that ET decreases with mowing height, most researchers agree that a taller cut allows development of a plant that is a more efficient water user (i.e., better turf quality after a given amount of water is transpired), primarily because it has a deeper root system. Deep roots serve to pull water up from moist subsurface layers when the surface is drying down. Tall fescue, for example, is one turfgrass species that avoids drought by tapping into deep soil water reservoirs. Lowering mowing height (within the preferred range of heights for a given species) to achieve lower ET rates may be reasonable on sites where a relatively deep-rooted turf species is growing in shallow soil. For example, tall fescue that has a root zone only 6 inches (15 cm) deep may be encouraged to use less water by mowing at the lower end of the recommended range. However, when good growing conditions exist, the beneficial effects of high mowing on turfgrass rooting and corresponding drought resistance cannot be ignored.

Mowing frequency and mower blade sharpness also can influence ET. Greater intervals between mowing allow for greater leaf extension and more advective influences on ET as the time from the last mowing lengthens. Therefore, one should expect higher daily ET rates as the next mowing day approaches compared to those that might occur shortly after mowing. A Kentucky bluegrass blend mowed with a sharp blade used approximately 1.3 times more water than turf cut with a dull blade in Nebraska (Steinegger et al. 1983). Turf vigor was reduced where the dull blade was used, which likely resulted in less water demand.

Figure 8-11
Mowing with a dull blade reduces turfgrass vigor and water use rate.

Some sod-forming grasses are unique in the way an increase in mowing height affects water requirements. For example, creeping bentgrass often exhibits wilt more quickly in collars than on putting surfaces. This is curious, for one would suspect that deeper rooting should delay wilt. Bentgrass, however, produces a dense stolon mat, particularly at mowing heights above 1.5 inches (3.8 cm). Roots

Figure 8-12
Creeping bentgrass collars commonly decline before the lower-mown putting surface. Roots elevated in the surface organic layer may be susceptible to desiccation and heat stress.

become elevated in this stolon mat and are susceptible to summer and winter desiccation. As such, more intensive cultivation may be required on collars compared to the lower-mown putting surface.

Undoubtedly, other factors may also contribute to the greater tendency for creeping bentgrass collars to wilt, including greater potential for soil compaction on collars and wicking of water out of a sand-based medium by a surrounding fine-textured soil.

A similar propensity to develop elevated roots in a stolon mat likely exists for bermudagrasses (particularly the new ultradwarf types), and more intensive cultivation may also be needed for these grasses, particularly at heights commonly used on putting green collars.

Temperature Stresses

Researchers have demonstrated that there is a direct correlation between carbohydrate reserves and tolerance to heat and cold. Regarding freezing injury, it is common for turf professionals managing bermudagrass and other warm-season grasses in the southern United States to raise mowing heights in late summer and early autumn to maximize leaf area for photosynthesis and encourage the accumulation of carbohydrates prior to the onset of low winter temperatures. An accumulation of carbohydrates prior to the onset of winter may help with survival in at least two ways. First, complex carbohydrates, such as starch, may be converted into simple sugars during acclimation and serve an important role in preventing cell damage resulting from extracellular freezing. As discussed earlier, tissue damage arising from extracellular freezing actually results from dehydration. As discussed in Chapter 3, an increase in soluble sugars may help to reduce the water potential of the cell, limiting the movement of water to extracellular spaces. The result may be reduced cell dehydration and better winter survival. Centipedegrass acclimated to cold temperatures had 69 percent better survival at 25°F (–4°C) than nonacclimated turf (Fry et al. 1993), with a positive correlation observed between stolon survival and sucrose content. In this case, sucrose may have served as an osmoticum that helped to maintain lower plant water potential and minimize water movement to extracellular spaces.

Maximizing stored carbohydrate levels in warm-season grasses by raising the mowing height also provides a source of energy for maintenance respiration and spring green-up. Dormant warm-season grasses have no capacity to produce photosynthates, but respiration continues, albeit at a relatively slow rate, throughout winter. During spring green-up, the reserve carbohydrate pool must be accessed in order for the plant to produce new vegetative growth. It is clear that any cultural strategy the turfgrass manager uses to increase the level of reserve carbohydrates, including raising the mowing height, will increase the probability of winter survival.

Sod-forming warm-season grasses, such as bermudagrass, zoysiagrass, centipedegrass, and St. Augustinegrass, accumulate more thatch as mowing height increases. For example, Meyer zoysiagrass had 13 to 25 percent more thatch annually over five years when maintained at 1.5 inches (3.8 cm) versus 0.75 inches (1.9 cm) (Dunn, Sheffer, and Halisky 1981). Therefore, there is a greater tendency for crowns and roots to become elevated in thatch at higher mowing heights, increasing the likelihood of freezing injury during low temperature exposure. Hence, although higher mowing heights may serve to increase reserve carbohydrate levels, thatch management is critical in these grasses to keep the potential for freezing injury to a minimum.

Mowing height and the resulting level of stored carbohydrates also play an important role in heat tolerance in cool-season grasses. The stored carbohydrates serve as an important energy source during high summer temperatures, when the potential exists for respiration rates to exceed rates of photosynthesis. The carbohydrate pool prevents starvation and decline during summer months. Golf course superintendents growing bentgrass where summer stress is a problem should consider mowing at the highest allow-

Figure 8-13
Higher mowing heights on lateral-spreading grasses can lead to thatch accumulation. Increased thatch results in crowns and roots that are elevated above the soil surface, and more susceptible to temperature extremes (drawing by Angie Settle).

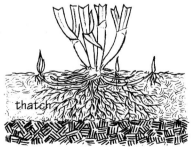

Higher mowing ⇒ increased thatch   Lower mowing ⇒ decreased thatch

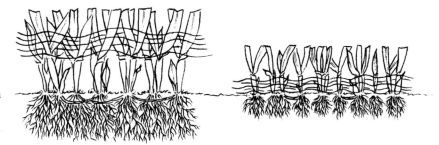

Figure 8-14
In higher-mowed turf, highest temperatures occur in the canopy (left), not at the crown level as may occur in lower-mowed turf (right) (drawing by Angie Settle).

Higher temperature at mid-canopy   Higher temperature at crown

able height in fall and spring to maximize carbohydrate storage prior to midsummer stress.

Turf maintained at the higher end of the recommended range of mowing heights will generally exhibit better vigor and is less likely to thin and decline in quality. The higher canopy shades the soil and keeps the soil surface cooler. Turf at lower heights may begin to thin, which will subsequently lead to elevated soil temperatures, root death, and additional decline.

Shade Turf growing in shade should be mowed as high as aesthetically acceptable. Reduced light intensity and quality under tree shade require that the plant be provided maximal opportunity to intercept incoming light. This will allow plants to maximize photosynthetic capability under difficult growing conditions. Roots of shade-grown turf are competing with trees for water and nutrients, and mowing high improves rooting and provides turf with the best possible ability to tap into soil resources.

INTERACTIONS WITH TURFGRASS PESTS

Weeds Turf maintained at the higher end of its recommended mowing height range will generally exhibit best tolerance to weed encroachment. A higher turf canopy improves turf vigor and creates an inferior environment for weeds to become established. When tall fescue was under severe pressure from smooth crabgrass in Maryland, turf mowed at 1.25 inches (3.2 cm) had nearly 80 percent crabgrass cover by the end of the season, whereas that maintained at 3.5 inches (8.8 cm) had only 3 percent crabgrass cover (Dernoeden, Carroll, and Krouse 1993). Likewise, increasing the mowing height of Merion Kentucky bluegrass from 1.5 inches (3.8 cm) to 4 inches (10.2 cm) in Missouri resulted in a 49 percent reduction in weed coverage (Table 8-2) (Minner 1993).

Bermudagrass encroachment into tall fescue was also exacerbated by low mowing heights (Brede 1992). Tall fescue mowed at 0.75 inches (1.9 cm) had a greater number of bermudagrass crowns and stolon coverage than turf maintained at 2.25 inches (5.7 cm).

Turf maintained at the lower end of the suggested range of mowing heights may begin to thin in early summer as temperatures rise, photosynthesis slows, and respiration increases. Drought may also contribute to thinning, as roots of plants at this mowing height will be relatively shallow. When density decreases, the microclimate in the turf canopy shifts to favor weed establishment. The soil surface will receive more direct sunlight and warm quickly and to higher temperatures. Some weed species, such as crabgrass, require light for germination. Furthermore, it is not uncommon for turf managers to irrigate thinning, drought-stressed turf, but in so doing, germinating weed seedlings benefit. Turf maintained at higher mowing heights may never experience the thinning that is

Figurte 8-15
Turf maintained at a lower mowing height had greater smooth crabgrass infestations (light areas) than higher mowed turf.

observed at the lower mowing height. Therefore, the favorable microclimate for weed establishment never develops.

In some cases, mowing can be detrimental to weeds. For example, weeds that commonly infest newly established stands of turf, such as lamb's-quarters (*Chenopodium album*), redroot pigweed (*Amaranthus retroflexus*), and henbit (*Lamium amplexicaule*), exhibit poor tolerance to mowing. Hence, once mowing commences on the newly established turf, these weeds may decline quickly.

Clipping management may also influence weed populations. Populations of weeds that are prolific seed producers may be reduced if seed-containing clippings are removed rather than returned. In Michigan, removing clippings from a mixed stand of fairway-height creeping bentgrass and annual bluegrass (Fig. 2-4) resulted in a 12 percent decrease in annual bluegrass compared to returning clippings (Gaussoin and Branham 1989) (Table 8-3). Clipping removal also reduced the number of viable seeds in the underlying soil by 60 percent. As such, a long-term program of clipping collection may help to reduce annual bluegrass infestations in fairway-height creeping bentgrass.

Insects Little research has been done to evaluate insect behavior response to any turf cultural practice, including mowing. Researchers in Kentucky observed that total Japanese beetle grub biomass in tall fescue mowed at 7 inches (18 cm) was 55 percent lower than that maintained at 3 inches (7.6 cm) (Potter et al. 1996). They suggested that maintaining turf at the higher end of the recommended mowing

Table 8-3

Changes in annual bluegrass populations in a mixed stand of creeping bentgrass and annual bluegrass as affected by clipping management in Michigan (after Gaussoin and Branham 1989)

Clipping Management	Change in Annual Bluegrass (%)			
	1984	1985	1986	Combined
Returned	0.7*	−7.5	−3.4*	−10*
Removed	−5.3	−8.1	−8.8	−22.1

* Means in a column are significantly different ($P < 0.05$).

height during periods of peak flights of adults may help to reduce grub infestations.

Mowing height did not have a large effect on black cutworm (Fig. 6-9) in creeping bentgrass, but clippings disposal did (Williamson and Potter 1997). Cutworms lay their eggs on the tips of leaf blades during the evening. Mowing removed nearly all of these eggs, but proper disposal was important to ensure that eggs did not hatch and result in young cutworms returning to the green. It is common for golf course employees to empty mower baskets on green banks or other surrounds. Greater attention to clipping management is a key to reducing black cutworm damage on greens.

Diseases
Mowing height can impact turfgrass response to diseases in multiple ways. One would expect that an increase in mowing height would allow for better plant vigor, resulting from increased photosynthetic capacity. In general, this is the case. Kentucky bluegrass maintained at 3 inches (7.6 cm) had higher carbohydrate levels and less summer patch (Fig. 6-33) damage than turf maintained at 1.5 inches (3.8 cm) (Davis and Dernoeden 1991). Similarly, once disease was evident in lower-mowed turf, increasing the height to 3 inches (7.6 cm) sped recovery time.

Warm-season grasses have also demonstrated favorable responses to mowing at the higher end of the recommended range during disease activity. Large patch (Fig. 6-22) in Meyer zoysiagrass produced patches of greater diameter and caused more turf injury when turf was mowed at 0.5 inches (1.3 cm) or 1 inch (2.5 cm) compared to 1.8 inches (4.5 cm) (Green et al. 1994) (Table 8-4).

Mixed results have been reported concerning mowing height effects on foliar blighting pathogens in perennial ryegrass and tall fescue. Brown patch (Fig. 6-16) was more severe in perennial ryegrass maintained at 1.8 inches (4.5 cm) compared to 0.7 inches (1.7 cm) in two of three years evaluated (Fidanza and Dernoeden 1996). In Georgia, brown patch severity in tall fescue was greater at 3.5 inches (8.9 cm) than at 1.5 inches (3.8 cm) in one year of evaluation, and the opposite was true the following year (Burpee 1995). Conflicting results regarding brown patch incidence in tall fescue at varying mowing heights have also been reported by Kentucky researchers (Vincelli and Powell 1996, 1997). Tall fescue canopy density has been shown to have a direct influence on brown patch

Table 8-4

Influence of mowing height on development of large patch disease in Meyer zoysiagrass (after Green et al. 1994)

Mowing Height (inches [cm])	AUDPC[1]	
	Patch Diameter	**Turf Damage**
0.5 (1.3)	1250 a[2]	158 a
1.0 (2.5)	1120 a	107 b
2.0 (5.1)	647 b	38 c

[1] AUDPC = area under the disease progress curve; represents the total amount of disease that occurred over the entire season. Higher numbers indicate greater damage.

[2] Numbers followed by different letters in a column are statistically different from one another ($P < 0.05$).

development. Swards that are denser are likely to experience more disease (Giesler, Yuen, and Horst 1996a). This is due in part to longer periods of leaf wetness and higher relative humidities in denser canopies (Giesler, Yuen, and Horst 1996b). As stated previously, turfgrasses that are mowed at lower heights within the preferred range will have higher shoot densities and greater leaf succulence than those maintained at higher heights. This would lead one to believe that mowing lower may result in greater disease pressure, but the aforementioned results suggest that this is not always the case. Results suggest that Pythium blight (Fig. 6-24) in tall fescue may be favored by lower mowing heights, however. The disease was more severe in tall fescue maintained at 1 inch (2.5 cm) compared to 2.5 inches (6.4 cm), especially when irrigation was applied daily (Settle, Fry, and Tisserat 2001)

One would suspect that root-infecting diseases may be suppressed at higher mowing heights. Indeed, Maryland researchers found that Kentucky bluegrass exhibited less summer patch (Fig. 6-33) injury when maintained at a 3-inch (7.6 cm) height than at 1.5 inches (3.8 cm). Not all data support higher mowing heights for reducing diseases caused by root pathogens, however. In Oklahoma, seeded bermudagrasses maintained at 0.5 inches (1.3 cm) had smaller patches caused by spring dead spot (Fig. 6-31) than turf mowed at 1.5 inches (3.8 cm) (Martin et al. 2001).

Table 8-5

Summary of research results from projects that compared mowing height effects on turfgrass diseases. The citation is listed in the respective mowing height column where least disease occurred

Disease	Turfgrass	Strategy That Reduces Disease Symptoms	
		Low Mowing	**High Mowing**
Bermudagrass decline	Bermudagrass		Elliott 1997
Dollar spot	Creeping bentgrass	No effect of mowing height observed (Bruneau et al. 2001)	
Brown patch	Perennial ryegrass	Conflicting results: sometimes less at lower heights, other times at higher mowing heights (Fidanza and Dernoeden 1996).	
	Tall fescue	Conflicting results: sometimes less disease at lower mowing heights, other times at higher mowing heights (Burpee 1995; Vincelli and Powell 1996, 1997)	
Gray leaf spot	Perennial ryegrass	No effect of mowing height observed (Williams et al. 2001)	
Pythium blight			Settle, Fry, and Tisserat 2001
Large patch	Zoysiagrass		Green et al. 1994
Spring dead spot	Bermudagrass	Martin et al. 2001	
Summer patch	Kentucky bluegrass		Davis and Dernoeden 1991

Turf managers are often hesitant to return clippings in turf swards where diseases are active. Research to date indicates that diseases may be influenced by clipping management, but their contribution seems to be due to a nutritional influence rather than one of spreading the pathogen from one area to another. Dollar spot was reduced by returning clippings in perennial ryegrass, whereas brown patch was exacerbated (Dunn et al. 1996). These responses were likely due to nitrogen contributed by clippings to the turf, for dollar spot is favored by lower nitrogen levels, while brown patch is favored by higher nitrogen levels. Collecting or leaving clippings in place did not consistently affect the severity of dollar spot in creeping bentgrass in Kentucky (Williams et al. 1996). Infection levels in brown-patch-infested tall fescue were no different whether clippings were returned or collected (Settle, Fry, and Tisserat 2001). In Texas, no differences in disease incidence in St. Augustinegrass, bermudagrass, or tall fescue occurred whether clippings were returned with a mulching mower or collected (Colbaugh, Hipp, and Knowles 1992).

REFERENCES

Brede, A. D. 1992. Cultural factors for minimizing bermudagrass invasion into tall fescue turf. *Agron. J.* 84:919–22.

Bruneau, A. H., C. A. Bigelow, R. J. Cooper, and D. C. Bowman. 2001. Performance of creeping bentgrass cultivars maintained at two mowing heights and under two fungicide regimes in North Carolina. *Int. Turfgrass Soc. Res. J.* 9:835–42.

Burpee, L. 1995. Interactions among mowing height, nitrogen fertility, and cultivar affect the severity of Rhizoctonia blight of tall fescue. *Plant Dis.* 79:721–26.

Colbaugh, P. F., B. W. Hipp, and T. Knowles. 1992. Influence of clipping recycling on disease incidence in three turfgrass species. *Phytopathology* 82:1109.

Davis, D., and P. Dernoeden. 1991. Summer patch and Kentucky bluegrass quality as influenced by cultural practices. *Agron. J.* 83:670–77.

Dernoeden, P., M. Carroll, and J. Krouse. 1993. Weed management and tall fescue quality as influenced by mowing, nitrogen, and herbicides. *Crop Sci.* 33:1055–61.

Dunn, J., D. Minner, B. Fresenburg, and S. Bughrara. 1996. Clippings disposal and fertilization influence disease in perennial ryegrass turf. *HortScience* 31:1180–81.

Dunn, J. H., K. M. Sheffer, and P. M. Halisky. 1981. Thatch and quality of Meyer zoysiagrass in relation to management. *Agron. J.* 73:949–52.

Elliott, M. L. 1997. Bermudagrass decline: Transmission of the causal agent *Gaeumannomyces graminis* var. *graminis* by vegetative planting material. *Int. Turfgrass Soc. Res. J.* 7:329–34.

Feldhake, C., R. Danielson, and J. Butler. 1983. Turfgrass evapotranspiration. I. Factors influencing rate in urban environments. *Agron. J.* 75:824–30.

Fidanza, M., and P. H. Dernoeden. 1996. Interaction of nitrogen source, application timing, and fungicide on Rhizoctonia blight in ryegrass. *HortScience* 31:389–92.

Fry, J. and J. Butler. 1989. Annual bluegrass and creeping bentgrass evapotranspiration rates. *HortScience* 24:269–71.

Fry, J., N. Lang, P. Clifton, and F. Meier. 1993. Freezing tolerance and carbohydrate content of low-temperature-acclimated and nonacclimated centipedegrass. *Crop Sci.* 33:1051–5.

Gaussoin, R. E., and B. E. Branham. 1989. Influence of cultural factors on species dominance in a mixed stand of annual bluegrass/creeping bentgrass. *Crop Sci.* 29:480–84.

Giesler, L. J., G. Y. Yuen, and G. L. Horst. 1996a. Tall fescue canopy density effects on brown patch disease. *Plant Dis.* 80:384–88.

———. 1996b. The microclimate in tall fescue turf as affected by canopy density and its influence on brown patch disease. *Plant Dis.* 80:389–94.

Green, D., J. Fry, J. Pair, and N. Tisserat. 1994. Influence of management practices on Rhizoctonia large patch disease in zoysiagrass.*HortScience* 29:186–88.

Juska, F., and A. Hanson. 1961. Effects of interval and height of mowing on growth of Merion and Common Kentucky bluegrass. *Agron. J.* 53:385–88.

Liu, X., and B. Huang. 2002. Mowing effects on root production, growth, and mortality of creeping bentgrass. *Crop Sci.* 42:1241–50.

Martin, D. L., G. E. Bell, J. H. Baird, C. M. Taliaferro, N. A. Tisserat, R. M. Kuzmic, D. D. Dobson, and J. A. Anderson. 2001. Spring dead spot resistance and quality of seeded bermudagrasses under different mowing heights. *Crop Sci.* 41:451–56.

Minner, D. 1993. Mowing requirements of turfgrass species. *Grounds Maintenance* 28 (5):12–14, 16–17.

Potter, D., A. J. Powell, P. Spicer, and D. Williams. 1996. Cultural practices affect root-feeding white grubs in turfgrass. *J. Econ. Entom.* 89:156–64.

Settle, D., J. Fry, and N. Tisserat. 2001. Development of brown patch and pythium blight in tall fescue as affected by irrigation frequency, clipping removal, and fungicide application. *Plant Dis.* 85:543–46.

Spak, D., J. DiPaola, and C. Anderson. 1993. Tall fescue sward dynamics. I. Seasonal patterns of turf shoot development. *Crop Sci.* 33:300–4.

Steinegger, D., R. Shearman, R., T. Riordan, E. Kinbacher. 1983. Mower blade sharpness effects on turf. *Agron. J.* 75:479–80.

Vincelli, P., and A. J. Powell. 1996. Impact of mowing and nitrogen fertility on brown patch of tall fescue, 1995. *Biol. and Cultural Tests* 11:34.

———. 1997. Impact of mowing height and nitrogen fertility on brown patch of tall fescue, 1996. *Biol. and Cultural Tests* 12:129.

Williams, D. W., P. B. Burrus, and P. Vincelli. 2001. Severity of gray leaf spot in perennial ryegrass as influenced by mowing height and nitrogen level. *Crop Sci.* 41:1207–11.

Williams, D. W., A. J. Powell, P. Vincelli, and C. T. Daugherty. 1996. Dollar spot on bentgrass as influenced by displacement of leaf surface moisture, nitrogen, and clipping removal. *Crop Sci.* 36:1304–9.

Williamson, C., and D. Potter. 1997. Oviposition of black cutworm on creeping bentgrass putting greens and removal of eggs by mowing. *J. Econ. Entom.* 90:590–94.

9

Fertilization

NUTRITION AND GROWTH RESPONSES

A basic understanding of required nutrients, nutrient uptake, and deficiency symptoms is useful in developing a turfgrass fertilization program. There are seventeen essential elements, with average concentrations required by the turfgrass plant varying depending upon the nutrient.

Table 9-1
Elemental tissue content sufficiency (after Jones 1980)

Element	Tissue Content Sufficiency Range
Nitrogen (N)	2.75–3.5% (27.5–35 g/kg)
Phosphorus (P)	0.3–0.55% (3.0–5.5 g/kg)
Potassium (K)	1–2.5% (10.0–25.0 g/kg)
Calcium (Ca)	0.3–1.25% (5.0–12.5 g/kg)
Magnesium (Mg)	0.2–0.6% (2.0–6.0 g/kg)
Sulfur (S)	0.2–0.45% (2.0–4.5 g/kg)
Iron (Fe)	35–100 ppm (35–100 mg/kg)
Manganese (Mn)	25–150 ppm (25–150 mg/kg)
Zinc (Zn)	20–55 ppm (20–55 mg/kg)
Copper (Cu)	5–20 ppm (5–20 mg/kg)
Boron (B)	10–60 ppm (10–60 mg/kg)
Molybdenum (Mo)	Unknown
Chlorine (Cl)	Unknown

Macronutrients　There are nine macronutrients required by the turfgrass plant. Tissue concentration levels of these nutrients are required at levels ≥1,000 ppm (mg/kg) on a dry weight basis. These elements include carbon (C), hydrogen (H), oxygen (O), nitrogen (N), potassium (K), phosphorus (P), calcium (Ca), magnesium (Mg), and sulfur (S). The plant obtains three of these (carbon, hydrogen, oxygen) from carbon dioxide and water, the remainder must be absorbed from the soil solution.

Nitrogen (N)　Nitrogen is a vital constituent of many essential substances in plant growth and function, including the chlorophyll molecule, amino acids, proteins, enzymes, and nucleic acids (DNA). It is the most important nutrient in the turf fertility program. Nitrogen deficiency is commonly observed in the field. Symptoms include yellowing of older leaves and eventually leaf dieback from the leaf tip down. Prolonged deficiency results in a decline in turf density.

Nitrogen levels in turfgrass shoots range from 2 to 4 percent. Among its many other functions, nitrogen is essential for chlorophyll production; hence turf exhibits a darker green color after nitrogen

Table 9-2

Nitrogen fertilizer classes, modes of nitrogen release, and examples of fertilizers

Fertilizer Class	Mode of Nitrogen Release	Examples
Fast Release:		
Synthetic inorganic	Soluble in water	Ammonium sulfate, ammonium nitrate
Slow Release:		
Synthetic organic	Soluble in water	Urea
Synthetic organic	Hydrolysis	Isobutylidene diurea (IBDU)
Synthetic organic	Diffusion	Polymer coated ureas
Synthetic organic	Microbial breakdown	Sulfur-coated urea, urea formaldehyde (and related products)
Natural organic	Microbial breakdown	Composted sewage sludge, animal manure

application. Because it has many important functions in the plant, dramatic growth responses occur after nitrogen application.

The source of nitrogen can influence plant growth almost as much as the rate of application. Ultimately, the turfgrass root absorbs nitrogen as nitrate (NO_3^-) or ammonium (NH_4^+). Nitrogen

Figures 9-1 and 9-2
Nitrogen-deficient turf appears chlorotic and lacks density as evident with buffalo-grass (Fig. 9-1, top) and creeping bentgrass (Fig. 9-2, bottom).

sources vary in the processes required to reach these usable forms. Likewise, fertilizer costs vary depending upon manufacturing and shipping costs. Synthetic inorganic nitrogen sources are soluble in water, whereas synthetic organic fertilizers require hydrolysis or microbes to assist in nitrogen release. Natural organic fertilizers also require microbial activity for nitrogen release.

The ideal nitrogen source would be one that releases the exact amount of nitrogen required by the plant, exactly when it needs it. Unfortunately, such a product has yet to be developed. Instead, turf extension specialists attempt to predict what kind of timing scenarios are best for turfgrass performance depending upon the nitrogen source used.

Standard nitrogen recommendations for cool-season grasses take into account the fact that the shoot growth curve has its highest spike in spring and a smaller peak in the autumn. To avoid promoting additional growth and depleting carbohydrates, the majority of nitrogen on cool-season grasses is applied in autumn. Comparatively lesser amounts of nitrogen are applied to cool-season grasses in the spring, and little or none is applied during summer months.

Because nitrogen stimulates shoot development, routine applications of nitrogen during turf establishment can lead to rapid canopy closure. There is a tendency among turfgrass managers, particu-

Figure 9-3
Benefits of autumn-emphasized N fertilization of cool-season grasses include early spring green-up as observed on the right-hand side of this Kentucky bluegrass lawn in Colorado.

larly those managing sports turfs, to believe that because nitrogen is so effective at promoting shoot growth, applying more than standard rates is beneficial, maximizing growth rate and promoting canopy closure. However, several research projects have demonstrated that more is not always better in regard to nitrogen. In Nebraska, performance of bentgrass greens established using an accelerated versus controlled grow-in program were evaluated for several years (Gaussoin et al. 1999). Bentgrass greens on the accelerated program received a pre-planting application of 6 pounds of nitrogen per 1,000 square feet (294 kg/ha) incorporated into the seedbed, whereas the control received 3 pounds per 1,000 square feet (147 kg/ha). Post-seeding rates were 6.1 pounds of nitrogen per 1,000 square feet (299 kg/ha) per month for the accelerated program and 3.5 pounds of nitrogen per 1,000 square feet (172 kg/ha) per month for the controlled program. After seeding in May, bentgrass receiving nitrogen on the accelerated grow-in schedule had 84 percent coverage by early July compared to 63 percent coverage in the controlled program. However, late in the first year of establishment, and during midsummer of the second season of evaluation, bentgrass receiving nitrogen in the accelerated grow-in program experienced an outbreak of Pythium blight and injury resulting from direct high temperature stress.

Negative responses have also been observed when high nitrogen rates have been used to hasten coverage of newly established stands of warm-season grasses. Meyer zoysiagrass established as plugs exhibited a negative response in coverage, stolon number, and response to drought as nitrogen increased from 1 to 7 pounds per 1,000 square feet (49 to 343 kg/ha) per year during the season of establishment (Fry and Dernoeden 1987). A slight positive response to increasing nitrogen levels was observed the second year of establishment, however. The level of seeded buffalograss coverage that was achieved in Kansas, Nebraska, and Oklahoma by applying nitrogen at 3 pounds per 1,000 square feet (147 kg/ha) was as good or better than the result of treating with nitrogen at 6 pounds per 1,000 square feet (294 kg/ha) (Frank et al. 2002).

This work with cool- and warm-season grasses indicates that although nitrogen is important in encouraging cover during establishment, excessive nitrogen levels may not result in more rapid coverage and may ultimately have deleterious effects on the turf. Negative turf responses to excessive nitrogen rates may or may not

Table 9-3

Effect of nitrogen rate on percentage of buffalograss coverage after seeding at 2 pounds pure live seed per 1,000 square feet (98 kg/ha) on June 14 in Stillwater, Oklahoma (after Frank et al. 2002)

N Rate (lb/1,000 ft²)[1]	Weeks after Seeding		
	4	7	11
0	13 ab[2]	23 ab	48 b
1	14 a	23 ab	55 ab
3	16 a	28 a	61 a
6	10 b	20 b	48 b

[1] 1 lb = 49 kg/ha, 3 lb = 147 kg/ha; 6 lb = 294 kg/ha.

[2] Means in columns for nitrogen rates followed by the same letter are not significantly different according to Fisher's LSD at the 5 percent level.

reveal themselves in the initial season. For example, bermudagrass fertilized with high levels of nitrogen in the transition zone to stimulate growth and coverage may appear to be healthy and of high quality at the end of the initial growing season, and then be subject to winter injury due to reduced carbohydrates levels.

The benefits of nitrogen application following stand loss or thinning shouldn't be ignored, however. After stresses such as drought,

Figure 9-4
Late summer and autumn applications of nitrogen to this bermuda- grass athletic field in Kansas resulted in severe winter injury.

heat, winter injury, or traffic have taken their toll, a nitrogen application is commonly used to stimulate recovery once environmental conditions are favorable for growth.

Although excessive nitrogen levels can create succulent tissues and reduce tolerance to wear, moderate levels of nitrogen have been shown to enhance wear tolerance in both warm- and cool-season grasses (Trenholm, Carrow, and Duncan 2001; Carroll and Petrovic 1991b). Greater shoot density resulting from nitrogen helps to cushion the underlying crowns when traffic is imposed. Hence, the amount of traffic a particular turf area receives should help to govern the amount nitrogen applied. For example, a low-maintenance lawn may require little nitrogen, whereas a high-use athletic field may require a relatively high level.

As shoot growth increases after nitrogen application, carbohydrates are consumed and reserves are reduced. In work with greenhouse-grown sod plugs of Kentucky bluegrass, nitrogen-fertilized turf had lower total nonstructural carbohydrate levels than unfertilized turf (Watschke and Waddington 1975). Creeping bentgrass, Kentucky bluegrass, and annual bluegrass were also found to have lower levels of reducing sugars, sucrose, and fructans in root, stem, and leaf tissues when fertilized at relatively high versus low nitrogen rates in the greenhouse (Westhafer, Law, and Duff 1982). Reductions in carbohydrate levels following nitrogen applications may be important as they relate to heat tolerance in cool-season grasses and freezing tolerance in warm-season grasses. Both stresses cause more injury on carbohydrate-depleted turfs.

Warm-season grasses seem to vary in carbohydrate response to nitrogen fertilization. Floradwarf bermudagrass exhibited decreasing total nonstructural carbohydrates with increasing nitrogen under short days, whereas a similar response was observed in Tifdwarf bermudagrass under long days (Trenholm et al. 1998). Increasing centipedegrass nitrogen fertilization levels from 2 to 4 or 6 pounds per 1,000 square feet (98 to 196 or 294 kg/ha) in the field resulted in a significant reduction in TNC levels in stolons (Walker and Ward 1973). For this reason, delivery of nitrogen over a longer period of time in small amounts will help to prevent carbohydrate depletion. This may be accomplished by using products that release nitrogen slowly (e.g., synthetic organic or natural organic fertilizers) or "spoon-feeding" techniques with synthetic inorganic fertilizers.

Nitrogen also has important effects on rooting, succulence, and thatch accumulation. Increasing nitrogen levels have been shown to reduce rooting, even within a recommended range of application (Madison 1962). However, nitrogen is obviously needed to maintain density and produce the leaf tissue that will provide photosynthates to roots. Application of nitrogen above a recommended level will stimulate shoot development at the expense of roots. In Kentucky, poorer December rooting of creeping bentgrass occurred in nitrogen-fertilized versus unfertilized turf; however, by the following June, nitrogen-fertilized turf had higher root weights than unfertilized turf (Powell, Blaser, and Schmidt 1967). Increased rooting was also observed in bermudagrass as nitrogen levels increased from 0 to 1 pound per 1,000 square feet (49 kg/ha) (Horst, Baltensperger, and Firkner 1985).

Nitrogen increases leaf succulence (water content) and results in a plant with thinner cell walls. Perennial ryegrass fertilized with nitrogen at up to 12.8 pounds per 1,000 square feet (625 kg/ha) on a sand medium had increasing leaf moisture levels as nitrogen increased (Canaway 1985). It was suggested that ryegrass receiving high nitrogen levels may be more susceptible to wear stress because leaf water content is higher. Higher leaf water content may also lead to reduced resistance to pathogens. This may also explain why increasing nitrogen levels make some cool-season grasses more susceptible to certain diseases, such as brown patch.

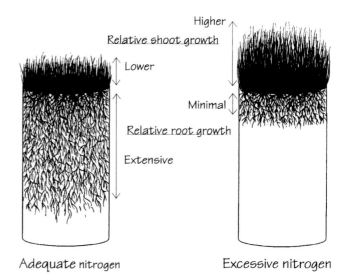

Figure 9-5
Excessive nitrogen promotes shoot growth at the expense of roots (drawing by Angie Settle).

Because nitrogen promotes the formation of stem tissue, such as tillers, rhizomes, and stolons, thatch accumulation may occur. When the production of tissue exceeds the rate at which it breaks down, accumulation results. Sod-forming grasses are more prone to form thatch than bunchgrasses, and particular attention may be required to control it when high nitrogen levels are used on these grasses. Meyer zoysiagrass fertilized with nitrogen at 1 pound per 1,000 square feet (49 kg/ha) had thatch depths 25 to 116 percent greater than that of unfertilized turf in Missouri (Weston and Dunn 1985). Applying high levels of nitrogen to grasses that have thatch accumulation tendencies, such as zoysiagrass and centipedegrass, can quickly lead to their demise, due in large part to the greater temperature and moisture extremes experienced by elevated crowns (see Chapter 10).

Phosphorus Phosphorus is a constituent of several important compounds in plant cells, including sugar phosphate for energy storage and transfer in the respiration and photosynthesis processes, nucleic acid for genetic materials, and phospholipids in cell membranes. A phosphorus deficiency in the field would most commonly be observed in turf growing on sand-based root zones that contain little or no organic matter. Symptoms include purpling of leaves that almost

Figure 9-6
Leaf purpling is a common symptom of a P deficiency as exhibited by creeping bentgrass growing in a 100% sand medium.

makes the turf appear wilted, and possibly poor spring green-up and growth.

Bentgrass growing on a sand medium in Colorado exhibited poor quality, due primarily due to a purplish color of the turf, over an eight-year period when no phosphorus was applied (Fry, Harivandi, and Minner 1989). However, turf receiving phosphorus at 0.1 pound per 1,000 square feet (5 kg/ha) per month exhibited no phosphorus deficiency and good quality. Because phosphorus is a component of the high-energy molecules ATP and ADP, it is clearly important for many of the shoot and root growth processes that occur in the plant.

Phosphorus is particularly critical when establishing turf on soils that test low in the element. Visible increases in establishment rate can be seen if phosphorus is amended on soils testing deficient. Buffalograss, for example, exhibited an increase in establishment rate when phosphorus was applied to soils with low existing phosphorus levels (Frank et al. 2002) (Table 9-4). On soils that had adequate phosphorus levels prior to planting, no effect of phosphorus on buffalograss establishment rate was observed. Similarly, phosphorus incorporated at 2.5 pounds per 1,000 square feet (123 kg/ha) into a soil testing high (172 pounds per acre (193 kg/ha)] in phosphorus had no effect on the rate of Meyer zoysiagrass establishment from vegetative plugs in Maryland (Fry and Dernoeden 1987).

Although research results are limited, some information suggests that phosphorus is also important in promoting turfgrass rooting. Rooting of Kentucky bluegrass (Watschke et al. 1977) and

Table 9-4

Effect of phosphorus rate on percent buffalograss coverage after seeding at 2 pounds pure live seed per 1,000 square feet (98 kg/ha) on June 14 in Stillwater, Oklahoma (after Frank et al. 2002)

Phosphorus Rate (lb per 1000 ft²)[1]	Weeks after Seeding		
	9	10	11
0	44 b[2]	47 b	50 b
1	51 a	54 a	57 a

[1] 1 lb/ft² = 49 kg/ha.

[2] Means followed by the same letter are not significantly different according to Fisher's LSD at the 5 percent level.

annual ryegrass (Rechcigl 1992) were increased by application of phosphorus.

Phosphorus has come under increasing scrutiny for its potential role as a water contaminant resulting from stormwater runoff in urbanized settings. Application of phosphorus to home lawns and commercial turf is strictly regulated in Minnesota's Twin Cities. In some cases, soil test results providing evidence of a phosphorus deficiency must be available in order for a phosphorus application to be made. Evidence garnered from turf research with phosphorus indicates that if soil tests indicate levels are low, it should be supplemented at the time of establishment. Applications to established turf should be made frugally, based upon soil test results.

Potassium Potassium activates more than forty enzymes and is especially important in the photosynthesis and respiration processes. It also plays an important role in the regulation of stomata opening and water uptake by influencing osmotic potential of cells. Visible potassium deficiencies in the field are rare, even when soil and tissue concentrations are relatively low. Potassium deficiencies are most likely on sand-based root zones that have poor nutrient retention capacities. Symptoms include chlorosis of older leaves and dieback at the leaf tip and along the margin.

Tissue levels of potassium are second only to the levels of nitrogen. Potassium is also more mobile than phosphorus in soils, particularly on sand-based soils, and it is common for K_2O (the form in which potassium is most often delivered in fertilizers) to be applied at levels nearly equal to nitrogen on high-maintenance turf. Potassium has been linked to increased wear tolerance and resistance to drought and temperature stresses. The best evidence for the contribution of potassium to wear resistance was recently provided by Shearman and Beard (2002). In their field test, done on a USGA-specification green with an initial potassium level of 180 ppm (mg/liter), creeping bentgrass tissue potassium, wear tolerance, load-bearing capacity, and total cell wall content increased linearly as potassium application increased from 0 to 8.2 pounds per 1,000 square feet (400 kg/ha) per season (Table 9-5). Hence, the benefits of potassium on improving creeping bentgrass wear tolerance on a sand-based system were clearly demonstrated.

Table 9-5
Potassium effects on turfgrass wear stress tolerance, tissue potassium content, shoot density, verdure, load-bearing capacity and total cell wall (TCW) content of creeping bentgrass grown on a USGA specification near Mead, Nebraska (after Shearman and Beard 2002)

Potassium Treatment[1] (lb/1,000 ft²/yr)	Wear Tolerance[2] (no. revolutions)	LBC[3] (newtons/45 cm²)	Tissue Potassium[4] (%)	TCW[5] (g/dm²)
0	400	14	1.4	1.45
2.0	455	20	1.88	1.79
4.1	500	25	2.25	1.9
6.1	535	28	2.73	1.98
8.2	595	32	3.01	2.07
LSD (0.05)	30	2	0.21	0.21
Linear	*	*	*	*

* Indicates linear response (i.e., as potassium increases a corresponding increase in the measured variable occurred) at phosphorus ≤ 0.05.

[1] Potassium treatments were applied in eight applications made every three weeks, beginning in May and ending in Sept. Urea (46-0-0) was applied in six treatments of 0.5 pounds nitrogen per 1,000 square feet (25 kg/ha) applied every four weeks and one treatment of 1 pound nitrogen per 1,000 square feet (49 kg/ha) applied in late autumn, for a total of 4 pounds nitrogen per 1,000 square feet (196 kg/ha) per season. Convert pounds per 1,000 square feet to kg/ha by multiplying by 49.

[2] Turfgrass wear tolerance expressed as number of revolutions of a wear simulator required to reach an endpoint where all leaf blades were shredded and only leaf sheaths and stems remained.

[3] Load-bearing capacity (LBC) is an indicator of the resilience of the turf.

[4] Tissue potassium was determined after all treatments had been applied for the growing season.

[5] Total cell wall (TCW) content.

Micronutrients   Eight micronutrients are required by the plant in concentrations of ≤100 ppm (mg/kg) on a dry weight basis. These include iron (Fe), manganese (Mn), copper (Cu), molybdenum (Mo), zinc (Zn), boron (B), chloride (Cl), and cobalt (Co). Of the micronutrients, iron is the most important in fertility management in turfgrass systems.

Iron (Fe)   Iron is an essential element in chlorophyll synthesis and a constituent of several enzymes. It is the most important micronutrient in turfgrass management. Iron deficiencies are common in soils with a high pH, in sandy soils, and in cold, wet soils in early spring. Frequent removal of clippings, excessive phosphorus application, and

Figure 9-7
Iron-deficient
Kentucky bluegrass in
this photo had good
density, but exhibited
iron chlorosis (lighter
areas in photograph).
Darker areas received
an iron application.

overliming also induce iron deficiency. An iron deficiency can be corrected by application of ferrous sulfate or chelated forms of iron as a foliar spray. Iron deficiency symptoms include interveinal leaf chlorosis, beginning on youngest leaves first, which may progress to a bleached white appearance in severe cases. Turf also may appear mottled with chlorotic areas. Turf density may be relatively good.

WATER USE AND DROUGHT RESISTANCE

Evapotranspiration rates increase with increasing nitrogen level, due to the production of more leaves and an increase in total leaf surface area. In addition, nitrogen-fertilized turf has a faster vertical elongation rate, which leads to greater water use rates and a greater effect of wind on ET as the canopy grows taller. Nitrogen also increases leaf surface area, which contributes to higher ET rates. Nitrogen-deficient Kentucky bluegrass had an ET rate approximately 14 percent lower than turf receiving supplemental nitrogen in a greenhouse test (Sills and Carrow 1983). Likewise, lysimeter-grown Kentucky bluegrass receiving nitrogen at 0.8 pounds per

1,000 square feet (40 kg/ha) in May had an ET rate 14 percent lower than turf receiving the same amount of nitrogen each month between May and September (Feldhake, Danielson, and Butler 1983). Applying a total of 4.3 or 8.6 pounds N per 1,000 square feet (211 or 421 kg/ha) over a period of two years increased the ET rate of a mixture of orchardgrass, smooth bromegrass, tall fescue, and creeping red fescue compared to turf receiving less nitrogen (Krogman 1967).

No information is available on the influence of phosphorus and potassium on turfgrass ET rates. Potassium may enhance rooting, which could increase water available for uptake, and possibly ET (Kneebone, Kopec, and Mancino 1992).

Moderate nitrogen levels enhance drought resistance, but excessive nitrogen reduces drought resistance by reducing the root-to-shoot ratio. The quality of nitrogen-deficient Kentucky bluegrass declined more rapidly during drought than that of turf receiving adequate nitrogen (Feldhake, Danielson, and Butler 1984).

Little is known about how phosphorus influences drought resistance. Phosphorus has the potential to enhance rooting, and therefore adequate levels should be present to maximize drought resistance.

Potassium serves an important role in stomatal opening and closing and has been reported to significantly increase drought resistance in Kentucky bluegrass (Erusha 1990). Potassium fertility also had a significant effect on the concentration of osmotically active solutes in Kentucky bluegrass leaves, which likely influences leaf water and osmotic potential and leaf folding during drought (Carroll and Petrovic 1991a). Application of potassium to Tifway bermudagrass at 1 or 2 pounds per 1,000 square feet (49 or 98 kg/ha) reduced leaf-firing damage and encouraged greater recovery following drought stress (Miller and Dickens 1997) (Table 9-6). Tall fescue cultivars that maintained higher potassium concentrations in shoot tissues were also found to be more drought resistant (Huang 2001).

TEMPERATURE STRESSES

Freezing   Because nitrogen has a dramatic effect on growth rate, plant succulence, and thatch formation, it has the potential to significantly influence temperature stress tolerance. Turf fertilized with high levels of

Table 9-6

Leaf-firing damage (LFD) and drought recovery of Tifway bermudagrass at three levels of potassium fertility (after Miller and Dickens 1997)

Potassium Rate (lb/1,000 ft²)[1]	LFD (%)	Recovery (%)
0	68	43
1	28	83
2	23	87
LSD[2]	23	20

[1] Convert lb/1,000 ft² to kg/ha by multiplying by 49.

[2] Fisher's protected LSD ($P \leq 0.05$)

nitrogen may develop succulent tissues that are sensitive to freezing. Although cool-season grasses are generally considered relatively freezing resistant, some, such as perennial ryegrass and annual bluegrass, can suffer significant freezing injury. Research in this area seems to support the recommendation to maintain moderate nitrogen fertilization levels where freezing injury is a concern. Perennial ryegrass fertilized with 3 pounds nitrogen per 1,000 square feet (148 kg/ha) and sampled as plugs from the field in April exhibited over 7 percent more leakage of cells from crowns compared to plants that weren't fertilized (Welterlen and Watschke 1985) (Table 9-7).

In areas where freezing stress is a concern with warm-season grasses, late-fall nitrogen fertilization should be avoided. Likewise, late-spring nitrogen applications to heat-sensitive cool-season grasses may result in greater summer stress injury.

Fertilizers containing potassium are commonly advertised as "winterizers" that enhance freezing resistance, but not all research has supported this claim. Several researchers observed reduced injury to warm-season grasses with potassium application (Reeves, McBee, and Bloodworth 1970; Gilbert and Davis 1971; Palmertree, Ward, and Pluenneke 1973). Other studies have provided results suggesting that potassium has little or no influence on freezing tolerance. Field-grown Tifgreen bermudagrass receiving nitrogen-to-potassium ratios that resulted in leaf tissue potassium levels ranging from 1.55 to 1.85 percent exhibited no differences in freezing tol-

Table 9-7

Relative conductivity (RC) of perennial ryegrass tissue extracts obtained in April from field-sampled turf receiving two nitrogen levels the previous fall in State College, Pennsylvania (after Welterlen and Watschke 1985)

Test Temperature (°F)[1]	N Rate (lb/1,000 ft²)[2]	RC (%)[3]
23	0	39.8[4]
	3	47.0
18.5	0	53.5
	3	61.4
14	0	65.2
	3	72.7

[1] 23, 18.5, and 14°F = –5, –7.5, and –10°C.

[2] 3 pounds nitrogen per 1,000 square feet = 147 kg/ha.

[3] Relative conductivity is a measure of cell leakage. Higher numbers indicate greater freezing injury.

[4] Conductivity readings between nitrogen rates at all temperatures are significantly different ($P < 0.05$).

erance (Peacock, Bruneau, and DiPaola 1997). Similarly, Tifdwarf bermudagrass receiving potassium at 0 to 8 pounds per 1,000 square feet (0 to 392 kg/ha) per growing month had leaf tissue levels that ranged from 8,900 to 17,300 ppm (mg/kg) dry weight (Miller and Dickens 1996). Despite differences in tissue potassium levels, however, there were no differences in tolerance of rhizomes to freezing when sampling was done from October through March in Alabama. Because no benefit was afforded from using high rates of potassium, these researchers suggested that maintaining adequate soil test levels of potassium may be all that is required to maximize bermudagrass freezing resistance.

Heat It is a standard recommendation that the majority of nitrogen fertilizer be applied in autumn, in part to avoid reducing summer heat stress. Spring nitrogen fertilizer applications promote shoot growth during the time of year when it most naturally is occurring at a rapid rate. Excessive nitrogen application promotes growth and respiratory consumption of carbohydrates and may be detrimental to summer survival of cool-season grasses. As discussed in Chapter 8, carbohydrate depletion is a major contributor to summer decline of creeping bentgrass and most likely other cool-season grasses as well. When the rate of respiration rate exceeds the rate of photosynthesis and carbohydrate reserves are depleted, turf quality declines.

Use of slow-release fertilizers in spring also helps to prevent excessive shoot growth and improve heat tolerance. Other macronutrients should be maintained at adequate soil test levels to maximize heat tolerance.

Shade Little research data are available on fertility requirements of shade-grown turf. In Michigan, creeping bentgrass receiving nitrogen at 3 to 3.8 pounds per 1,000 square feet (147 to 186 kg/ha) per year had 3.3 to 7.2 percent greater cover under 80 percent shade than turf receiving nitrogen at 4.3 to 4.8 pounds per 1,000 square feet (211 to 235 kg/ha) per year (Goss et al. 2002) (Table 9-8). It is generally accepted that nitrogen requirements for shaded turf are lower than those for turf growing in full sun. Shaded turf is succulent and prone to diseases; high nitrogen levels exacerbate these conditions. Adequate soil test levels of phosphorus and potassium should be present to provide the plant with the best opportunity to grow.

Table 9-8

Nitrogen effects on creeping bentgrass cover under shade in 1998 and 1999 at East Lansing, Michigan. Shade treatments began on July 14, 1998, and May 27, 1999, and were removed in October of each year (after Goss et al. 2002)

	Cover (%)[1]			
Nitrogen[2]	**9/23/1998**	**6/7/1999**	**7/14/1999**	**9/14/1999**
Low	72.2 a[3]	92.8 a	81.1 a	89.2 a
High	65.0 b	86.1 b	70.0 b	82.5 b

[1] Percentage cover of creeping bentgrass was rated visually on a 0 to 100 percent scale, where 0 percent = bare soil and 100 percent = complete turfgrass cover.

[2] Low and high nitrogen levels were 0.2 and 0.4 pounds per 1,000 square feet (10 and 20 kg/ha), respectively, applied at fourteen- to twenty-one-day intervals during the growing season.

[3] Means followed by the same letter in each column are not significantly different ($P \leq 0.05$) according to Fisher's protected means separation test.

Figure 9-8
Turf growing in the shade has lower nitrogen requirements than that in full sun (drawing by Angie Settle).

Shaded sites—lower nitrogen   Full sun—higher nitrogen

INTERACTIONS WITH TURFGRASS PESTS

Weeds   Turf receiving adequate levels of nitrogen is generally most resistant to weed invasion. Tall fescue receiving 4 pounds nitrogen per 1,000 square feet (196 kg/ha) per year had approximately 30 percent less crabgrass cover than that receiving 2 pounds per 1,000 square feet (98 kg/ha) per year in Maryland (Dernoeden, Carroll, and Krouse 1993). In Illinois, less broadleaf weed cover was also reported where nitrogen was applied at 2 to 4 pounds per 1,000 square feet (98 to 196 kg/ha) per year compared to nonfertilized turf (Voigt, Fermanian, and Haley 2001).

Nitrogen levels can influence the encroachment of sod-forming grasses into cool-season turfs. A tall fescue lawn receiving 5 pounds nitrogen per 1,000 square feet (245 kg/ha) per year experienced more bermudagrass invasion than turf receiving 1 pound per 1,000 square feet (49 kg/ha) (Brede 1992).

 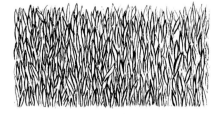

Figure 9-9
Nitrogen-deficient turf is prone to weed invasion (drawing by Angie Settle).

Low nitrogen—weed-infested

Adequate nitrogen—weed-resistant

High nitrogen levels applied to high-maintenance turf may foster an increase in annual bluegrass (Fig. 2-4) populations. In one of three years in Michigan, applying nitrogen at 6 pounds per 1,000 square feet (294 kg/ha) per year resulted in about 4 percent more annual bluegrass than where nitrogen was applied at 2 pounds per 1,000 square feet (98 kg/ha) per year (Gaussoin and Branham 1989). By the end of the third year, however, annual bluegrass populations were similar regardless of nitrogen application level.

Turf deficient in nitrogen is more susceptible to an invasion by weeds capable of fixing nitrogen, such as white clover (Fig. 6-6).

Nutrients other than nitrogen generally have less effect on weed encroachment. Annual bluegrass is an exception in that nutritional modifications applied to the soil or foliarly can impact its growth. Phosphorus applications increased the encroachment of annual bluegrass in creeping bentgrass golf putting greens in Washington (Goss, Brauen, and Orton 1975). The same researchers found that acidifying soil with sulfur reduced establishment of annual bluegrass. Monthly foliar applications of iron (0.03 pounds per 1,000 square feet [1.47 kg/ha]) plus magnesium (0.03 pounds per 1,000 square feet [1.47 kg/ha]) reduced annual bluegrass populations by 65 percent and provided complete control of roughstalk bluegrass in Ohio (Bell, Odorizzi, and Danneberger 1997). However, the same treatments were ineffective when evaluated on a golf course that had perennial types of annual bluegrass present.

Insects   The little work that has been done on the influence of fertilization on insects indicates there may be some effects. Acidifying the soil with aluminum sulfate (25 pounds per 1,000 square feet [1,225 kg/ha) reduced numbers of root-feeding white grubs in tall fescue

(Potter et al. 2000). In the same test, adult beetles seem to be attracted to natural organic fertilizers, such as manures, which may increase grub infestations.

Diseases Nitrogen influences turf diseases by affecting leaf succulence and susceptibility to infection, soil pH, and the rate at which the plant may outgrow symptoms. Low nitrogen levels are commonly associated with dollar spot (Fig. 6-18), red thread (Fig. 6-27), and rust (Fig. 6-28). High nitrogen levels can promote brown patch (Fig. 6-16), Pythium blight (Fig. 6-25 and Fig. 6-26), and snow mold (Fig. 6-23). Several researchers have reported greater brown patch infection in tall fescue and perennial ryegrass with increasing levels of nitrogen (Watkins and Wit 1993; Dunn, Minner, and Bughrara 1996; Vincelli and Powell 1996). *Rhizoctonia solani* is presumably better able to penetrate succulent leaves that contain cells with thin walls.

Nitrogen source can have a pronounced effect on turfgrass response to diseases. Quick-release nitrogen sources may result in more succulent tissue and lead to greater infection. In perennial ryegrass, for example, turf fertilized at 3 pounds nitrogen per 1,000 square feet (147 kg/ha) per year with the quick-release nitrogen source sodium nitrate suffered up to 30 percent more brown patch injury than turf treated with the slow-release fertilizer sulfur-coated urea (Fidanza and Dernoeden 1996).

There is some thought that the use of organic fertilizers may reduce turfgrass diseases by encouraging proliferation of beneficial microbes. Presumably, the microbes involved in breaking down the organic products may be antagonistic to common turfgrass pathogens. The results of work evaluating organic fertilizers for disease suppression have been mixed, however. In New York, the use of various compost-amended topdressings was effective in suppressing dollar spot on creeping bentgrass putting greens (Nelson and Craft 1992); however, suppression may have resulted from the increased N delivered in the composts and fertilizers and not from an increase in organisms antagonistic to the dollar spot pathogen.

In Kansas, five organic fertilizers were compared to urea for their effects on disease suppression in four creeping bentgrass cultivars with a range of dollar spot susceptibility (Lee, Fry, and Tisserat 2002).

Table 9-9
Summary of research results from projects that compared nitrogen level effects on turfgrass diseases

| Disease | Turfgrass | Strategy That Increases Disease Symptoms | |
		Low Nitrogen	High Nitrogen
Dollar spot	Perennial rye	Dunn, Minner, and Bughrara 1996	
	Creeping bentgrass	Golembiewski and Danneberger 1998 Watkins et al. 2001b	
Brown patch	Perennial rye	Watkins et al. 2001a	Dunn, Minner, and Bughrara 1996 Fidanza and Dernoeden 1996 Settle et al. 2001
	Tall fescue		Burpee 1995 Vincelli and Powell 1997
	Creeping bentgrass		Bloom and Couch 1960
Gray leaf spot	Perennial rye		Williams, Burrus, and Vincelli 2001
Pythium blight	Creeping bentgrass		Gaussoin et al. 1999
Rust	Perennial rye	Watkins 1996	
Snow mold	Colonial bentgrass		Madison, Petersen, and Hodges 1960
Spring dead spot	Bermuda		McCarty, Lucas, and DiPaola 1992
Red thread	Perennial rye	Cahill, Murray, and Dernoeden 1983 Tredway, Soika, and Clarke 2001	

Compared to plots receiving urea, less disease occurred in plots where two of the fertilizers were applied, but more dollar spot was observed on turf fertilized with five of the organic nitrogen sources (Table 9-10). Creeping bentgrass fertilized with urea in Pennsylvania also had equal or better turf quality and dollar spot suppression compared to turf receiving natural organic fertilizer (Landschoot and McNitt 1997). In Maryland, nine nitrogen sources were applied to fairway-height Southshore creeping bentgrass over six years, and dollar spot was evaluated the last three years. Ringer Lawn Restore (a poultry waste product) and urea suppressed dollar spot (Davis and Dernoeden 2002). Com-Pro, a composted sewage sludge, increased dollar spot. Other nitrogen sources evaluated had no effect on dollar spot relative to urea, nor were any of them consistently associated with higher levels of soil microbial activity.

Less information is available on the potential effects of organic fertilizers on diseases in grasses other than creeping bentgrass. In work with Rebel tall fescue, there was no less brown patch observed in turf treated with the organic fertilizer Turf Restore (derived primarily from meals of feathers, soybeans, blood, and bones) compared to turf treated with urea (Peacock and Daniel 1992).

Clearly, there are benefits to using natural organic fertilizers, including their slow release of nitrogen and the fact that a waste product is utilized. Nevertheless, most of the research conducted to date does not support the claim that the use of organic products in place of synthetic organic fertilizers results in less disease.

Acid-reacting fertilizers have been shown to reduce the incidence of root-infecting pathogens that cause spring dead spot (Fig. 6-32), summer patch (Fig. 6-33), and take-all patch (Fig. 6-34). Ammonium sulfate and ammonium chloride can be used to suppress take-all patch (Dernoeden 1987) and enhance spring green-up and quality of bermudagrass infested with spring dead spot (Dernoeden, Crahay, and Davis 1990). In the latter test, extent of spring dead spot injury was positively correlated with soil pH. Summer patch injury on Kentucky bluegrass in Maryland was reduced by as much as 10 percent when turf was fertilized with sulfur-coated urea compared to urea (Davis and Dernoeden 1991). The benefits afforded by the sulfur-coated product were thought to be due more to its slow-release properties than to its potential acidifying effects on the soil.

Table 9-10

Effects of nitrogen sources on turfgrass diseases

	Grass	Nitrogen Source	Description	Average Increase (+) or Decrease (–) in Symptoms Compared to Urea-Treated Turf[1]	Source
Dollar spot	Crenshaw creeping bentgrass	Milorganite (6-0.9-0)	Composted sewage sludge	47% (–)	Lee, Fry, and Tisserat 2002
		Nature Safe (8-1.3-4.2)	Feather, meat, blood, and bone meals	25% (+)	
		Nature Safe (10-0.9-6.6)	Feather, meat, blood, and bone meals	16% (+)	
		Sustane (10-0.4-1.7)	Composted turkey litter	11% (–)	
		Sustane with Iron (5-0.9-3.3)	Composted turkey litter	20% (+)	
	Penncross creeping bentgrass	Sustane (10-0.4-1.7)	Composted turkey litter	47% (+)	
	Providence creeping bentgrass	Nature Safe (8-1.3-4.2)	Feather, meat, blood, and bone meals	56% (+)	
	Southshore creeping bentgrass	Com-Pro (1-2-0)	Composted sewage sludge	128% (+)[2]	Davis and Dernoeden 2002
		Ringer Lawn Restore	Poultry manure	65% (–)[2]	
	Creeping bentgrass/ annual bluegrass	Organic fertilizer CP	Plant and animal by-products	81% (–)[3]	Nelson and Craft 1992
	Penncross creeping bentgrass	Harmony 14-3-6	Poultry manure	35% (+)	Landschoot and McNitt 1997
		Sustane 5-2-4	Composted turkey litter	35% (+)	
		Milorganite 6-2-0	Composted sewage sludge	40% (+)	

Continued on next page

Table 9.10 (*continued*)

	Grass	Nitrogen Source	Description	Average Increase (+) or Decrease (–) in Symptoms Compared to Urea-Treated Turf[1]	Source
Spring dead spot	Tufcote bermuda-grass	Ammonium sulfate	Synthetic inorganic	21% (–)	Dernoeden, Crahay, and Davis 1990
		Ammonium chloride	Synthetic inorganic	18% (–)	
Summer patch	S-21 Kentucky bluegrass	Sulfur-coated urea	Synthetic organic	8% (–)	Davis and Dernoeden 1991
Take-all patch	Creeping bentgrass	Ammonium chloride and ammonium sulfate	Synthetic inorganic	9% (–)[4]	Dernoeden 1987

[1] Averages based upon dates when treatments were significantly ($P < 0.05$) different from urea-treated turf.

[2] Values are in comparison to untreated turf.

[3] Fertilizer was applied as topdressing at 30 percent (by volume) of a fine sand mixture.

[4] These were the only fertilizers that reduced disease to an acceptable level, but were not statistically different than urea.

The use of phosphorus and potassium in combination with nitrogen has also been shown to reduce the incidence of some turf diseases. Phosphorus and potassium applied in combination with nitrogen reduced dollar spot (Bloom and Couch 1960), take-all patch (Goss and Gould 1967), and stripe smut (*Ustilago striiformis*) (Hull, Jackson, and Skogley 1979). In perennial ryegrass, use of phosphorus (1.5 pounds per 1,000 square feet [74 kg/ha] per year) and potassium (3 pounds per 1,000 square feet (147 kg/ha] per year), in conjunction with nitrogen, reduced brown patch blighting in Maryland on soil that tested high (3.6 pounds per 1,000 square feet [176 kg/ha]) and medium (2 lb per 1,000 square feet [98 kg/ha]) in phosphorus and potassium, respectively, before application (Fidanza and Dernoeden 1996). Hence, a disease reduction benefit was realized by the addition of supplemental phosphorus and potassium even when soil tests indicated levels were adequate. Deficiencies of either of these nutrients warrant their application to reduce the potential for some diseases. However, current environmental regulations in some areas of the United States may limit the additions of phosphorus when soil tests indicate adequate levels are present.

Little information has been published on the potential effects of micronutrients on turfgrass disease responses. A 15 percent reduction in take-all patch in creeping bentgrass occurred when manganese was applied at 1.82 pounds per acre (2.04 kg/ha) every four weeks from March through November in New Jersey (Hill et al. 1999). It is thought that manganese may serve to increase the plant's disease resistance by enhancing production of phenolics and ligneous compounds.

Silicon, a nonessential element, has demonstrated some positive effects on reducing diseases in St. Augustinegrass and creeping bentgrass. Gray leaf spot (Fig. 6-19) in St. Augustinegrass was reduced 9 to 28 percent by silicon (Brecht et al. 2001). North Carolina researchers reported a 20 to 30 percent reduction in brown patch and dollar spot when soluble potassium silicate was applied to creeping bentgrass (Anonymous 1997). Two years of evaluating the influence of granular calcium silicate on creeping bentgrass and tall fescue in Kansas revealed no benefit in reducing dollar spot or brown patch (Zhang et al. 2003).

REFERENCES

Anonymous. 1997. Effect of soluble silica on brown patch and dollar spot of creeping bentgrass. *North Carolina Turfgrass*. Aug.-Sept., pp. 34–36.

Bell, G. E., E. Odorizzi, and T. K. Danneberger. 1997. Controlling annual bluegrass and rough bluegrass in creeping bentgrass fairways: A nutritional approach. *Agron. Abst.*, p. 122.

Bloom, J. R., and H. B. Couch. 1960. Influence of environment on diseases of turfgrasses. I. Effect of nutrition, pH, and soil moisture on Rhizoctonia brown patch. *Phytopathology* 50:532–35.

Brecht, M. O., L. E. Datnoff, T. A. Kucharek, and R. T. Nagata. 2001. Effect of silicon and chlorothalonil on suppression of gray leaf spot in St. Augustinegrass. *Phytopathology* 91:11.

Brede, A. D. 1992. Cultural factors for minimizing bermudagrass invasion into tall fescue turf. *Agron. J.* 84:919–22.

Burpee, L. 1995. Interactions among mowing height, nitrogen fertility, and cultivar affect the severity of Rhizoctonia blight of tall fescue. *Plant Dis.* 79:721–26.

Cahill, J. V., J. J. Murray, and P. H. Dernoeden. 1983. Interrelationships between fertility and red thread fungal disease of turfgrasses. *Plant Dis.* 67:1080–3.

Canaway, P. M. 1985. The response of renovated turf of *Lolium perenne* (perennial ryegrass) to fertilizer nitrogen II. Above-ground biomass and tiller numbers. *J. Sports Turf Research Institute* 61:100–3.

Carroll, M., and M. Petrovic. 1991a. Nitrogen, potassium, and irrigation effects of water relations of Kentucky bluegrass leaves. *Crop Sci.* 31:449–53.

———. 1991b. Wear tolerance of Kentucky bluegrass and creeping bentgrass following nitrogen and potassium applications. *HortScience* 26:851–53.

Davis, D., and P. Dernoeden. 1991. Summer patch and Kentucky bluegrass quality as influenced by cultural practices. *Agron. J.* 83:670–77.

Davis, J. G., and P. H. Dernoeden. 2002. Dollar spot severity, tissue nitrogen, and soil microbial activity in bentgrass as influenced by nitrogen source. *Crop Sci.* 42:480–88.

Dernoeden, P. H. 1987. Management of take-all patch of creeping bentgrass with nitrogen, sulfur, and phenyl mercury acetate. *Plant Dis.* 71:226–29.

Dernoeden, P. H., M. J. Carroll, and J. M. Krouse. 1993. Weed management and tall fescue quality as influenced by mowing, nitrogen, and herbicides. *Crop Sci.* 33:1055–61.

Dernoeden, P. H., J. N. Crahay, and D. B. Davis. 1990. Spring dead spot and bermudagrass recovery as influenced by nitrogen source and potassium. *Crop Sci.* 31:1674–80.

Dunn, J. H., D. D. Minner, and S. S. Bughrara. 1996. Clippings disposal and fertilization influence disease in perennial ryegrass. *HortScience* 31:1180–81.

Erusha, K. 1990. Irrigation and potassium effects on a Kentucky bluegrass fairway turf. Ph.D. dissertation, Dept. of Horticulture, University of Nebraska.

Feldhake, C. M., R. E. Danielson, and J. D. Butler. 1983. Turfgrass evapotranspiration. I. Factors influencing rate in urban environments. *Agron. J.* 75:824–30.

_____. 1984. Turfgrass evapotranspiration. II. Responses to deficit irrigation. *Agron. J.* 76:85–89.

Fidanza, M. A., and P. H. Dernoeden. 1996. Brown patch severity in perennial ryegrass as influenced by irrigation, fungicide, and fertilizers. *Crop Sci.* 36:1631–38.

Frank, K. W., R. E. Gaussoin, J. D. Fry, M. D. Frost, and J. H. Baird. 2002. Nitrogen, phosphorus, and potassium effects on seeded buffalograss establishment. *HortScience* 37:371–73.

Fry, J. D., and P. H. Dernoeden. 1987. Growth of zoysiagrass from vegetative plugs in response to fertilizers. *J. Amer. Soc. Hort. Sci.* 112:286–89.

Fry, J. D., M. A. Harivandi, and D. D. Minner. 1989. Creeping bentgrass response to P and K on a sand medium. *HortScience* 24:623–24.

Gaussoin, R. E., and B. E. Branham. 1989. Influence of cultural factors on species dominance in a mixed stand of annual bluegrass/creeping bentgrass. *Crop Sci.* 29:480–84.

Gaussoin, R. E., R. Drijber, W. Powers, R. C. Shearman, M. Aslan, M. R. Vaitkus, and L. A. Wit. 1999. Grow-in and cultural impacts on USGA putting greens and their microbial communities. Turfgrass Research Report, University of Nebraska.

Gilbert, W. B., and D. L. Davis. 1971. Influence of fertility rations on winter hardiness of bermudagrass. *Agron. J.* 63:591–93.

Golembiewski, R. C., and T. K. Danneberger. 1998. Dollar spot severity as influenced by trinexapac-ethyl, creeping bentgrass cultivar, and nitrogen fertility. *Agron. J.* 90:466–70.

Goss, R. M., J. H. Baird, S. L. Kelm, and R. N. Calhoun. 2002. Trinexapac-ethyl and nitrogen effects on creeping bentgrass grown under reduced light conditions. *Crop Sci.* 42:472–79.

Goss, R. L., S. E. Brauen, and S. P. Orton. 1975. The effects of N, P, K and S on *Poa annua* L. in bentgrass putting green turf. *J. Sports Turf Res. Inst.* 51:74–82.

Goss, R. L., and C. J. Gould. 1967. Some interrelationships between fertility levels and Ophiobolus patch disease in turfgrasses. *Agron. J.* 59:149–51.

Hill, W. J., J. R. Heckman, B. B. Clarke, and J. A. Murphy. 1999. Take-all patch suppression in creeping bentgrass with manganese and copper. *HortScience* 34:891–92.

Horst, G. L, A. A. Baltensperger, and M. D. Firkner. 1985. Effects of N and growing season on root-rhizome characteristics of turf-type bermudagrasses. *Agron. J.* 71:553–55.

Huang, B. 2001. Nutrient accumulation and associated root characteristics in response to drought stress in tall fescue cultivars. *HortScience* 36:148–52.

Hull, R. J., N. Jackson, and C. R. Skogley. 1979. Influence of nutrition on stripe smut severity in Kentucky bluegrass turf. *Agron. J.* 71:553–55.

Jones, J. R., Jr. 1980. Turf analysis. *Golf Course Management* 48 (1):29–32.

Kneebone, W. R., D. M. Kopec, and C. F. Mancino. 1992. Water requirements and irrigation. Pp. 441–72 in D. V. Waddington, R. N. Carrow, and R. C. Shearman, eds., *Turfgrass*. Madison, WI: Crop Science Society of America.

Krogman, K. K. 1967. Evapotranspiration by irrigated grass as related to fertilizer. *Canadian J. Plant Sci.* 47:284–87.

Landschoot, P. J., and A. S. McNitt. 1997. Effects of nitrogen fertilizers on suppression of dollar spot disease of *Agrostis stolonifera* L. *Int. Turfgrass Soc. Res. J.* 8:905–11.

Lee, J., J. Fry, and N. Tisserat. 2002. Creeping bentgrass disease incidence as affected by cultivar, a plant defense activator, and organic fertilizers. Kansas State University Agricultural Experiment Station, Report of Progress no. 894.

Madison, J. H. 1962. Effects of mowing irrigation, and nitrogen treatments on *Agrostis palustris* Huds., Seaside and *Agrostis tenuis* Sibth., Highland on population, yield, rooting, and cover. *Agron. J.* 54:407–12.

Madison, J. H., L. J. Petersen, and T. K. Hodges. 1960. Pink snowmold on bentgrass as affected by irrigation and fertilizer. *Agron. J.* 52:591–92.

McCarty, L. B., L. T. Lucas, and J. M. DiPaola. 1992. Spring dead spot occurrence in bermudagrass following fungicide and nutrient applications. *HortScience* 27:1092–3.

Miller, G. L., and R. Dickens. 1996. Potassium fertilization as related to cold resistance in bermudagrass. *Crop Sci.* 36:1290–5.

———. 1997. Water relations of two *Cynodon* turf cultivars as influenced by potassium. *Int. Turfgrass Soc. Res. J.* 8:1298–1306.

Nelson, E. B., and C. M. Craft. 1992. Suppression of dollar spot on creeping bentgrass and annual bluegrass turf with compost-amended topdressings. *Plant Dis.* 76:954–58.

Palmertree, H. D., C. Y. Ward, and R. H. Pluenneke. 1973. Influence of mineral nutrition on the cold tolerance and soluble protein fraction of centipedegrass. Pp. 500–7 in E. C. Roberts, ed., *Proceedings of the Second International Turfgrass Research Conference.* Blacksburg, VA, and Madison, WI: American Society of Agronomy and Crop Science Society of America.

Peacock, C. H., A. H. Bruneau, and J. M. DiPaola. 1997. Response of *Cynodon* cultivar Tifgreen to potassium fertilizers. *Int. Turfgrass Soc. Res. J.* 8:1308–13.

Peacock, C. H., and P. F. Daniel. 1992. A comparison of turfgrass response to biologically amended fertilizers. *HortScience* 27:883–84.

Potter, D. A., R C. Williamson, K. F. Haynes, and A. J. Powell. 2000. Cultural control, risk assessment, and environmentally responsible management of scarab grubs and cutworms in turfgrass. In J. M. Clark and M. P. Kenna, eds., *Fate and Management of Turfgrass Chemicals.* Washington, DC: American Chemical Society.

Powell, A. J., R. E. Blaser, and R. E. Schmidt. 1967. Effect of nitrogen on winter root growth of bentgrass. *Agron. J.* 59:529–30.

Rechcigl, J. E. 1992. Response of ryegrass to limestone and phosphorus. *J. Prod. Agric.* 5:602–7.

Reeves, S., G. McBee, and M. Bloodworth. 1970. Effect of N, P, and K tissue levels and late fall fertilization on the cold hardiness of Tifgreen bermudagrass. *Agron. J.* 62:659–62.

Settle, D., J. Fry, and N. Tisserat. 2001. Effects of irrigation frequency on brown patch in perennial ryegrass. *Int. Turfgrass Soc. Res. J.* 9:710–13.

Shearman, R. C., and J. B. Beard. 2002. Potassium nutrition effects on *Agrostis stolonifera* L. wear stress tolerance. Pp. 667–75 in E. Thain, ed., *Science and Golf IV: Proceedings of the World Scientific Congress of Golf.* London: Routledge.

Sills, M. J., and R. N. Carrow. 1983. Turfgrass growth, N use and water use under soil compaction and N fertilization. *Agron. J.* 75:488–92.

Tredway, L. P., M. D. Soika, and B. B. Clarke. 2001. Red thread development in perennial ryegrass in response to nitrogen, phosphorus, and potassium fertilizer applications. *Int. Turfgrass Soc. Res. J.* 9:715–22.

Trenholm, L. E., R. N. Carrow, and R. R. Duncan. 2001. Wear tolerance, growth, and quality of seashore paspalum in response to nitrogen and potassium. *HortScience* 36:780–83.

Trenholm, L. E., A. E. Dudeck, J. B. Sartain, and J. L. Cisar. 1998. Bermudagrass growth, total nonstructural carbohydrate concentration, and quality as influenced by nitrogen and potassium. *Crop Sci.* 38:168–74.

Vincelli, P., and A. J. Powell. 1997. Impact of mowing height and nitrogen fertility on brown patch and tall fescue, 1996. *Biol. and Cult. Tests* 12:129.

Voigt, T. B., T. W. Fermanian, and J. E. Haley. 2001. Influence of mowing and nitrogen fertility on tall fescue turf. *Int. Turfgrass Soc. Res. J.* 9:953–56.

Walker, R. H., and C. Y. Ward. 1973. Influence of N and K nutrition on net photosynthesis, dark respiration, and carbohydrates in centipedegrass. Pp. 196–208 in E. C. Roberts, ed., *Proceedings of the Second International Turfgrass Research Conference.* Blacksburg, VA and Madison, WI: American Society of Agronomy and Crop Science Society of America.

Watkins, J. E. 1996. Nitrogen fertilization's effect on turfgrass disease injury. *Turfgrass Trends* 5 (11):1–5.

Watkins, J. E., R. E. Gauossoin, K. W. Frank, and L. A. Wit. 2001. Brown patch severity and perennial ryegrass quality as influenced by nitrogen rate and source and cultivar. *Int. Turfgrass Soc. Res. J.* 9:723–28.

Watkins, J. E., R. C. Shearman, R. E. Gaussoin, W. K. Cecil, M. Vaitkus, and L. A. Wit. 2001. An integrated approach to dollar spot management on a bentgrass fairway. *Int. Turfgrass Soc. Res. J.* 9:729–35.

Watkins, J. E., and L. A. Wit. 1993. Effect of nitrogen level and cutting height on brown patch severity, 1992. *Biol. and Cultural Tests* 8:124.

Watschke, T. L., and D. V. Waddington. 1975. Effect of nitrogen fertilization on the recovery of Merion Kentucky bluegrass from scalping and wilting. *Agron. J.* 67:559–63.

Watschke, T. L., D. V. Waddington, D. J. Wehner, and C. L. Forth. 1977. Effect of P, K, and lime on growth, composition and P absorption by Merion Kentucky bluegrass. *Agron. J.* 69:825–28.

Welterlen, M. S., and T. L. Watschke. 1985. Influence of drought stress and fall nitrogen fertilization on cold deacclimation and tissue components of perennial ryegrass turf. Pp. 831–40 in F. Lemaire, ed., *Proceedings of the Fifth International Turfgrass Research Conference.* Versailles: INRA.

Westhafer, M. A., J. T. Law Jr., and T. D. Duff. 1982. Carbohydrate quantification and relationships with N nutrition in cool-season turfgrasses. *Agron. J.* 74:270–74.

Weston, J. B., and J. H. Dunn. 1985. Thatch and quality of Meyer zoysia in response to mechanical cultivation and nitrogen fertilization. Pp. 449–58 in F. Lemaire, ed., *Proceedings of the Fifth International Turfgrass Research Conference.* Versailles: INRA.

Williams, D. W., P. B. Burrus, and P. Vincelli. 2001. Severity of gray leaf spot in perennial ryegrass as influenced by mowing height and nitrogen level. *Crop Sci.* 41:1207–11.

Zhang, Q., J. Fry, K. Lowe, and N. Tisserat. 2003 Evaluation of calcium silicate for brown patch suppression in tall fescue. Kansas State University Agricultural Experiment Station, Report of Progress no. 911.

10

Cultivation

In row crops, cultivation refers to plowing, discing, or performing some other operation on fallow ground. In turf, however, cultivation refers to some operation done on an actively growing turf to disturb the underlying soil or the vegetation itself. For example, core aerification might be done to alleviate compaction, or vertical mowing may be done to remove thatch; both are considered turf cultivation practices.

SOIL COMPACTION

Soil Physical Properties

Turf growing on athletic fields is subjected to wear and compaction stresses. Wear results from the direct abrasive effects of cleats, golf cart tires, et cetera, on the plant. Soil compaction is a separate stress that results when changes occur to the turfgrass root zone that negatively affect plant growth. Turf managers employ cultural practices directly focused on reducing turf stress that results from compaction. Fine-textured soils high in silt and clay content are most susceptible to compaction. Sandy soils are more resistant to compaction, which is one reason why sports turf root zones commonly contain high levels of sand.

For example, consider a hypothetical "normal" loam soil (composed of about equal parts of sand and fine-textured soil) that is composed of about 50 percent solids (45 percent mineral, 5 percent organic) and 50 percent pore space (25 percent air, 25 percent water) (Fig. 10-2). After compaction, whether from foot traffic, golf carts, or

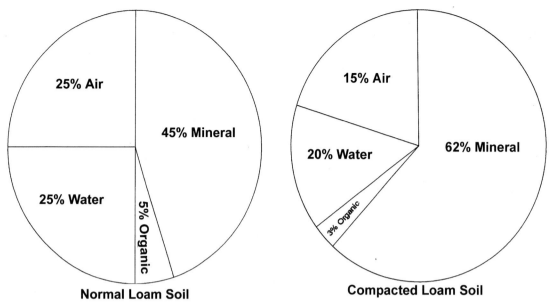

Figure 10-1
Solids and pore space in a normal (left) and compacted (right) loam soil.

some other means, solids will constitute a larger proportion of the soil makeup. In our hypothetical example, a compacted loam now has 65 percent solids (62 percent mineral, 3 percent organic) and 35 percent pore space (15 percent air, 20 percent water).

Degree of soil compaction can be measured as bulk density, calculated as:

$$\text{weight of soil (g)} \div \text{volume of soil (cm}^3).$$

The denominator, soil volume, accounts for the volume of pore space as well as the volume occupied by solids. When a particular soil is compacted, there are more solids in a given volume of soil and less pore space; therefore, bulk density increases as compaction increases. Because particles in coarse-textured soils are heavier, bulk densities of noncompacted sandy soils are higher than those of fine-textured soils. Fine-textured soils are compacted more easily, however, so the potential increases in bulk density are greater on these soils.

Soil compaction affects turfgrass growth in many ways, most of which are detrimental to plant growth. Research has demonstrated

Figure 10-2
Athletic field managers are constantly battling soil compaction, which is worse in the areas of greatest traffic. (Photo courtesy of Dr. Steve Keeley.)

that shoot growth, rooting, total nonstructural carbohydrate levels, and water use rates are all influenced by the degree of soil compaction. Much of the groundbreaking work on turf responses to compaction was presented in Carrow (1980) and O'Neill and Carrow (1983) and is included in Table 10-1.

Shoot Growth

Compaction reduces clipping production and turfgrass coverage. In most species, a reduction in shoot density is observed, although perennial ryegrass has exhibited an increase in density under compaction stress (Carrow 1980). It is believed that the increase in turf density may be due to an increase in plant ethylene production in soils during compaction stress. Variability in sizes of individual plants has also been observed during compaction, with some, such as tall fescue, increasing in size, and others, such as Kentucky bluegrass, decreasing in size (Carrow 1980).

Total Nonstructural Carbohydrates

When exposed to compaction during midsummer, total nonstructural carbohydrates in Kentucky bluegrass, tall fescue, and perennial ryegrass were reduced (Carrow 1980). This reduction in

Table 10-1

Turfgrass growth responses to compaction stress

Grass	Description	Quality	Shoot Growth	Root Growth	Water Use	Reference
Kentucky bluegrass	Field study; silt loam; smooth power roller applied 0, 12, or 24 passes per week for 8 weeks; study began in mid-June in Kansas	Slight decline in quality, particularly with 24 passes per week	Coverage was reduced by 9 percent with 24 passes per week; shoot density declined with compaction; total nonstructural carbohydrates declined 50 percent from 12 to 24 pass treatments; size of individual plants decreased with compaction	Root weight reduced by 32 percent at 0 to 10 cm during compaction but 27 percent higher in autumn in this zone	Not evaluated	Carrow 1980
Tall fescue		Significant decline with increasing compaction	Coverage reduced by 33 percent during compaction; shoot density declined with compaction; total nonstructural carbohydrates declined 35 percent from 12 to 24 pass treatment; size of individual plants declined with compaction	Rooting increased by 28 percent at 0 to 10 cm as passes increased from 0 to 12 per week	Not evaluated	Carrow 1980
Perennial ryegrass		Slight decline with increasing compaction	No effect on coverage; shoot density increased with compaction; total nonstructural carbohydrates declined 28 percent from 12 to 24 passes	Rooting reduced by 39 percent at 10 to 20 cm and by 18 percent at same depth in autumn in turf receiving 12 passes per week	Not evaluated	Carrow 1980

Grass	Description	Quality	Shoot Growth	Root Growth	Water Use	Reference
Perennial ryegrass	Greenhouse study; soil 1 part sand, 2 parts silt loam; compaction levels of none, moderate, and heavy applied every 2 weeks	Declined with duration and intensity of compaction	Density was reduced late in the study; clipping production reduced with increasing compaction	Heavy compaction increased rooting in the 0 to 5 cm zone and reduced rooting at 10 to 25 cm	Compaction reduced water use rate	O'Neil and Carrow 1983
Tifway bermuda-grass	Compacted sandy loam; smooth power roller, 20 passes in April, 10 passes every other week until mid-September	Generally no effect on quality	Verdure and individual shoot weight declined; shoot density increased; clippings reduced 29 to 74 percent	Reduced rooting at 0 to 10 cm by 20 percent, 20 to 20 cm by 77 percent, 20 to 60 cm by 64 percent	Reduced water extraction, primarily near the soil surface	Wiecko, Carrow, and Karnok 1993
Penncross creeping bentgrass	Modified sandy loam; water-filled vibrating roller (51 kPa static pressure), 1–2 passes per day over plots	Reduced quality, particularly in midsummer	No effect as measured by ashing	Reduced rooting, particularly at depths from 7.6 to 22.8 cm	Not evaluated	Murphy, Rieke, and Erickson 1993

TNC makes it more difficult for the turf to recover, especially if compaction is coupled with other stresses, such as wear (which will occur in conjunction with compaction), heat stress, or pests. Although a reduction in TNC occurred during the stress period, Carrow (1980) found that turf growing in compacted soil had TNC levels comparable to turf growing in noncompacted soil when good growing conditions returned in autumn.

Root Growth Rooting is either reduced or altered by compaction stress. The inability of roots to function normally is the primary factor leading to turf quality decline during compaction. Although the compaction may be

Table 10-2
Estimates of minimum soil bulk densities for different soil types at which rooting becomes restricted (after USDA 1996)

Texture	Bulk Density (g/cm³)
Coarse, medium, fine, and loamy sands	1.8
Sandy loams	1.75
Silt loams	1.55
Clay	1.4

focused in the upper few centimeters of the root zone, the higher bulk density in this region increases soil strength and makes it more difficult for roots to penetrate (Table 10-2). It is not unusual to find that total root production may not be greatly affected, but a greater proportion of roots will be confined to the surface few inches (several cm) because they cannot penetrate through a compacted layer high in soil strength. Physiologically, roots function poorly because less oxygen is available for respiration as a result of less porosity in the zone where roots are growing. Over an extended period of time, anoxia experienced by roots will result in their demise, which subsequently results in a loss of shoots.

Water Use Lower water use rates have been reported when cool-season grasses are under compaction stress. This is likely due to slower shoot vertical elongation rates and reduced density.

AERIFICATION

There are now many types of equipment that are capable of modifying compacted soil under growing turf in order to improve growing conditions. Aerifiers employ hollow or solid tines or jets of water propelled at high pressure to disturb the soil underlying established turf, increasing the infiltration of air into the soil. Aerifiers come in all shapes and sizes and vary in the number of holes they create in the surface, depth of penetration, and degree of surface disturbance. In some cases, aerifiers are drills that are capable of

Figures 10-3 and 10-4
Aerifiers may remove cores of soil (Fig. 10-3, top) or penetrate with solid tines (Fig. 10-4, bottom).

penetrating to depths of 12 inches (30 cm), and others support large knives that cut into the surface in an attempt to break through compacted soil. In many cases this results in improved soil physical properties, such as reduced bulk density, increased porosity, and higher water infiltration rates (Table 10-3). By improving the suitability of these soils for turfgrass growth, aerifiers are capable of improving shoot and root growth.

Shoot Growth   Bermudagrass and creeping bentgrass have exhibited fairly rapid shoot growth responses to aerification when they are growing on compacted soils. Hollow tine aerifiers, deep drills, water injectors, and soil slicers have all shown the capability for improving shoot growth (Table 10-3). Hollow tine aerifiers may cause a short-term decline in turf quality, or decline in verdure, because they remove a portion of the turf canopy. The positive responses of shoots to aerification are almost surely due to an improved growing environment for roots, which have been directly impacted by the poor soil conditions.

Root Growth   The goal of aerification is to reduce soil strength and increase soil porosity so that roots may flourish. In Georgia, rooting of Tifway bermudagrass was increased in at least one of two years by a slicer, hollow and solid tine aerifiers, and a deep drill (Wiecko, Carrow, and Karnok 1993) (Table 10-3). In some cases, rooting was improved well below the penetration depth of the aerifier used. For example, the hollow tine aerifier penetrated to a depth of 3 inches (7.6 cm), but rooting at depths of 7.8 to 24 inches (20 to 60 cm) was improved by 38 percent in one year of the evaluation. By reducing bulk density and soil strength to the depth of aerifier penetration, roots are given the opportunity to elongate and flourish at deeper soil depths.

Bentgrass root weight density has been shown to be negatively affected by hollow tine, solid tine, and water injection aerifiers despite increases in shoot growth and improvements in soil physical conditions (Murphy, Rieke, and Erickson 1993; Murphy and Rieke, 1994). Hollow tine aerifiers will remove a portion of surface roots, due to the nature of the operation. Solid tine and water injection aerifiers create a physical force that likely injures roots that are in the path of the penetrating tines or water jets. These short-term reductions in surface rooting do not negate the positive effects that these aerification procedures have on improving bentgrass quality, however. On cool-season grasses, and bentgrass more specifically, the potential stress that results from aerification procedures must

Table 10-3

Turfgrass growth responses to different types of aerifiers

Aerifier	Grass	Description	Shoot growth	Root growth	Other	Reference
Solid and hollow tine	Soil preparation before sodding Kentucky bluegrass	Compacted sandy loam; 1.3 cm diam. tines; spacing 7.5 cm; depth 7.5 cm	Not measured	Rooting strength resulting from hollow tine was comparable to tilled soil; solid tine increased rooting strength over tilling or hollow tine	Under dry soil conditions (2 to 4 percent by wt.), both reduced bulk density, but benefit not evident after 10 months.	Lee and Rieke, 1993
Aerway slicer	Tifway bermudagrass	Compacted sandy loam; 1.6 × 5 cm tines; spacing 18 cm; depth 18 cm	Higher verdure than turf on com-pacted soil	Increased by 50–120 percent at 20–60 cm		Wiecko et al. 1993
Hollow tine		Compacted sandy loam; 1.6 cm diam.; spacing 5 cm; depth 7.6 cm	Slight decline in quality shortly after treatment	Increased by 38 percent at 20–60 cm in 1 of 2 years	Reduced bulk density at 0 to 5 and 5 to 10 cm in 1 of 2 years.	
Solid tine		Compacted sandy loam; 1.6 cm diam.; spacing 5 cm; depth 7.6 cm;		Increased rooting at 20–60 cm the first year but reduced it the second year	Reduced bulk density at 0 to 5 cm in 1 of 2 years.	
Deep drill		Compacted sandy loam; 1.6 cm diam.; spacing 13 cm; depth 25 cm	Higher verdure than turf on compacted soil	Increased rooting by ~40 percent at 20–60 cm	Increased deep water extraction by 28 to 85 percent	

Continued on next page

Table 10-3 (*Continued*)

Aerifier	Grass	Description	Shoot growth	Root growth	Other	Reference
Hollow tine	Penncross creeping bentgrass	Modified loamy sand; 1.3 cm diam.; spacing 5.7 × 6.3 cm; depth 5–7 cm	Increased shoot growth by 16 percent the first week after treatment	Decreased root weight density by 12 percent 4 weeks after 3 treatments and by 26 percent 6 weeks after imposing 5 treatments (compared to untreated)	Three treatments reduced soil bulk density and increased soil porosity to a 7.6 cm depth and reduced soil strength to a 6 cm depth; superior to water injection for thatch control	Murphy and Rieke 1994
Water injection		Modified loamy sand; 1.2 mm diam. water streams at 20 MPa pressure; 7.6 cm spacing	Increased shoot growth by 42 percent the first week after treatment	On one occasion rooting was reduced ~10 percent when measured 40 weeks after 3 treatments had been imposed; on other occasions, no different from untreated check	Total porosity increased at 7.6 to 15.2 cm compared to untreated check and hollow tine; soil strength reduced to a 10 cm depth	
Solid tine	Penneagle creeping bentgrass	Modified loamy sand; 1.3 cm diam. tines	Shoot tissue was comparable to the control.	Surface root weight density 20 percent lower in cultivated turf by the end of the study	Enhanced the development of a compacted layer at the lower end of the cultivation zone	Murphy, Rieke, and Erickson 1993
Hollow tine			Reduced total shoot tissue by 34 percent		Increased air porosity by 21 percent more than solid tine cultivation	

Figure 10-5
Aerification has the potential to promote rooting. Note how roots are proliferating in the area where the aerification tine penetrated.

be taken into account. Core aerification imposes greater stress on the plant and should be avoided when temperatures are above the optimum for plant growth. Water-injection and solid tine aerifiers, despite their potential for causing root injury, are less invasive than hollow tine aerifiers and can be applied when temperatures exceed the optimal range.

Hard Pan Formation

Aerifiers are generally more effective at improving growing conditions if used when the soil is relatively moist. Some simply will not penetrate dry, hard soil. As such, there is the potential for soil compaction at the base of, and surrounding, the penetrating tine. This potential would seem to be greater for solid tine aerifiers, which create a hole without removing any soil. In fact, solid tine aerifiers have shown a propensity to increase soil strength below the depth of the penetrating tine (Murphy, Rieke, and Erickson 1993).

Hollow tine aerifiers are also capable of increasing soil bulk density and creating a hard pan below the depth of penetration (Petrovic 1979). Maximum bulk density was found to be within the region 0.039 to 0.078 inches (1 to 2 mm) in lateral distance from the edge of the coring hole. Bulk density decreased linearly to a lateral distance up to 0.47 inches (12 mm) from the hole. In this case, the

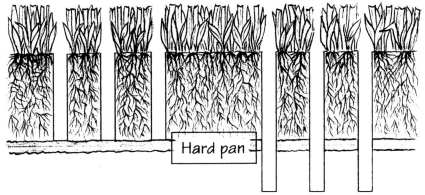

Figure 10-6
There is the risk of developing a hardpan soil layer if aerification is done routinely to the same depth. Varying the depth of penetration can help to prevent, or eliminate, a hard pan (drawing by Angie Settle).

degree of compaction was greater at the base of the core than along the edges. Furthermore, the higher bulk density at the base of the core persisted after ninety-three days of evaluation, whereas the walls of the holes had collapsed by this time. The potential for soil compaction with hollow and solid tine aerifiers suggests that the depth of penetration be varied to minimize the negative effects that repeated aerification at the same depth may have on soil physical properties and root growth.

Effects on Environmental Stresses

Almost no scientific information has been published on the interactions between soil cultivation and environmental stresses. There is little doubt that improved rooting following aerification (which has been documented) should result in increased drought resistance, especially on compacted soils in which rooting was restricted. Furthermore, significant improvements in turf performance may be realized after cultivating sloped or bermed areas by encouraging water infiltration.

Although research has not substantiated the effects of cultivation on heat stress on cool-season grasses, or freezing stress on warm-season grasses, cultivation practices that impose significant stress on the plant should be avoided when the plant is not actively growing or the likelihood of temperature injury is greater. For example, creeping bentgrass at putting green height may respond negatively to midsummer core aerification. The combined stresses of heat and disturbance by cultivation can result in turf decline. Less invasive cultivators, such as water injectors and small solid tine (needle tine) aerifiers, impose less stress and can be used during summer heat on cool-season grasses.

It is also possible that freezing injury could be greater in sensitive warm-season turfs if open aerification holes are present during cold winter temperatures. Holes allow for the infiltration of cold air that could cause lower soil temperatures at the crown level, which could increase the potential for injury from low temperatures. Similarly, open aerification holes during winter on creeping bentgrass greens could increase the potential for winter desiccation injury. Aerification of warm-season grasses and bentgrass should be done before growth slows to a point where turf recovery will not occur before winter.

Cultivation of shade-grown turf should be done only when it is clear that soil compaction is affecting growth. Plants in shaded areas are tender and succulent and have low carbohydrate levels. Hence, injury due to the cultivation may be greater, and recovery will be significantly slower.

Interactions with Pests

Weeds

The two greatest concerns regarding the interaction of cultivation and weed control are the potential for breaking the pre-emergence herbicide barrier, potentially leading to an increase in annual grassy weed encroachment, and the timing of cultivation and its potential effects on weed encroachment. Pre-emergence herbicides create an invisible chemical barrier at the soil surface that controls germinating annual grass seedlings. Theoretically, there is concern that any disturbance of the soil surface could reduce the efficacy of the pre-emergence herbicide. In Michigan, core cultivation (1 or 3 passes) and vertical mowing were done on an annual bluegrass (Fig. 2-4) turf at the time of herbicide application, or four weeks after application (Branham and Rieke 1986). Large crabgrass (Fig. 6-2) control was not affected by the cultivation treatments. Similarly, in Georgia core cultivation of bermudagrass performed one, two, three, or four months after pre-emergence herbicide application had no effect on large crabgrass control (Johnson 1987). These results suggest that routine core aerification does not reduce the efficacy of pre-emergence herbicides.

Cultivation performed at the time when a particular weed pest is likely to emerge may increase the encroachment of that weed. For example, intensive core cultivation or vertical mowing in mid- to late spring in the absence of a pre-emergence herbicide may increase encroachment of annual grasses. Annual bluegrass germinates in late summer and early autumn, and cultivation at this time of the year could increase its populations. Any cultural practice performed in the fall that opens up the turf canopy could also facilitate encroachment of annual bluegrass. For example, seeding new creeping bentgrass greens in autumn resulted in higher levels of annual bluegrass than seeding in spring (Murphy, Honig, and Lawson 1999). Conversely, Michigan researchers reported that hollow tine cultivation in spring and fall, or spring, summer, and fall, had no effect on encroachment of a perennial-type annual bluegrass into a creeping bentgrass golf green (Karcher, Rieke, and Makk 2001).

Some weed species, including annual bluegrass, goosegrass (Fig. 6-3), broadleaf plantain (Fig. 6-7), and prostrate knotweed (Fig. 6-8), have the ability to tolerate high soil strength and low oxygen levels associated with soil compaction. As such, relieving soil compaction to improve competitiveness of the desirable turfgrass should ultimately reduce populations of these weed species.

Insects　It is possible that disturbing the soil surface in some way may affect the suitability of a turf area for adult insects that lay eggs, or the development of insects in the soil. Compacting soil with a heavy roller at the beginning of the beetle flight of Japanese beetles and southern masked chaffers (Fig. 6-13), or when grubs were third instars, had no effect on subsequent soil densities of larvae (Potter et al. 1996). Furthermore, core cultivation performed just prior to beetle flight also had no effect on grub densities (Potter et al. 1996).

There is little doubt that the physical force of penetrating aerifier tines increases the mortality of grubs and other subsurface-feeding insects that are in their path. Weekly or biweekly use of a water injector aerifier reduced earthworm castings on a creeping bentgrass golf green compared to turf aerified twice annually with a hollow-tine cultivator (Karcher, Rieke, and Makk 2001). The authors surmised that the earthworms were physically injured by the water jets, or the soil environment was altered and was less conducive to them, or a combination of both. A water-injector aerifier had no effect on nematode populations in a creeping bentgrass/annual bluegrass mixture (Wick and Reid 1995).

Strap-on sandals that have solid tines protruding from their base are marketed as home lawn aerifiers and an alternative to insecticides for controlling grubs. Researchers in Colorado observed up to a 50 percent reduction in grub populations if a total of two spike insertions occurred per square inch (2.5 cm), which required walking over the area three to five times (Mason 1999).

Diseases By promoting water infiltration and reducing soil surface wetness, it is likely that core aerification has the potential to reduce the incidence of numerous foliar diseases that are most pronounced in low, wet areas that drain poorly, including brown patch (Fig. 6-16), large patch (Fig. 6-22), Pythium blight (Fig. 6-25), and others. More specific research has been done on the influence of cultivation on root-infecting pathogens, however.

Figure 10-7
Severe disturbance of the soil surface with aerification and vertical mowing was shown to reduce the symptoms of the spring dead spot the following year.

Cultivation has been evaluated for its effects on spring dead spot (Fig. 6-32) in bermudagrass and summer patch (Fig. 6-33) in Kentucky bluegrass, both caused by root-infecting pathogens. Core aerification had no effect on summer patch levels in Kentucky bluegrass when fungicides were used to suppress the disease (Wetzel and Fry 1999). In untreated turf, however, blighting was greater in turf that had been aerified (47 percent of plot area damaged) compared to that which had not (36 percent of plot area damaged).

Symptoms of spring dead spot in bermudagrass in Kansas were completely eliminated if sod was harvested and turf was allowed to regrow from rhizomes (Tisserat and Fry 1997). In addition, hollow tine aerification followed by vertical mowing done twice each summer reduced disease severity. Neither aerification nor vertical mowing done alone was as effective as the two combined.

THATCH, VERTICAL MOWING, AND TOPDRESSING

Thatch Grasses that are rhizomatous or stoloniferous have a propensity to develop thatch, an accumulation of living and dead organic material above the soil surface. Organic accumulation occurs in the turf canopy when growing plants contribute living tillers, rhizomes, and stolons. Organic material is also added when older vegetative material dies. The microbial community at the soil surface degrades dead organic material and helps to minimize thatch accumulation. Thatch may become excessive when production of organic material and its degradation are not in balance. This can arise from cultural practices that promote excessive production of vegetation, such as high nitrogen levels, or factors that reduce the activity of beneficial thatch-degrading microbes, such as cold temperatures or compacted soils.

Thatchy turf is susceptible to drought; low and high temperature stresses; and all turfgrass pests. When thatch contains moisture, roots proliferate in it. In turf areas with excessive thatch (greater than 1 inch deep), crowns and some roots are elevated above the soil surface. Once the thatch dries and the roots have no water available, wilt occurs quickly. Extended periods without water cause death of roots and shoots. Thatch is hydrophobic and is very difficult to wet again once it dries.

Figure 10-8
Thatch results from accumulation of living and dead plant material above the soil surface.

Figure 10-9
A thatchy bermuda-grass putting green in Hawaii is susceptible to desiccation and scalping.

Soil is an excellent buffer for temperature fluctuations, but thatch is not. Elevated crowns experience higher and lower temperatures throughout the year than crowns growing at or just below the soil surface. Therefore, high and low temperature injury are exacerbated on thatchy sites. Temperatures experienced by growing

Figure 10-10
A plug from Penncross creeping bentgrass (left), which did not have a distinct organic layer at the surface, suffered less winter desiccation injury than A-4 bentgrass (right), which did.

points elevated slightly above the soil surface in thatch can be significantly lower or higher than those experienced by crowns at or below the soil surface. Zoysiagrass mowed at 1.5 inches (3.8 cm) in Missouri that did not receive an annual mechanical thatch removal experienced 81 percent winter injury, whereas turf mowed at 0.75 inches (1.9 cm) that had thatch removed experienced no injury (Dunn, Sheffer, and Halisky 1981).

Vertical Mowing

Vertical mowing refers to the use of equipment that uses vertically oriented blades rotating on a crankshaft, set at a desired depth of penetration, to disrupt the turf and/or organic layer lying above the soil surface. It is used to alter growth of the grass plant to improve playability, remove excessive organic material (thatch), or prepare a seedbed.

The severity of the vertical mowing operation depends upon how the characteristics of the vertical blades and their attachment to the rotating shaft, the spacing between the blades, and the depth at which the knives are set to penetrate the surface. Groomers, verticutters, and power rakes (listed in increasing order of the

Figures 10-11 and 10-12 The excessive thatch in this St. Augustine turf (Fig. 10-11, top) resulted in winter injury (Fig. 10-12, bottom), as crowns were elevated above the soil surface.

severity with which they operate) all use vertical mowing to accomplish a desired result.

Groomers are used almost exclusively on bentgrass and bermudagrass putting greens. They are attached to the front of reel mowing units and serve to "tickle" the turf canopy and encourage

Figures 10-13, 10-14, and 10-15
A vertical mower (Fig. 10-13, above, left), power rake (Fig. 10-14, above, right), and groomer (Fig. 10-15, opposite).

leaf sheaths to stand more erect prior to being cut. This helps to prevent leaf sheaths from lying horizontally rather than being mowed. Repeatedly mowing bentgrass and bermudagrass in the same direction can result in the formation of grain. Ultimately the concern is that when bentgrass and bermudagrass plants all lean in the same direction, that influences the way a golf ball rolls. Because grooming is not an aggressive procedure, it is often done through much of the growing season. In areas where high temperature stress on bentgrass is common, groomers may be removed during summer months.

A verticutter uses rigid, vertically oriented blades that are fixed to a crankshaft to disturb the turf or the soil surface. Some verticutter units can be interchanged with reels on mowers to reduce grain and help control accumulation of organic matter in high quality bentgrass and bermudagrass. Vertical mowing was evaluated on Penncross creeping bentgrass in Nebraska to evaluate its effects on turf quality, golf ball roll speed, and turf rooting.

Table 10-4

Influence of aerification and verticutting on thatch depths (inches) in Meyer zoysiagrass in Columbia, Missouri (after Weston and Dunn 1985)

Treatment[1]	1980	1981
Control	1.14 a[2]	0.81 a
Aerification	1.08 a	0.70 b
Verticutting	1.07 a	0.65 b
Aerification plus verticutting	0.99 b	0.57 c

1 Means are an average of treatments imposed in June, June and July, and June, July, and August. Aerification holes were 3 inches (7.6 cm) deep and on 2-inch (5.1 cm) centers.

2 Means within columns followed by the same letter are not statistically different ($P < 0.05$). To convert depth in inches to mm, multiply by 25.4.

Applying treatments once or twice monthly had no effect on any of the parameters measured (Salaiz, Horst, and Shearman 1995). In Canada, weekly or monthly vertical mowing reduced thatch depth on a seven-year-old Penncross creeping bentgrass green by about 2 mm after one season (Eggens 1980). Weekly vertical mowing increased winter injury.

Verticutters can also be used on other sod-forming grasses to mechanically remove thatch. Reports vary on the effectiveness of verticutting on thatch removal. In Missouri, verticutting Meyer zoysiagrass resulted in no effect on thatch depth in one year but reduced depth by 20 percent in the second year (Table 10-4) (Weston and Dunn 1985). In the same test, a combination of aerification plus verticutting resulted in a 29 percent reduction in thatch depth.

Thatch depth of DeAnza zoysiagrass was reduced from 1.21 inches (30.7 mm) when no vertical mowing was employed to 1.08 inches (27.4 mm) when four vertical mowings were imposed at five-week intervals in California (Cockerham et al. 1997). Use of a vertical mower twice annually on centipedegrass in Georgia resulted in a 15 to 17 percent reduction in thatch (Johnson, Carrow, and Burns 1988). In another Georgia study, verticutting a bermudagrass lawn twice annually reduced thatch by 8 percent. In Alabama, verticutting bermudagrass putting greens twice annually was as effective in controlling thatch as verticutting every other week during the growing season (White and Dickens 1984).

The power rake is a variant of the vertical mower that uses closely spaced vertical blades that hang loosely until centrifugal force affects their position around the rotating shaft. This equipment is used for turf renovation and is capable of severely disturbing the turf surface.

Topdressing Topdressing refers to the application of a light layer of soil onto an actively growing turf. It is used primarily to level an uneven surface, modify the soil profile near the surface (when done in conjunction with aerification), and reduce thatch. On sites where turf is growing on fine-textured soils, topdressing may be done with a similar soil, or with sand if the objective is to modify the soil profile.

For turf growing on sand-based systems, topdressing is done with a sand that, preferably, has the same physical characteristics as that used in root zone construction. Use of a sand that is finer in texture than the underlying root zone can, over time, result in a layer that is capable of perching water, as often is done near the base of sports turf root zones when gravel lies under the finer-textured root

Figure 10-16
This athletic field is being top-dressed to level low spots and change the soil surface profile.

Figure 10-17
Infrequent topdressing, or use of sand of a size significantly different from the root zone mix, can result in an accumulation of layers as observed here.

zone to encourage water retention. It is not desirable to have a similar situation near the soil surface, however.

The layering that results can restrict water movement, result in anaerobic conditions, and eventually have deleterious effects on turf performance. Black layer, the name given to symptoms that result when poor drainage leads to anaerobic soil conditions and a corresponding black color in the soil, is an indicator that significant root zone problems exist and changes are needed. The black color is associated directly or indirectly with the presence of sulfur in irrigation water and soil. Hydrogen sulfide gas gives black-layered areas a rotten egg odor. Black layer can be prevented by using a topdressing with the same particle size and physical properties as the sand used for construction and avoiding overwatering. Other important factors in managing black layer include (Carrow, Waddington, and Rieke 2001):

- Improving drainage to remove excess water
- Establishing an intensive cultivation program to enhance air exchange
- Avoiding composts and organic matter that might contain mineral fines
- Checking irrigation water for sulfur and fines
- Reducing the use of sulfur that might be contained in fertilizers

Topdressing also assists in the reduction of thatch. Much debate continues on the mechanisms whereby adding a layer of soil or sand results in less surface organic matter, but it has been shown to be the case. Topdressing Penncross creeping bentgrass putting green growing on a loamy sand for ten consecutive years resulted in a significant decline in the amount of organic matter per unit volume of soil (Table 10-5) (Couillard, Turgeon, and Rieke 1997). Bentgrass growing in nontopdressed plots had significantly more organic matter near the soil surface than did turf that received topdressing. The reduction in thatch was proposed to be due to dilution of the thatch by the added topdressing material in combination with a stimulation of thatch degradation in topdressed turf. Although it has not been well documented, it seems that the addition of the sand or soil layer creates a more favorable environment

Figure 10-18
Poor drainage over an extended period of time can result in black layer. (Photo courtesy of Steve Wilson.)

Table 10-5

*Influence of ten years of topdressing on organic matter content (mg/cm³)
under Penncross creeping bentgrass putting green in Michigan (after
Couillard, Turgeon, and Rieke 1997)*

Depth (inches)[1]	80 Percent Sand/20 Percent Peat[2]	Control
0–0.5	40.9 a	77.5 a
0.5 –1	47.3 ab	69.2 a
1 – 1.1	52.8 b	53.8 b
1.1 –2	53.1 b	40.2 c

[1] Convert inches to cm by multiplying × 2.54.

[2] Means followed by the same letter in a column are not significantly different
($P < 0.01$).

for thatch-decomposing microbes to flourish. One suggested theory
is that a higher relative humidity is maintained in the thatch of
topdressed turf, which is favorable for microbes.

Similar benefits of reducing thatch in bentgrass with topdressing
were observed in Penncross in Canada, where thatch depths were
57 percent shallower in topdressed versus untreated turf (Eggens
1980). In Iowa, sand topdressings in November improved spring
recovery of Penncross for up to fifty days compared to untreated
turf (Christians, Diesburg, and Nus 1985).

Topdressing has also been proven to benefit turf mowed at
heights greater than those employed on putting greens. Meyer
zoysiagrass topdressed with soil had higher surface root weights
and reduced mat weights compared to untreated turf (Dunn et al.
1995). After four years of topdressing a Tifway bermudagrass lawn
with sand, thatch was reduced by 44 percent with one annual application and 62 percent for two annual applications (Carrow, Johnson, and Burns 1987).

Although it has not been well documented, it seems logical that
topdressing could only help to minimize environmental stress
injury on sod-forming cool- and warm-season grasses. Creeping
bentgrass growing with roots elevated in an organic layer, as is
common at mowing heights of ~0.5 inches (1.2 cm), could be protected from desiccation and high temperature injury by more consistent topdressing to protect exposed roots. The same applies to

thatchy warm-season grasses that have elevated crowns and roots. Topdressing helps to protect roots from drying winds and insulate crowns from freezing temperatures in winter.

Topdressing may also influence turfgrass pests, particularly diseases. In New York, use of sand topdressings in combination with composts or organic fertilizers (ratio of 70 parts sand to 30 parts compost or fertilizer by volume) reduced dollar spot to levels comparable to fungicide-treated creeping bentgrass turf (Nelson and Craft 1992). It was not clear, however, whether disease suppression arose from a biologically suppressive property of the compost or the nitrogen contained, for nitrogen has been shown to lessen the symptoms of dollar spot. Surprisingly, two separate projects have inexplicably reported that using sand topdressing on creeping bentgrass resulted in an increase in dollar spot (Fermanian, Haley, and Burns 1985; Cooper and Skogley 1981).

REFERENCES

Brady, N. C. 1974. *The nature and properties of soils*. New York: Macmillan.

Branham, B. E., and P. E. Rieke. 1986. Effects of turf cultivation practices on the efficacy of preemergence grass herbicides. *Agron. J.* 78:1089–91.

Carrow, R. N. 1980. Influence of soil compaction on three turfgrass species. *Agron. J.* 72:1038–42.

Carrow, R. N., B. J. Johnson, and R. E. Burns. 1987. Thatch and quality of Tifway bermudagrass turf in relation to fertility and cultivation. *Agron. J.* 79:524–30.

Carrow, R. N., D. V. Waddington, and P. E. Rieke. 2001. *Turfgrass soil fertility and chemical problems: Assessment and management*. Chelsea, MI: Ann Arbor Press.

Christians, N. E., K. L. Diesburg, and J. L. Nus. 1985. Effects of nitrogen fertilizer and fall topdressing on the spring recovery of *Agrostis palustris* Huds. greens. Pp. 459–68 in F. Lemaire, ed., *Proceedings of the Fifth International Turfgrass Research Conference*. Versailles: INRA.

Cockerham, S. T., V. A. Gibeault, S. B. Ries, and R. A. Khan. 1997. Verticutting frequency and mowing height for management of DeAnza and Victoria zoysia. *Int. Turfgrass Soc. Res. J.* 8:419–26.

Cooper, R. J., and C. R. Skogley. 1981. An evaluation of several programs for *Agrostis palustris* Huds. and *A. canina* L. putting green turf. Pp. 129–36 in R. W. Sheard, ed., *Proceedings of the Fourth International Turfgrass Research Conference.* Guelph, Ontario: Ontario Agricultural College and International Turfgrass Society.

Couillard, A., A. J. Turgeon, and P. E. Rieke. 1997. New insights into thatch biodegradation. *Int. Turfgrass Soc. Res. J.* 8:427–35.

Dunn, J. H., D. D. Minner, B. F. Fresenburg, S. S. Bughrara, and C. H. Hohnstater. 1995. Influence of core aerification, topdressing, and nitrogen on mat, roots, and quality of Meyer zoysiagrass. *Agron. J.* 87:891–94.

Dunn, J. H., K. M. Sheffer, and P. M. Halisky. 1981. Thatch and quality of Meyer zoysiagrass in relation to management. *Agron. J.* 73:949–52.

Eggens, J. L. 1980. Thatch control in creeping bentgrass turf. *Can. J. Plant Sci.* 60:1209–13.

Fermanian, T. W., J. E. Haley, and R. E. Burns. 1985. The effects of sand top-dressing on heavily thatched creeping bentgrass turf. Pp. 439–48 in F. Lemaire, ed., *Proceedings of the Fifth International Turfgrass Research Conference.* Versailles: INRA.

Johnson, B. J. 1987. Effect of core cultivation on preemergence herbicide activity in bermudagrass. *HortScience* 22:440.

Johnson, B. J., R. N. Carrow, and R. E. Burns. 1988. Centipedegrass decline and recovery as affected by fertilizer and cultural treatments. *Agron. J.* 80:479–86.

Karcher, D. E., P. E. Rieke, and J. F. Makk. 2001. Cultivation effects on surface qualities of an *Agrostis palustris* putting green. *Int. Turfgrass Soc. Res. J.* 9 (2):532–36.

Lee, D. K. and P. E. Rieke. 1993. Soil cultivation effects on establishment of *Poa pratensis* L. sod. *Intl. Turfgrass Soc. Res. J.* 7:437–43.

Mason, S. 1999. Grub control options for home lawns. University of Illinois Extension, Homeowners Column. Available at www.urbanext. uiuc.edu/champaign/homeowners/hc990731.html.

Murphy, J. A., J. A. Honig, and T .J. Lawson. 1999. Seeding date and bentgrass cultivar effects on annual bluegrass invasion. *1999 Annual Agronomy Meeting Abstracts* 91:140.

Murphy, J. A., and P. E. Rieke. 1994. High pressure water injection and core cultivation of a compacted putting green. *Agron. J.* 86:719–24.

Murphy, J. A., P. E. Rieke, and A. E. Erickson. 1993. Core cultivation of a putting green with hollow and solid tines. *Agron. J.* 85:1–9.

Nelson, E. B., and C. M. Craft. 1992. Suppression of dollar spot on creeping bentgrass and annual bluegrass turf with compost-amended topdressings. *Plant Dis.* 76:954–58.

O'Neil, K. J., and R. N. Carrow. 1983. Perennial ryegrass growth, water use, and soil aeration status under soil compaction. *Agron. J.* 75:177–80.

Petrovic, A. M. 1979. The effects of vertical operating hollow tine cultivation on turfgrass soil structure. Ph.D. dissertation, Dept. of Crop and Soil Science, Michigan State University.

Potter, D. A., A. J. Powell, P. G. Spicer, and D. W. Williams. 1996. Cultural practices affect root- feeding white grubs in turfgrass. *J. Econ. Entom.* 89:156–64.

Salaiz, T. A., G. L. Horst, and R. C. Shearman. 1995. Mowing height and vertical mowing frequency effects on putting green quality. *Crop Sci.* 35:1422–5.

Tisserat, N., and J. Fry. 1997. Cultural practices to reduce spring dead spot severity in *Cynodon dactylon*. *Int. Turfgrass Res. Soc. J.* 8:931–36.

USDA. 1996. Soil quality resource concerns: Compaction. Soil Quality Information Sheet. USDA Natural Resources Conservation Service, Washington, DC.

Weston, J. B., and J. H. Dunn. 1985. Thatch and quality of Meyer zoysia in response to mechanical cultivation and nitrogen fertilization. Pp. 449–58 in F. Lemaire, ed., *Proceedings of the Fifth International Turfgrass Research Conference*. Versailles: INRA.

Wetzel, H. III, and J. Fry. 1999. Effects of aerification and fungicide application on the development of summer patch disease in Mystic Kentucky bluegrass. 1999 Turfgrass Research. Kansas State University Agriculture Experiment Station, Report of Progress no. 836.

White, R. H,. and R. Dickens. 1984. Thatch accumulation in bermudagrass as influenced by cultural practices. *Agron. J.* 76:19–22.

Wick, R. L., and T. Reid. 1995. Evaluation of Hydroject 3000 aerification as a means of reducing plant parasitic nematodes, 1993. *Biol. and Cult. Tests for Control of Plant Dis.* 10:32.

Wiecko, G., R. N. Carrow, and K. J. Karnok. 1993. Turfgrass cultivation methods: Influence on soil physical, root/shoot, and water relationships. *Int. Turfgrass Soc. Res. J.* 7:451–57.

11

Plant Growth Regulators and Biostimulants

A plant growth regulator (PGR) is a natural or manufactured chemical that, when applied to a turf stand, affects shoot growth by inhibiting cell division, disrupting amino acid production, or influencing plant hormone production. Until the 1990s, when trinexapac-ethyl (TE, Primo) was made available, careful thought was given to any PGR usage on moderate to high quality turf. PGR application often resulted in turf discoloration and growth suppression was sometimes inconsistent. Trinexapac-ethyl has revolutionized PGR use on turf and is now used as routinely as nitrogen in the cultural programs of many turfgrass managers maintaining high-quality turf areas.

SHOOT RESPONSES

Cell division inhibitors (type I): Mefluidide (Embark and Embark Lite), maleic hydrazide (Royal Slo-Gro). Some herbicides are also used at low rates to produce a type I growth regulating effect.

Absorption: Foliar
Mode of action: Inhibit cell division

Other: Good seedhead suppressors, but phytotoxicity can be a concern if overlap occurs. Mefluidide is sometimes used on annual bluegrass to suppress seedheads and produce a more robust, stress-resistant plant.

These growth-inhibiting compounds are absorbed primarily by foliage, rapidly stopping cell division and differentiation in meristematic areas. Type I PGRs are good seedhead suppressors, but they must be applied before the seedhead emerges to be effective. Growth suppression usually occurs within three or four days of application and persists for three to four weeks, depending upon application rate (Murphy et al. 2001). Uniform application is important with type I regulators, as overapplication may result in phytotoxicity and under application will result in nonuniform growth. Maleic hydrazide is used primarily on low-maintenance turf areas to suppress growth. Mefluidide is used in low- to medium-maintenance turf and can also be used to suppress annual bluegrass seedhead development in fairway-height creeping bentgrass.

The herbicides imazameth (Plateau), sethoxydim (Vantage), chlorsulfuron (Corsair), and glyphosate (Roundup), although not true PGRs, have type I PGR-like activity when used at low rates. These are commonly used on low-maintenance warm-season turfs in the southern United States for growth and seedhead suppression.

Gibberellic acid inhibitors (type II): Ethephon (Proxy), flurprimidol (Cutless), paclobutrazol (TGR Turf Enhancer), trinexapac-ethyl (Primo). Some fungicides also have type II growth regulating effects.

Absorption: Root, with the exception of trinexapac-ethyl, which is foliar- and crown-absorbed.

Mode of action: Inhibit cell elongation by reducing production of gibberellic acid.

Other: Do not suppress seedheads well; may reduce seedhead numbers or create dwarfed seedheads. Trinexapac-ethyl is used routinely to reduce mowing requirements and improve quality of high-maintenance turf. Flurprimidol and paclobutrazol are used to reduce annual bluegrass populations in creeping bentgrass golf greens.

Figures 11-1 and 11-2
Carpetgrass seedheads were reduced (Fig. 11-1, top) by using low application rates of sethoxydim, an herbicide with Type I PGR activity, compared to untreated turf (Fig. 11-2, bottom).

Growth regulators in this group interfere with the synthesis of gibberellin, a growth-promoting hormone, and reduce cell elongation and subsequent plant organ expansion. Although vertical growth rate is reduced, seedhead production and lateral growth continue. Plant response to application is slower than for type I PGRs, but may persist for a longer period of time. Type II growth regulators differ in the specific locale in the gibberellin biosynthesis pathway where they are inhibitory. Flurprimidol (Cutless) and paclobutrazol (TGR Turf Enhancer) inhibit gibberellin early in the pathway, whereas trinexapac-ethyl is inhibitory later in the pathway. In general, PGRs that inhibit gibberellin early in the pathway are more phytotoxic than trinexapac-ethyl.

Ethephon is considered a type II growth regulator because it inhibits gibberellin production, but it has a unique mode of action. It is metabolized into ethylene in plant leaves, which inhibits elongation of stems by affecting gibberellin production, but provides only partial seedhead suppression.

The fungicides propiconazole (Banner), tradimefon (Bayleton), and fenarimol (Rubigan) also produce a type II growth-regulating response. Application of propiconazole at 1.3 pounds active ingredient (a.i.) per acre (1.5 kg/ha a.i.) one week prior to harvest increased Kentucky bluegrass sod strength by 23 percent and rooting strength of new sod by 64 percent (Goatley and Schmidt 1991).

Turf treated with nearly any PGR (although less so with ethephon) experiences a post-inhibition resurgence of growth during which shoot elongation rate is faster than if no PGR had been applied. Sequential PGR applications that extend suppression help to prevent this problem.

ROOT RESPONSES

The potential effects of PGRs on turfgrass rooting can be viewed from two different perspectives. Some would suggest that reducing foliage and flower production allows the plant to redirect energy into root production. Others might comment on the potential phytotoxic effects of some PGRs and suggest that this might reduce rooting. In fact, there is evidence to support both points of view.

Research approaches to evaluating PGR effects on rooting have differed. Some have applied to PGRs to field-grown turf and sampled root biomass or evaluated rooting with a mini-rhizotron. Others have treated sod or plugs in the greenhouse and evaluated root development. One would expect that results from projects evaluating the rooting dynamics of field-grown turf would be most representative of what a turf manager could expect after applying a PGR. Rarely would a PGR be applied to newly laid sod; nevertheless, results from both types of studies should be considered when evaluating the potential effects of PGRs on rooting.

Ohio researchers used a rhizotron, which allows viewing of root growth progression along a glass window in situ in the field, to observe annual bluegrass (*Poa annua* ssp. *reptans*) roots after mefluidide application. An increase in root elongation of annual bluegrass of up to 0.31 inches (8 mm) per week was observed between April and September after applying mefluidide at 0.06 or 0.12 pounds a.i. per acre (0.07 or 0.12 kg/ha a.i.) (Cooper et al. 1987) (Table 11-1). Researchers inferred that the plant was expending less energy to produce seedheads and had more carbohydrates to devote to root production after mefluidide application.

Neither flurprimidol at 0.75 pounds a.i. per acre (0.84 kg/ha a.i.) nor mefluidide at 0.30 pounds a.i. per acre (0.34 kg/ha a.i.) influenced rooting of Kentucky-31 tall fescue when applied shortly after sodding turf in a greenhouse (McCarty, Miller, and Colvin 1990). Mefluidide seemed to enhance rooting during periods of the study. Mefluidide was also reported to increase root length density of Kentucky-31 tall fescue in an Arkansas field study sixty-four days after treatment at 0.27 pounds a.i. per acre (0.30 kg/ha a.i.) (Beyrouty, West, and Gbur 1990).

Marcum and Jiang (1997) evaluated tall fescue root elongation and distribution in clear root tubes after applying PGRs to sod plugs in the greenhouse. Mefluidide, ethephon, paclobutrazol, and trinexapac-ethyl applied at the label rate all reduced rooting to some degree. Ethephon was most inhibitory to tall fescue in this test, reducing maximum rooting depth by over 85 percent compared to untreated turf.

Table 11-1

Effect of mefluidide (applied on March 31) on the average weekly root elongation rate (mm) of annual bluegrass in Columbus, Ohio, in 1983 (after Cooper et al. 1987)

Treatment	Application Rate (lb/acre a.i.)[1]	April 6	May 25	June 29	July 27	August 10	August 31
Mefluidide	0.06	10.3 a[2]	7.8 a	5.4 a	6.5 ab	8.5 a	7.9 a
	0.12	10.3 a	7.5 ab	5.3 a	7.1 a	9.3 a	8.9 a
Untreated	—	5.6 b	4.8 c	4.2 a	3.0 b	0.5 b	8.6 a

[1] To convert to kg/ha a.i., multiply this number by 1.12.

[2] Means followed by the same letter in a column are not significantly different ($P < 0.05$)

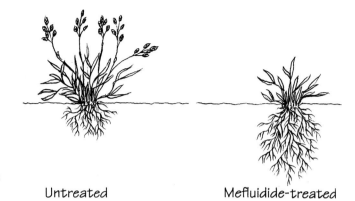

Figure 11-3
By reducing annual bluegrass seedhead production with mefluidide, the plant is able to direct more energy to root growth (drawing by Angie Settle).

Untreated   Mefluidide-treated

Rooting of newly laid Kentucky bluegrass sod, as measured by tensile strength (force required to lift the sod), was increased by up to 34 percent eight weeks after harvest when trinexapac-ethyl was applied at the label rate two weeks before harvest (Bingaman, Christians, and Gardner 2001).

In Kansas, researchers evaluated root biomass production of fairway-height perennial ryegrass after trinexapac-ethyl (0.17 pounds a.i. per acre [0.192 kg/ha a.i.]), ethephon (3.0 pounds a.i. per acre [3.363 kg/ha a.i.]), mefluidide (0.12 pounds a.i. per acre [0.134 kg/ha a.i.]), and paclobutrazol (0.5 pounds a.i. per acre [0.553 kg/ha a.i.]) were applied twice each summer for two consecutive years (Jiang and Fry 1998). Only trinexapac-ethyl did not reduce root length density at one or more sampling depths over three sampling dates. Greatest reduction in rooting occurred in turf where mefluidide was applied and caused a significant level of phytotoxicity.

North Carolina researchers published the only evaluation of creeping bentgrass rooting responses to repeated PGR application (Fagerness and Yelverton 2001). They applied three rates of paclobutrazol and one level of trinexapac-ethyl for twenty-four consecutive months beginning in April. None of the treatments enhanced bentgrass rooting, and paclobutrazol at 0.5 pounds a.i. per acre (0.56 kg/ha a.i.), twice the label rate, reduced root biomass. Researchers concluded that golf course superintendents should not be concerned about root reductions brought about by regular applications of paclobutrazol or trinexapac-ethyl at label rates.

To summarize research addressing PGR effects on turfgrass rooting, there have been only three reported increases in rooting after application. Mefluidide increased rooting of tall fescue (Beyrouty, West, and Gbur 1990) and annual bluegrass (Cooper et al. 1987). Rooting strength of newly laid Kentucky bluegrass sod was increased by trinexapac-ethyl application (Bingaman, Christians, and Gardner 2001). In all other published reports of PGR effects on turfgrass rooting, they have been shown to have no effect or to reduce it.

EFFECTS ON ENVIRONMENTAL STRESSES

Water Use and Drought Resistance

Plant growth regulator-treated cool- and warm-season grasses have lower ET rates resulting from reduced leaf area and a shorter, slower-growing turf canopy that is less affected by wind. Tall fescue ET was reduced over a six-week period in the greenhouse by mefluidide, ethephon, and trinexapac-ethyl, but not paclobutrazol (Marcum and Jiang 1997). Field studies in the mid-1980s in Nebraska demonstrated that flurprimidol and mefluidide reduced Kentucky bluegrass ET for thirty-five to forty-two days in the field, but then turf exhibited a growth flush and higher ET than untreated plants (Doyle and Shearman 1985).

St. Augustinegrass ET was reduced by an average of 18 percent in the greenhouse when flurprimidol and mefluidide were applied. Flurprimidol was more effective at reducing ET than mefluidide, and the effect was prolonged when turf was growing on relatively dry soil (suppression for a total of fifteen weeks) compared to that maintained near field capacity (suppression for a total of five weeks) (Green, Kim, and Beard 1990).

Any PGR that has demonstrated a propensity to increase rooting may also increase drought avoidance characteristics. Likewise, a reduction in rooting following PGR application may bring about reduced drought resistance. Perennial ryegrass managed under golf course fairway conditions in the greenhouse and treated with selected PGRs exhibited better drought resistance than nontreated turf (Jiang and Fry 1998). In particular, ethephon and trinexapac-ethyl improved turf quality during dry-down in the greenhouse (Table 11-2). The same drought-enhancing PGR benefits were not

Table 11-2
Turf quality of PGR-treated perennial ryegrass during dry-down in the greenhouse (after Jiang and Fry 1998)

PGR	Application Rate (lb a.i. per acre)[1]	Weeks after Treatment[2]		
		3	6	9
Trinexapac-ethyl	0.17	7.4 a[3]	7.5 a	6.6 a
Ethephon	3	7.9 a	7.8 a	6.3 ab
Mefluidide	0.12	3.9 b	3.1 c	3.3 c
Paclobutrazol	0.5	7.0 a	5.8 b	4.3 c
Untreated	—	7.0 a	5.8 b	4.4 bc

[1] To convert to kg/ha, multiply this number by 1.12.

[2] Irrigation ceased two weeks after PGR application.

[3] Quality was rated visually on a 0 to 9 scale, 9 = best. Means in a column followed by the same letter are not significantly different ($P < 0.05$).

observed in the field, however, where high temperature stress may have masked positive drought responses.

The natural plant hormone abscisic acid (ABA) has also been shown to have the potential to enhance turf drought resistance. ABA levels naturally increase in leaves of plants exposed to drought stress and are associated with protecting the plant from drought damage. ABA seems to induce the closure of stomata, which reduces water lost through transpiration and also increases

Figure 11-4
In this greenhouse study, perennial ryegrass treated with trinexapac-ethyl (far left) or ethephon (to the right of trinexapac-ethyl) had better quality during dry down than untreated turf (second in from right).

the conductance of water from roots to leaves. Kentucky bluegrass treated with foliar applications of ABA had better quality during dry-down in a growth chamber test than untreated turf (Wang, Huang, and Xu 2003). These researchers concluded that ABA improved the ability of the leaf cells to adjust osmotically to drought stress, improved leaf turgor, and reduced damage to cell membranes and the photosynthetic system. At present, there are no commercially available formulations of ABA labeled for use on turf.

Temperature Stresses

Plant growth regulators that reduce the ability of the plant to produce and store carbohydrates may increase the potential for freezing or heat stress injury. Similarly, PGRs that enhance carbohydrate production may increase survival during periods of temperature stress.

Freezing

Wisconsin researchers (Rossi and Buelow 1997) theorized that using trinexapac-ethyl to suppress annual bluegrass shoot growth might serve to increase energy reserves and improve winter survival. When trinexapac-ethyl was applied at the label recommended rate, no improvement in winter injury occurred. When ultralow rates (1.5 to 6 percent of the label rate) of trinexapac-ethyl were used, however, annual bluegrass plants were more robust and exhibited better spring recovery, although levels of winter injury were still unacceptable.

Observations that trinexapac-ethyl-treated bermuda retained its color longer into autumn led North Carolina researchers to investigate the PGR's influence on bermuda freezing tolerance. Tifway bermuda treated with an early fall application of trinexapac-ethyl, or three summer applications, had 19 to 34 percent better stolon survival when turf was harvested in October, subjected to –5°C in a freezer, and evaluated for recovery (Fagerness et al. 2002). Trinexapac-ethyl-treated turf sampled in November had cold tolerance that was similar to untreated bermuda.

Zenith and Z-9 zoysiagrass treated with two rates of trinexapac-ethyl at four-week intervals between August and October exhibited no differences in freezing tolerance compared to untreated turf when rhizomes were sampled in February and exposed to freezing temperatures (Dunn, Warmund, and Fresenburg 2001). Results with zoysia and bermuda provide no clear evidence that PGRs can be used to enhance freezing tolerance of warm-season grasses.

Heat   There is little information on the influence of PGRs on turfgrass heat tolerance. Work that has been done focused on the influence of trinexapac-ethyl on the heat tolerance of Kentucky bluegrass sod. Treating Kentucky bluegrass with trinexapac-ethyl at 0.21 pounds a.i. per acre (0.24 kg/ha a.i.) two weeks before harvest enhanced sod survival during shipping (Heckman et al. 2001a). Stacks of sod that had been treated with trinexapac-ethyl before harvest were up to 18°F (10°C) cooler than stacks of untreated sod after storing for forty-eight hours. Trinexapac ethyl applied before harvest also improved the sod tensile strength by 30 percent and quality by 17 percent at twenty-four hours after harvest. The improved performance of trinexapac-ethyl-treated sod was thought to be due to reduced respiration rates, which would result in lower temperatures in stacked sod. Although trinexapac-ethyl has a positive influence on reducing sod stack temperatures, trinexapac-ethyl-treated Kentucky bluegrass was found to have slightly poorer heat tolerance than nontreated turf (Heckman et al. 2001b). It was noted that trinexapac-ethyl is in the same chemical class as the cycohexanedione herbicides, which are known to interfere with lipid biosynthesis, and this may have influenced membrane responses to heat.

Shade   Qian and colleagues (1998) were the first to report that applications of trinexapac-ethyl improved turfgrass shade tolerance. They grew Diamond zoysia in boxes in the greenhouse and exposed the turf to shade levels of 40 percent, 75 percent, and 88 percent. Turf growing under the 75 percent and 88 percent shade levels that received multiple trinexapac-ethyl applications at 0.043 pounds a.i. per acre (0.045 kg/ha a.i.) had better quality, greater rhizome mass, higher canopy net photosynthesis rates, and higher nonstructural carbohydrate levels than untreated turf. Further work indicated that the best approach to maintain quality of shaded Diamond zoysia was to apply trinexapac-ethyl monthly during active growth at 0.043 pounds a.i. per acre (0.045 kg/ha a.i.) or bimonthly at 0.09 pounds a.i. per acre (0.10 kg/ha a.i.) (Qian and Engelke 1999). In a Missouri field test, Meyer zoysia under 77 percent shade also responded positively to monthly applications of trinexapac-ethyl at 0.09 pounds a.i. per acre (0.10 kg/ha a.i.) (Ervin et al. 2002).

In the only work with trinexapac-ethyl on shaded cool-season turf, coverage of Penncross creeping bentgrass grown under 80 percent shade was increased by 6 to 33 percent when trinexapac-ethyl

Table 11-3

Trinexapac-ethyl (Primo) effects on creeping bentgrass cover under 80 percent shade in 1998 and 1999 in East Lansing, Michigan. Shade treatments began on July 14, 1998, and May 27, 1999, and were removed in October of each year (after Goss et al. 2002)

Trinexapac-ethyl Rate (pounds a.i. per acre)[2]	Cover (%)[1]			
	1998		1999	
	Sept. 23	June 7	July 14	Sept. 14
Untreated	63.3 b[3]	86.7 a	64.2 b	74.2 b
0.04	73.3 a	92.9 a	80.8 a	91.7 a
0.06	69.2 ab	88.8 a	81.7 a	91.7 a

[1] Percentage of cover of creeping bentgrass was rated visually on a 0 to 100 percent scale, where 0 percent = bare soil and 100 percent = complete turfgrass cover.

[2] To convert to kg/ha a.i., multiply by 1.12.

[3] Means followed by the same letter in each column for each main effect are not significantly different ($P \leq 0.05$) according to Fisher's protected means separation test.

Figure 11-5 Diamond zoysiagrass treated with trinexapac-ethyl (right) under 80% shade exhibited better quality than untreated turf (left). (Photo courtesy of Dr. Yaling Qian.)

was applied at 0.04 or 0.06 pounds a.i. per acre (0.04 or 0.07 kg/ha a.i.) (Goss et al. 2002) (Table 11-3). Bentgrass tillering was also increased up to 52 percent and fructose content was up to 40 percent higher where trinexapac-ethyl was applied to shaded bentgrass.

The studies have demonstrated that there are clear benefits to using trinexapac-ethyl when zoysia or bentgrass is grown under shade levels exceeding 75 percent. The mechanisms whereby trinexapac-ethyl improves the quality of shade-grown turf was defined by Tan and Qian (2003). A common growth response in shaded turf is the rather rapid elongation of shoots. Kentucky bluegrass cultivars subjected to 73 percent shade exhibited up to a 50 percent increase in gibberellic acids in leaf tissue. Since gibberellic acid naturally promotes shoot elongation, a single application of trinexapac-ethyl, a gibberellic acid inhibitor, at 0.09 pounds a.i. per acre reduced the concentration of gibberellic acid by 47 percent. As such, trinexapac-ethyl-treated turf is more compact, retains its density, and exhibits better quality in shaded environments. It should be noted that the work done with growth regulators on shade-grown turf has been conducted under artificial shade, not tree shade. More information is needed on how turf growing under tree shade responds to PGR application.

INTERACTIONS WITH TURFGRASS PESTS

Weeds   A side effect of the benefits of turf growth suppression is a reduced ability of the plant to compete with weeds that may encroach. Some of the weeds may be seedlings at the time of treatment and protected from PGR application by the overhanging turf canopy. Others may germinate after the PGR has been applied. Unfortunately, not all weeds are as sensitive to some PGRs as targeted turfgrass. For example, one test showed than the growth of bermudagrass was suppressed by 28 to 37 percent, whereas growth of goosegrass (Fig. 6-3) and purple nutsedge (*Cyperus rotundus*) was reduced by less than 13 percent following PGR application (Lowe and Whitwell 1997). Quick-growing weeds inhabiting a stand of PGR-treated turf necessitate frequent mowing and negate the positive growth suppression effects expected.

A Kentucky bluegrass-red fescue turf treated with PGRs for four consecutive years in Maryland had varying degrees of crabgrass (Fig. 6-2) infestation depending upon the PGR used (Dernoeden 1984). Turf treated with mefluidide at 0.5 pounds a.i. per acre (0.56 kg a.i. ha) twice annually had an average crabgrass infestation of 45 percent, whereas nontreated turf experienced only 8 percent encroachment. The increase in crabgrass was attributed to a concomitant reduction in turf density following mefluidide application. Application of flurprimidol or ethephon to the bluegrass-red fescue turf did not reduce density or increase crabgrass levels.

Paclobutrazol and flurprimidol, type II PGRs, are routinely applied to creeping bentgrass greens to suppress annual bluegrass (Fig. 2-4). Annual bluegrass growth is more adversely affected than that of creeping bentgrass following application of these PGRs.

For example, paclobutrazol was shown to inhibit photosynthesis and tissue production more in annual bluegrass than creeping bentgrass (Isgrigg, Yelverton, and Coble 1998). Bentgrass growth was also shown to recover about two weeks sooner than that of annual bluegrass growth following paclobutrazol application in the greenhouse. As such, creeping bentgrass theoretically has the opportunity to become more dominant in the stand following application paclobutrazol or flurprimidol. There is little evidence that other PGRs can be used to achieve the same objective. By suppressing annual bluegrass seedhead development, mefluidide-treated annual bluegrass becomes more vigorous and is less likely to decline (Cooper et al. 1987). Similarly, trinexapac-ethyl may have the potential to produce healthier annual bluegrass plants that do not give way to creeping bentgrass (Rossi 1997; Isgrigg and Yelverton 1999).

Work by Johnson and Murphy (1996) in Georgia demonstrates the reduction in annual bluegrass that might be expected using either paclobutrazol or flurprimidol. They applied three applica-

Untreated   Paclobutrazol-treated

Figure 11-6
Use of the Type II PGRs paclobutrazol and flurprimidol may help to reduce annual bluegrass populations on creeping bentgrass putting greens.

tions of each PGR in early spring and in autumn to a creeping bentgrass green with high levels of annual bluegrass (70 percent coverage) to provide a total of 1.6 pounds a.i. per acre (1.8 kg/ha a.i.) per year for two consecutive years. Annual bluegrass suppression provided by paclobutrazol at the end of the study was 72 percent, whereas that provided by flurprimidol was 47 percent. The suppression was not persistent, however, as four months after the last application annual bluegrass reduction in paclobutrazol-treated plots had dropped to 57 percent and that in plots receiving flurprimidol was 0 percent.

North Carolina researchers reported that the use of two spring and fall applications of paclobutrazol or flurprimidol resulted in a greater than 40 percent reduction in annual bluegrass by the end of

Figure 11-7
Creeping bentgrass treated with paclobutrazol is nearly free from annual bluegrass (lighter color in plots), whereas the nontreated plot in the center is infested (Photo courtesy of Dr. Fred Yelverton.)

the first year of application and at least 80 percent reduction by the end of the second year (Isgrigg and Yelverton 1999).

It is clear that the most effective use of these PGRs for annual bluegrass suppression occurs when they are applied in spring and fall and when the program is ongoing, allowing little opportunity for annual bluegrass recovery. It should be noted that flurprimidol has been shown to reduce germination and growth of creeping bentgrass seedlings (Gaussoin and Branham 1987; Haley and Fermanian 1989), and the same is likely true for paclobutrazol; any overseeding operation should account for this.

Diseases   Before the development of trinexapac-ethyl, there was concern that PGR-suppressed turf was more susceptible to diseases, or at least retained symptoms of infection longer because of an inability to produce new shoots to mask the infection. Rhode Island researchers found that the incidence of several diseases was increased after using PGRs but that leaf spot *(Bipolaris* spp.) was the greatest contributor to a reduction in turf quality (Pennucci and Jackson 1986). Of the PGRs evaluated for disease incidence, severity, and duration, the effects of mefluidide were equal to those of amidochlor; both of these were better than maleic hydrazide, which in turn was superior to flurprimidol, which was better than paclobutrazol.

There have been several reports of trinexapac-ethyl having a positive effect on disease occurrence in turf. Severity of gray leaf spot (Fig. 6-19) in perennial ryegrass was reduced when trinexapac-ethyl was applied in combination with the fungicides propiconazole or iprodione (Uddin and Soika 2000). Trinexapac-ethyl was also effective in reducing dollar spot (Fig. 6-18) in fairway-height creeping bentgrass (Golembiewski and Danneberger 1998).

On a bentgrass putting green in Georgia, paclobutrazol and flurprimidol reduced dollar spot levels, but trinexapac-ethyl did not. Applying trinexapac-ethyl four days before the fungicides chlorothalonil, iprodione, and propiconazole enhanced their activity.

Paclobutrazol had some positive effects in reducing disease in one of two years when applied alone or in combination with fungicides to tall fescue before the onset of brown patch (Fig. 6-16) (Burpee 1998).

BIOSTIMULANTS

The term *biostimulant* refers to products that may contain one or more of a broad range of purported active ingredients, including nutrients, organic acids, hormones, vitamins, microbial inoculants, plant extracts, and others (Karnok 2000). Work on biostimulants from a research perspective has been limited, in part due to the elusive nature of the products. Usually companies market products that contain a multitude of potential active ingredients, including nutrients. Evaluating such products in research is difficult, for if a response if observed, it often isn't clear which ingredient is responsible.

Some active ingredients contained in biostimulants are produced by turfgrasses and other plants. For example, cytokinins, including adenine and zeatin, are commonly extracted from seaweed (kelp) and incorporated into biostimulant formulations. Turf responses to cytokinin may include a delay of senescence and chlorosis, enhanced chloroplast development, promotion of cell division and elongation, and enhanced root elongation and root hair development (Horgan 1984). Under good growing conditions, the turfgrass plant may have adequate levels of all hormones to ensure normal growth, and little benefit will occur from application of additional hormones. However, when the plant is exposed to certain environmental and cultural stresses, levels of some hormones, such as cytokinins, may drop. Under these conditions, application of cytokinins or other plant hormones could help ameliorate the stress.

Humic acids may also be found in some biostimulants. Humic substances make up 65 to 70 percent of the organic matter found in soils (Hernando 1968) and accumulate when plant tissues degrade. Humic acids have been shown to increase cell membrane permeability (Hernando 1968; Visser 1985); increase oxygen uptake, respiration, and photosynthesis (Aitken, Acock, and Senn 1964); increase phosphorus uptake (Jelenic, Hajdukovic, and Aleksic 1966); increase root and cell elongation (Vaugham 1974); increase ion transport; and produce cytokininlike growth responses (Cacco and Civelli 1973).

Turf Growth Responses to Biostimulants   Schmidt and Chalmers (1993) found that nitrogen applied in conjunction with fortified seaweed extract, benzyladenine, or chelated iron improved Tifgreen bermudagrass color and enhanced postdormancy turf coverage. Application of seaweed extract and humic acid to creeping bentgrass increased summer root weights by 17 to 29 percent and enhanced photochemical activity and antioxidant superoxide dismutase activity under well-watered and drought-stressed conditions (Zhang et al. 2002). The authors suggested that application of these natural plant growth regulators before and during summer stress would improve bentgrass growth and quality.

Applications of seaweed extract and humic acid before harvest of tall fescue sod increased sod heat tolerance and resulted in up to a 35 percent increase in posttransplant root strength (Zhang, Ervin, and Schmidt 2003). The improvement in heat tolerance observed following biostimulant application may be due to the presence of cytokinin in the biostimulant. Heat stress was shown to reduce cytokinin biosynthesis in creeping bentgrass roots, and cytokinins are important in promoting heat stress (Liu and Huang 2002). Application of zeatin riboside, one type of cytokinin, into a creeping bentgrass root zone before or fourteen days into heat stress reduced injury. The zeatin riboside was shown to reduce leaf electrolyte leakage and increase activity of enzymes important in minimizing heat stress injury.

Biostimulants have obviously been shown to have some beneficial effects on turfgrass growth, including increased photochemical activity and rooting. Turf managers that have interest in these products should use the "buyer beware" approach, however, and make sure there are unbiased research results that support use of a particular product.

Biostimulants and Turf Diseases

Although the primary objective of a biostimulant application may not be to reduce disease incidence, it would be an added benefit. Some biostimulants are marketed as having the potential to reduce fungicide requirements by enhancing plant vigor. Only recently has any work been done in this area. An evaluation of twelve biostimulants for reducing dollar spot in creeping bentgrass in Kansas revealed that none of them suppressed disease compared to biweekly application of urea. During a year of high dollar spot pressure, nine of the biostimulant treatments increased dollar spot symptoms compared to biweekly applications of soluble nitrogen at 0.10 pounds per 1,000 square feet (4.9 kg/ha) (Lee, Fry, and Tisserat 2003b).

One group of biostimulants that show promise for reducing some turf diseases are plant defense activators. Plants have evolved numerous and complex defense mechanisms to survive attacks by fungal pathogens, most of which are triggered once the pathogen enters the plant. However, there are nonfungicidal organic chemicals that can be applied to plant leaves to stimulate defense responses. Research indicates that this induced resistance is likely associated with production of pathogenesis-related proteins (Hammerschmidt 1999). Acibenzolar-S-methyl (ASM, trade name Actigard) is a plant defense activator that induces systemic acquired resistance in plants and has antifungal activity (Cole 1999). The induced resistance is mediated via a salicylic-acid-dependent process and can be triggered by applying salicylic acid or ASM, which triggers a similar response (Hammerschmidt 1999). Acibenzolar-S-methyl applied at 0.031 pounds a.i. per acre (0.035 kg/ha a.i.) every fourteen days between mid-May and mid-September for two consecutive growing seasons reduced the number of dollar spot infection centers by 15 percent in Crenshaw, 24 percent in Penncross, and 29 percent in Providence creeping bentgrass, but had no effect on brown patch (Lee, Fry, and Tisserat 2003a) (Table 11-5). A similar ASM application to a blend of Crenshaw:Cato creeping bentgrass reduced dollar spot by 38 percent (Lee, Fry, and Tisserat 2003b). Although defense activators

Table 11-5
Dollar spot in four creeping bentgrass cultivars as influenced by the plant defense activator acibenzolar-S-methyl at Manhattan, Kansas (after Lee, Fry, and Tisserat 2003a)

Treatment	AUDPC[1]			
	Crenshaw	L-93	Penncross	Providence
Untreated	12,884 a[2]	1,415 a	2,414 a	2,798 a
ASM	10,923 b	1,161 a	1,830 b	1,986 b

[1] Area under the disease progression curve (AUDPC) represents counts of *Sclerotinia homoeocarpa* infection centers each year as follows: May 10 to Sep. 14, 2000; May 23 to Sep. 2001. AUDPC is expressed as number of infection centers times days. Means are of data combined from 2000 and 2001.

[2] Means followed by the same letter in a column are not significantly different ($P < 0.05$) according to a Fisher's protected LSD mean separation test.

such as ASM will not likely take the place of fungicides, they may have potential to reduce fungicide requirements.

REFERENCES

Aitken, J. B., B. Acock, and T. L. Senn. 1964. The characteristics of humic acids derived from leonardite. The South Carolina Agriculture Experiment Station, Clemson University, *Technical Bulletin* 1015:28.

Beyrouty, C. A., C. P. West, and E. E. Gbur. 1990. Root development of bermudagrass and tall fescue as affected by cutting interval and growth regulators. *Plant and Soil* 127:23–30.

Bingaman, B. R., N. E. Christians, and D. S. Gardner. 2001. Trinexapac-ethyl effects on rooting of Kentucky bluegrass sod. *Int. Turfgrass Soc. Res. J.* 9 (2):832–934.

Burpee, L. L. 1998. Effects of plant growth regulators and fungicides on Rhizoctonia blight of tall fescue. *Crop Prot.* 17:503–7.

Cacco, G., and G. Civelli. 1973. Effect of humic substances on the ion transport system in the roots. *Riv-Agron.* 7:127–31.

Cole, D. L. 1999. The efficacy of acibenzolar-S-methyl, an inducer of systemic acquired resistance, against bacterial and fungal diseases of tobacco. *Crop Prot.* 18:267–73.

Cooper, R. J., P. R. Henderlong, J. R. Street, and K. J. Karnok. 1987. Root growth, seedhead production, and quality of annual bluegrass as affected by mefluidide and a wetting agent. *Agron. J.* 79:929–34.

Dernoeden, P. 1984. Four-year response of a Kentucky bluegrass-red fescue turf to plant growth retardants. *Agron. J.* 76:807–13.

Doyle, J. M., and R. C. Shearman. 1985. Plant growth regulator effects on evapotranspiration of a Kentucky bluegrass turf. *Agron. Abst.* p. 315.

Dunn, J. H., M. R. Warmund, and B. S. Fresenburg. 2001. Cold tolerance of zoysiagrass as influenced by cutting height and Primo. University of Missouri, *Turfgrass 2001 Research and Information Report*, p. 27.

Ervin, E. H., C. H. Ok, B. S. Fresenburg, and J. H. Dunn. 2002. Trinexapac-ethyl restricts shoot growth and prolongs stand density of Meyer zoysiagrass fairway under shade. *HortScience* 37:502–5.

Fagerness, M. J., and F. H. Yelverton. 2001. Plant growth regulator and mowing height effects on seasonal root growth of Penncross creeping bentgrass. *Crop Sci.* 41:1901–5.

Fagerness, M. J., F. H. Yelverton, D. P. Livingston III, and T. W. Rufty Jr. 2002. Temperature and trinexapac-ethyl effects on bermudagrass growth, dormancy, and freezing tolerance. *Crop Sci.* 42:853–58.

Gaussoin, R. E., and B. E. Branham. 1987. Annual bluegrass and creeping bentgrass germination response to flurprimidol. *HortScience* 22:441–42.

Golembiewski, R. C., and T. K. Danneberger. 1998. Dollar spot severity as influenced by trinexapac-ethyl, creeping bentgrass cultivar, and nitrogen fertility. *Agron. J.* 90:466–70.

Goatley, J. M., Jr., and R. E. Schmidt. 1991. Biostimulator enhancement of Kentucky bluegrass sod. *HortScience* 26:254–55.

Goss, R. M., J. H. Baird, S. L. Kelm, and R. N. Calhoun. 2002. Trinexapac-ethyl and nitrogen effects on creeping bentgrass grown under reduced light conditions. *Crop Sci.* 42:472–79.

Green, R. L., K. S. Kim, and J. B. Beard. 1990. Effects of flurprimidol, mefluidide, and soil moisture on St. Augustinegrass evapotranspiration rate. *HortScience* 25:439–41.

Haley, J. E., and T. W. Fermanian. 1989. Flurprimidol effect on emergence and growth of annual bluegrass and creeping bentgrass. *Agron. J.* 81:198–202.

Hammerschmidt, R. 1999. Induced disease resistance: How do induced plants stop pathogens? *Physiol. Mol. Plant Pathol.* 55:77–84.

Heckman, N. L., G. L. Horst, R. E. Gaussoin, and K. W. Frank. 2001a. Storage and handling characteristics of trinexapac-ethyl treated Kentucky bluegrass sod. *HortScience* 36:1127–30.

Heckman, N. L., G. L. Horst, R. E. Gaussoin, and L. J. Young. 2001b. Heat tolerance of Kentucky bluegrass as affected by trinexapac-ethyl. *HortScience* 36:365–67.

Hernando, F. V. 1968. Effects of humic acid, extracted from manure by two methods, on maize plants. Effects on the roots. *Anales de Edafologia y Agrobiologia.* 34:983–90.

Horgan, R. 1984. Cytokinins. Pp. 53–75 in *Advanced plant physiology*. London: Pitman.

Isgrigg, J., III, and F. H. Yelverton. 1999. Transition of *Poa annua* ssp. *reptans* infested bentgrass putting greens to monoculture bentgrass using plant growth regulators and fungicides. *Proc. South. Weed Sci. Soc.*, pp. 76–77.

Isgrigg, J., III, F. H. Yelverton, and H. D. Coble. 1998. The effect of paclobutrazol on the relative growth of annual bluegrass and creeping bentgrass. *Proc. South. Weed Sci. Soc.*, p. 248.

Jelenic, D., B. M. Hajdukovic, and Z. Aleksic. 1966. The influence of humic substances on phosphate utilization from labeled superphosphate. Pp. 85–99 in *The use of isotopes in soil organic matter studies: Report of the FAO/IAEA Technical Meeting*. Oxford: Pergamon.

Jiang, H., and J. Fry. 1998. Drought responses of perennial ryegrass treated with plant growth regulators. *HortScience* 33:270–73.

Johnson, B. J., and T. R. Murphy. 1996. Suppression of a perennial subspecies of annual bluegrass (*Poa annua* spp. *reptans*) in a creeping bentgrass (*Agrostis stolonifera*) green with plant growth regulators. *Weed Tech.* 10:705–9.

Karnok, K. J. 2000. Promises, promises: Can biostimulants deliver? *Golf Course Management* 68:67–71.

Lee, J., J. Fry, and N. Tisserat. 2003a. Dollar spot in four bentgrass cultivars as affected by acibenzolar-S-methyl and organic fertilizers. *Plant Health Progress* doi:10.1094/PHP-2003-0626-01-RS. This is part of the Plant Health Network that can viewed at www.plantmanagementnetwork.org/php

———. 2003b. Dollar spot and brown patch incidence in creeping bentgrass as affected by acibenzolar-S-methyl and biostimulants. *HortScience* 31:1223–26

Liu, X., and B. Huang. 2002. Cytokinin effects on creeping bentgrass response to heat stress. II. Leaf senescence and antioxidant metabolism. *Crop Sci.* 42:466–72.

Lowe, D., and T. Whitwell. 1997. Primo, TGR and Cutless influence the growth of selected weeds. *Clemson Univ. Turfgrass Research Report*, pp. 105–7.

Marcum, K., and H. Jiang. 1997. Effects of plant growth regulators on tall fescue rooting and water use. *J. Turfgrass Management* 2:13–27.

McCarty, L. B., L. C. Miller, and D. L. Colvin. 1990. Tall fescue root growth rate following mefluidide and flurprimidol application. *HortScience* 25:581.

Murphy, T. R., T. Whitwell, L. B. McCarty, and F. H. Yelverton. 2001. Turfgrass plant growth regulators. Pp. 552–61 in L. B. McCarty, ed.,

Best golf course management practices. Upper Saddle River, NJ: Prentice-Hall.

Pennucci, A., and N. Jackson. 1986. Distinguishing phytotoxicity and pathogenicity by fungi in growth retardant treated turf. *Phytopath.* 76:657.

Qian, Y. L., and M. C. Engelke. 1999. Influence of trinexapac-ethyl on Diamond zoysiagrass in a shade environment. *Crop Sci.* 39:202–8.

Qian, Y. L., M. C. Engelke, M. J. V. Foster, and S. Reynolds. 1998. Trinexapac-ethyl restricts shoot growth and improves quality of Diamond zoysiagrass under shade. *HortScience* 33:1019–22.

Rossi, F. S., and E. J. Buelow. 1997. Exploring the use of plant growth regulators to reduce winter injury on annual bluegrass (*Poa annua* L.). *United States Golf Association Green Section Record* 35:12–15.

Schmidt, R. E., and D. R. Chalmers. 1993. Late summer to early fall application of fertilizer and biostimulants on bermudagrass. *Int. Turfgrass Soc. Res. J.* 7:715–21.

Tan, Z. G., and Y. L. Qian. 2003. Light intensity affects gibberellic acid content in Kentucky bluegrass. *HortScience* 38:113–16.

Uddin, W., and M. D. Soika. 2000. Effects of plant growth regulators, herbicides and fungicides on development of blast disease (gray leaf spot) of perennial ryegrass turf. *Phytopath.* 90:S78.

Vaugham, D. 1974. Possible mechanism for humic acid action on cell elongation in root segments of *Pisum sativum* under aseptic conditions. *Soil Biol. and Bioch.*6 (4):241–47.

Visser, S. A. 1985. Physiological action of humic substances on microbial cells. *Soil Biol. and Bioch.* 17:457–62.

Wang, Z., B. Huang, and Q. Xu. 2003. Effects of abscisic acid on drought responses of Kentucky bluegrass. *J. Amer. Soc. Hort. Sci.* 128:36–41.

Zhang, X., R. E. Schmidt, E. H. Ervin, and S. Doak. 2002. Creeping bentgrass physiological responses to natural plant growth regulators and iron under two regimes. *HortScience* 37:898–902.

Zhang, X., E. H. Ervin, and R. E. Schmidt. 2003. Seaweed extract, humic acid, and propiconazole improve tall fescue sod heat tolerance and posttransplant quality. *HortScience* 38:440–43.

About the Authors

Jack D. Fry, Ph.D., is a professor in the Department of Horticulture, Forestry and Recreation Resources at Kansas State University. Jack grew up in Overland Park, Kansas, where his father operated a service station for over thirty years. He is grateful to his parents, Claude and Marianne Fry, for the freedom and support they gave him to explore his passion through education.

Jack obtained a B.S. in horticulture from Kansas State University in 1982. He then traveled to the East Coast and received an M.S. in agronomy at the University of Maryland in 1984 under the guidance of Dr. Peter Dernoeden. There he studied methods for enhancing zoysiagrass establishment and conducted numerous projects related to integrated pest management. Dr. Dernoeden was an excellent mentor for developing research and writing skills.

Jack attended Colorado State University for the Ph.D. with Dr. Jackie Butler, receiving the degree in 1987. At CSU, his work focused on reducing water inputs in turfgrass systems. Dr. Butler was a true friend and demonstrated the importance of a strong university relationship with the turfgrass industry. He was a master at using humor to deliver important messages.

Jack presently holds a research and teaching appointment in turfgrass science at Kansas State, where he has been since 1991. From 1987 to 1991 he was an assistant professor of turfgrass science at Louisiana State University. At Kansas State, Jack helped establish a unique golf course management undergraduate curriculum and has taught the courses Turfgrass Management, Turfgrass Science, and Golf Course Operations. His research has focused on turfgrass response to environmental stresses, irrigation management, and integrated pest management. Jack served on the United States Golf Association Turfgrass and Environmental Research Committee in 1994, and has served as associate editor in the turf management area for the scientific journals *HortScience* and *Agronomy Journal*. In 2003–4, Jack served as chair of the C-5 (Turfgrass) division of the Crop Science Society of America.

Bingru Huang received a B.S. in agronomy from Hebei Agricultural University, China, in 1984 and an M.S. degree in crop science at Shandong Agricultural University, China, in 1987. She did her Ph.D. research from 1988 to 1991 at Texas Tech University under Dr. Howard Taylor, and studied root characteristics contributing to heat tolerance of wheat. After receiving her Ph.D., Dr. Huang took a postdoctoral position at the University of California, Los Angeles, where she investigated root physiological and anatomical traits conferring drought tolerance in desert plants. Dr. Huang then moved to the University of Georgia as a postdoctoral researcher to work on waterlogging stress physiology in wheat and drought stress physiology in turfgrasses.

Bingru is currently an associate professor at the Department of Plant Biology and Pathology, Rutgers University. Prior to her position at Rutgers, she was an assistant professor at Kansas State University from 1996 to 2000. Dr. Huang's current research focuses on the understanding mechanisms of plant tolerance to environmental stresses, with emphasis on drought and heat stress in turfgrasses. She is one of the few people who are exploring the physiological and biochemical basis of roots that can account for genetic variation in stress tolerance. She has authored or coauthored over ninety refereed journal articles, ten book chapters, and ninety non-refereed, technical publications, and has presented fifty-three invited lectures and seminars between 1991 and 2004. Dr. Huang is a Fellow of the America Society of Agronomy and is an Alfred Sloan Fellow. She was the recipient of the 1997 Young Crop Scientist Award of the Crop Science Society of America. She has served as associate editor for *Crop Science*.

Index

Index

Index

Index

Index

St. Augustinegrass (*continued*)
drought resistance of, 74, 77
evapotranspiration rate of, 156, 157, 283
excessive thatch in, 267
freezing injury in, 180
freezing resistance of, 86, 89, 90, 94–95
irrigation of, 177, 188
mowing height for, 196
plant growth regulators used with, 283
return of clippings and diseases in, 214
shade tolerance of, 121, 122
silicon application and disease reduction in, 241
Salicylic acid, 294
Salts, 174
Sand:
topdressing with, 270–271, 274
water holding capacity of, 166
Sandal aerifiers, 263
Sandy soils, compaction in, 249
Scalping, 202, 203
Seashore paspalum, 54
deficit irrigation of, 178
drought resistance of, 74
effect of shade on, 117
evapotranspiration rate of, 157
freezing resistance of, 86, 89, 90
shade and growth of, 114
Seaweed extract, 293
Sedges, 184
Seed stalks, 194
Sethoxydim, 278
Shade, 111–121
and carbohydrate depletion, 19
cultivation of turf in, 261
cultural practices affecting, 111
and fertilization, 233–234
genetic variability in tolerance for, 118–121
and growth of turfgrass, 111–116
and irrigation management, 183
light wavelengths received in, 11
in morning vs. afternoon, 114
mowing height for turf in, 208
perpetual, 114
and plant competition/allelopathy, 115–116
plant growth regulator use and tolerance of, 286–288
plant responses to, 116–117
and susceptibility to stresses/pests, 118
and turf microclimate, 115
Shoots, 195
aerification and growth of, 256

cool-season, air temperature for growth of, 22
cool-season, relative growth patterns for, 23
drought and growth of, 66
drought avoidance and changes in, 68
heat injury and density of, 98
irrigation frequency and growth of, 170–171
mowing and growth responses of, 195–198
mowing and longevity of, 194
and plant growth regulators, 277–280
rooting and growth of, 172
of shaded plants, 116, 117
soil compaction and growth of, 251
soil temperatures and growth of, 102, 103
warm-season, air temperature for growth of, 41
warm-season, relative growth patterns for, 41
water content of, 197
Silicon, 241
Silver crabgrass, 127
Smooth bromegrass, 89
Snow, protection by, 84, 85
Snow mold, 236, 237
Sod, trinexapac-ethyl-treated, 286
Sod-forming grasses. *See also specific grasses*
mowing height and thatch accumulation by, 207
mowing height and water requirements of, 205–206
nitrogen and encroachment of, 234
nitrogen and thatch formation with, 225
verticutters for, 269
Soils:
evapotranspiration and water content of, 154–155
and extracellular freezing, 84
phosphorus in, 226–227
physical properties of, 249–251
and root growth, 60
water content of, 159–161
water depletion rate and type of, 166–167
water holding capacity of, 166
Soil compaction, 249–254
and hard pan formation, 259–260
for insect control, 262
and physical properties of soil, 249–251
and root growth, 253–254
and shoot growth, 251

and total nonstructural carbohydrates, 251, 254
and water use, 254
Soil slicer aerifiers, 256, 257
Soil temperature, 102–104
Solid tine aerifiers, 256–259
Soluble sugars, 87, 88, 206
Southern climate turfgrasses, 41–48. *See also specific grasses*
bermudagrass, 41–44
buffalograss, 46–48
zoysiagrass, 44–46
Southern masked chaffers, 133–134
irrigation and peak flights of, 185
soil compaction and control of, 262
Split-root technique, 67
Spring dead spot, 146, 147
and acid-reacting fertilizers, 238
cultivation for control of, 264
and mowing height, 211, 213
and nitrogen, 237, 240
Starch, 5, 18, 87, 100
Statistics, interpretation of, x–xi
Stenotaphrum secondatum [Walt.] Kuntze, *see* St. Augustinegrass
Stolons, 195, 197
Stoloniferous grasses. *See also specific grasses*
freezing resistance of, 90
thatch development in, 264
Stomata, 4, 7, 13, 61–65
chemical signals controlling response of, 67–68
drought and conductance of, 67
opening/closing of, 62–63
potassium and function of, 227
relative humidity in, 64
transpiration and density of, 65
wax formation over, 68
Storage carbohydrates, 18–20, 87, 197
Stresses:
environmental, *see* Environmental stresses
mowing and tolerance of, 197
nitrogen application after, 222–223
related to cultural practices, *see* Cultural practices
Stripe smut, combination fertilization and, 240
Sucrose, 5, 18, 87, 100, 206
Sugar phosphate, 225
Sulfur (S), 218, 235, 238
Summer annual grasses, 128
cultural practices affecting, 127
and irrigation management, 184
Summer patch, 148–149
and acid-reacting fertilizers, 238
cultivation for control of, 264

effects of nitrogen on, 240
irrigation and suppression of, 186, 188
and mowing height, 211, 213
Sunlight, 11, 111–113. *See also* Light
Supina bluegrass, freezing injury in, 85
Syringing, 181–183

T

Take-all patch, 149
and acid-reacting fertilizers, 238
effects of nitrogen on, 240
and managanese application, 241
Tall fescue, 29–32
aluminum sulfate and grubs in, 235–236
biostimulant use with, 293
brown patch in, 186
deficit irrigation of, 177, 178
diseases in, 188, 211–214, 237, 238, 241
drought resistance of, 68, 69, 71, 72, 74–76
estimating ET for, 164–165
evapotranspiration rate of, 156, 157, 283
freezing resistance of, 95–96
frequency of irrigation and quality of, 178
heat resistance of, 104
insects and irrigation of, 185
irrigation of, 171, 172, 177, 178, 185, 188
minimum light duration for, 114
mowing frequency for, 202
mowing height for, 196, 204, 208–209, 211–213
nitrogen and weed resistance of, 234
nitrogen level and diseases of, 237
organic fertilizers and diseases in, 238
plant growth regulators used with, 281, 283
potassium fertilization of, 230
return of clippings and diseases in, 213–214
rooting of, 171, 172, 281
shade tolerance of, 119, 120
silicon application and disease reduction in, 241
and soil compaction stress, 251, 252
soil drying and root hair development in, 173
wilt-based irrigation for, 170
TDRs, *see* Time domain reflectometers
TE, *see* Trinexapac-ethyl
Temperature(s), 83–106
carbohydrate reserves and tolerance ~~of~~to, 206
for cool-season grass shoot growth, 22

cultural practices affecting, 83
and evapotranspiration, 154
freezing stress, 84–96
heat stress, 97–106
optimal, 11, 83
and photorespiration, 7
and photosynthesis, 11–12
plant growth regulators and stresses of, 285–286
potassium and stresses of, 227
and respiration, 17, 19
shade as moderator of, 115
thatch and stresses of, 264–266
for warm-season grass optimal growth, 9
Tensiometers, 159
Thatch, 264–267
control treatments for, 269
mowing height and accumulation of, 207
nitrogen and accumulation of, 225
topdressing for reduction in, 272
Time domain reflectometers (TDRs), 160–161
TNCs, *see* Total nonstructural carbohydrates
Tolerance:
drought, 71–73
freezing, 86–89
heat, 207–208
shade, 118–122, 286–288
temperature, 206
wear, 223, 227–228
Topdressing(s), 270–274
and black layer formation, 271
compost-amended, 236
for thatch reduction, 272
Total nonstructural carbohydrates (TNCs), 18, 100, 251, 253
Tradimefon, 280
Transition zone, 21–22
Transition zone turfgrasses, 41–48. *See also specific grasses*
bermudagrass, 41–44
buffalograss, 46–48
zoysiagrass, 44–46
Transpiration, 61–65. *See also* Evapotranspiration
definition of, 61
as heat avoidance mechanism, 103–104
physics of, 61–64
plant factors affecting, 64–65
Trinexapac-ethyl (TE), 277, 278, 280–289
Tropical climate turfgrasses, 49–55. *See also specific grasses*
bahiagrass, 52–53
centipedegrass, 51–52

freezing resistance of, 94–95
St. Augustinegrass, 49–50
seashore paspalum, 54
Tungsten lights, 11
Turfgrasses, 21–54. *See also specific grasses*
annual bluegrass, 24–25
bahiagrass, 52–53
bermudagrass, 41–44
buffalograss, 46–48
centipedegrass, 51–52
colonial bentgrass, 38–39
cool-season, 22–40
creeping bentgrass, 36–38
fine fescues, 32–33
perennial ryegrass, 33–36
roughstalk bluegrass, 27–28
St. Augustinegrass, 49–50
seashore paspalum, 54
for southern climates and transition zone, 41–48
tall fescue, 29–32
for tropical climates only, 49–55
velvet bentgrass, 39–40
warm-season, 41–54
zones of adaptation for, 21–22
zoysiagrass, 44–46

U

Unstirred layer, 63
Urea, 236, 238

V

Vapor pressure gradient, 63–64
and evapotranspiration, 154
and mowing height, 203
Vascular system, 61
Velvet bentgrass, 39–40
Vertical mowing, 261–262, 266–270
combined with aerification, 264
groomers for, 266–268
power rakes for, 266–268, 270
and thatch depth, 269
verticutters for, 266–270
Verticutters, 266–270
Visible spectrum, 112

W

Warm-arid zone, 21, 22
Warm-humid zone, 21, 22
Warm-Season (C_4) turfgrasses, 1, 41–54, 211–212. *See also specific types*
bahiagrass, 52–53
bermudagrass, 41–44
buffalograss, 46–48

Index